SHARED AGENCY

SHARED AGENCY

A Planning Theory of Acting Together

Michael E. Bratman

OXFORD
UNIVERSITY PRESS

Oxford University Press is a department of the University of Oxford.
It furthers the University's objective of excellence in research,
scholarship, and education by publishing worldwide.

Oxford   New York
Auckland   Cape Town   Dar es Salaam   Hong Kong   Karachi
Kuala Lumpur   Madrid   Melbourne   Mexico City   Nairobi
New Delhi   Shanghai   Taipei   Toronto

With offices in
Argentina   Austria   Brazil   Chile   Czech Republic   France   Greece
Guatemala   Hungary   Italy   Japan   Poland   Portugal   Singapore
South Korea   Switzerland   Thailand   Turkey   Ukraine   Vietnam

Oxford is a registered trade mark of Oxford University Press
in the UK and certain other countries.

Published in the United States of America by
Oxford University Press
198 Madison Avenue, New York, NY 10016

Library of Congress Cataloging-in-Publication Data
Bratman, Michael.
Shared agency : a planning theory of acting together / Michael E. Bratman.
    pages cm
Includes index.
ISBN 978-0-19-989793-3 (hardback : alk. paper)—ISBN 978-0-19-933999-0 (pbk. : alk. paper)
1. Agent (Philosophy) 2. Act (Philosophy) 3. Social interaction. 4. Social psychology. I. Title.
B105.A35B74   2013
302—dc23   2013013084

For Miles, Marion, Dylan, and Sylvia

CONTENTS

PREFACE

I began my 1987 book, *Intention, Plans, and Practical Reason*, with a question:

> What happens to our conception of mind and rational agency when we take seriously future-directed intentions and plans and their roles as inputs into further practical reasoning? (p. vii)

My answer was a way of thinking about our agency that departed in important ways from what was then a standard view, namely: the desire-belief model of our agency. The alternative I offered was the *planning theory* of intention and our agency.

In the present book I turn to a follow-up question:

> What happens to our understanding of small-scale cases of acting together—examples include singing duets, dancing together, conversing together, painting a house together, putting on a play together, performing a scientific experiment together, making a fresco together—when we take seriously the planning theory of our individual agency?

And what I have come to believe, in reflecting on this question, is that we are thereby led to a promising model of robust forms of small-scale shared intentional and shared cooperative agency, a model that builds on planning structures that we have independent reason to see as central to our individual agency. My main aim in this book is to lay out this planning model of our sociality in sufficient detail and with sufficient clarity so that we can assess its merits. This involves articulating in as clear a way as possible a web of building blocks—conceptual, metaphysical, and normative—that are both rooted in the planning theory and adequate for modeling robust forms of sociality. I am more confident about the overall contours of this theory than about the totality of details I have found it necessary to develop along the way. But to test the theory we need to try to provide such details. So that is what I have done—all the while endeavoring both to keep the overall conception in clear view and to articulate a range of resources that may be of use in related theoretical investigations.

Many (though not all) of the ideas to be presented here were initially sketched in a series of six essays originally published between 1992 and 2006, though there are also further developments and adjustments. These earlier essays are: Michael E. Bratman, "Shared Cooperative Activity," in *Faces of Intention* (New York: Cambridge University Press, 1999); Michael E. Bratman, "Shared Intention," in *Faces of Intention* (New York: Cambridge University Press, 1999); Michael E. Bratman, "Shared Intention and Mutual Obligation," in *Faces of Intention* (New York: Cambridge University Press, 1999); Michael E. Bratman, "I Intend That We J," in *Faces of Intention* (New York: Cambridge University Press, 1999); "Shared Valuing and Frameworks for Practical Reasoning," as reprinted in my *Structures of Agency* (New York: Oxford University Press, 2004); and Michael E. Bratman, "Dynamics of Sociality," *Midwest Studies in Philosophy: Shared Intentions and Collective Responsibility* XXX (2006): 1–15. Four more recent overview papers of mine—papers on which I draw in various ways in this book—are: "Shared Agency," in *Philosophy of the Social Sciences: Philosophical Theory and Scientific Practice*, ed. Chris Mantzavinos (Cambridge: Cambridge University Press, 2009); "Modest Sociality and the Distinctiveness of Intention," *Philosophical Studies* 144, no. 1 (2009): 149–165; "Agency, Time, and Sociality," *Proceedings and Addresses of the American Philosophical Association* 84, no. 2 (2010): 7–26; and "The Fecundity of Planning Agency," in *Oxford Studies in Agency and Responsibility, Volume 1*, ed. David Shoemaker. Oxford: Oxford University Press (2013): 47–69.

The thought that it might be worth trying to put these ideas together within a more systematic treatment came from my experience of trying to explain these ideas in a seminar organized by Philip Pettit at Princeton University's Center for Human Values. My thanks to Philip. My recent thinking about these matters has benefited from discussions with very many people; but let me mention in particular discussions with Scott Shapiro, especially when we both had the privilege of being Fellows at the Center for Advanced Study in the Behavioral Sciences in 2003–2004 while working on a joint project on shared agency, and discussions with Facundo Alonso and Margaret Gilbert. I learned a very great deal from a seminar on an earlier draft of this book at the Ohio State University Philosophy Department in March 2011 (organized by Abraham Sesshu Roth), from a workshop on the manuscript at Yale Law School in October 2011 (organized by Scott Shapiro), and from discussions of the manuscript in my graduate seminar at Stanford in winter term 2012. I am also much indebted to Maike Albertzart, Facundo Alonso, Stephen Butterfill, Luca Ferrero, Natalie Gold, Pamela Hieronymi, Shelly Kagan, Christopher Kutz, Kirk Ludwig, Abraham Roth, Carol Rovane, Olivier Roy, Kevin Toh, Paul Weirich, and Gideon Yaffe for written comments on earlier drafts of this manuscript. I also benefitted from comments from anonymous reviewers of an earlier draft of this manuscript. I have had many profitable conversations about central elements of this manuscript with many people in addition to those already mentioned. Though no doubt this is an (unintentionally!) incomplete list, let me thank, in particular, Samuel Asarnow, Joshua Cohen, Jules Coleman, Kit Fine, Randall Harp, Frank Hindriks, Christine Korsgaard, Daniel Markovits, Seamus Miller, Carlos Núñez, Philip Pettit, Grant Rozeboom, John Searle, Matthew Noah Smith, Michael Tomasello, and Han van Wietmarschen. Many thanks also to Samuel Asarnow for help in preparing the manuscript and the bibliography, and to Carlos Núñez for preparing the index. And I have benefited greatly from a pair of fellowships at the Stanford Humanities Center and, in the early years of this work on shared agency, support from Stanford's Center for the Study of Language and Information and a fellowship at the Center for Advanced Study in the Behavioral Sciences. I am deeply grateful to these many people and institutions for their invaluable aid and support.

And, as before, my deepest and most heartfelt thanks go to Susan, Gregory, and Scott.

SHARED AGENCY

1

SOCIALITY AND PLANNING AGENCY

1. Modest sociality and the continuity thesis

Human beings act together in characteristic ways, and these forms of shared activity matter to us a great deal. They matter to us intrinsically: think of friendship and love, singing duets, dancing together, and the joys of conversation. And they matter to us instrumentally: think about the usefulness of conversation and of how we frequently manage to work together to achieve complex goals, from building buildings to putting on a play to establishing results in the sciences. Such forms of sociality are deeply involved in our lives. And, indeed, some have conjectured that our capacities for certain forms of shared activity set us apart as a species.[1]

My project in this book is to reflect on such basic forms of sociality: What concepts do we need to understand them adequately? In what do these forms of sociality consist? How are they related to relevant forms of individual agency? What norms are central to such sociality? How precisely are these norms related to such sociality? How are these social norms related to norms that apply in the first instance to individual agency?

My pursuit in this book of these and related questions has a trio of interrelated aims, an underlying conjecture, and an important limitation.

The first aim is in the tradition of philosophy as conceptual articulation and innovation. The aim is to provide elements of a sufficiently clear and articulated framework of ideas to help support careful and fruitful theorizing about these basic forms of sociality both in philosophy and in the wide range of other domains and disciplines within which these phenomena are of significance.

The second aim is in the tradition of philosophical concerns with the metaphysics of human agency and its place in the natural world. What are the basic elements of the world that constitute our shared agency, how are these elements related to those that constitute our individual agency, and how are these elements located in the natural causal order?

Finally, my third aim is in the tradition of normative philosophy. Are there norms that are in some way fundamental to shared agency? If so, how precisely are they related to shared agency, and how are they related to norms of individual rationality?

My aims, then, are conceptual, metaphysical, and normative. And my pursuit of these aims is shaped by the conjecture that a rich account of individual planning agency facilitates the step to basic forms of sociality. We begin with an underlying model of individual planning agency, one I have called the *planning theory*.[2] And my guiding conjecture is that such individual planning agency brings with it sufficiently rich structures—conceptual, metaphysical, and normative—that the further step to basic forms of sociality, while significant and demanding, need not involve fundamentally new elements. There is here a deep *continuity* between individual and social agency. This is an aspect of the *fecundity of planning structures*, the idea that planning structures ground a wide range of fundamental practical capacities that are central to our human lives.[3]

I do not claim that planning agency by itself ensures the capacity for the forms of sociality that will be our focus. There will be theoretical room for planning agents who do not have this social capacity.[4] The claim is only that once such individual planning agency is on board, what further is needed to make the step to such sociality is—in a sense to be explained—conceptually, metaphysically, and normatively conservative. Nor do I claim that appeal to planning structures captures all of the stunning complexity of human agents. Forms of unplanned spontaneity and responsiveness play important roles in our agency. We have complex and frequently opaque emotional lives. We are prey to many different motivational pressures. Self-understanding is in many cases difficult. Wholeheartedness in thought and action can be elusive.[5] And much more could be said about, as Jennifer Rosner has put it, our messiness.[6] My claim is only that planning structures are one salient and theoretically important aspect of the psychology that underlies our agency. In the case of individual agency, such structures play a central role in characteristically human forms of cross-temporal organization and temporally extended agency. And my conjecture here is that versions of these planning structures are also an important part of basic forms of sociality. When we make a fresco together, or dance together, or converse together, or sing together, or build together, or experiment together, or run a give-and-go[7] together, or put on a play together, our activities are shared in ways that, in central cases, deeply involve such planning structures. At the bottom of our capacities both for distinctive forms of temporally extended agency and for distinctive forms of social agency is our capacity for planning agency.

This approach to our shared agency lies in the space between two important alternatives. The first is a commonsense version of the idea of Nash equilibrium in game theory. The idea is that in shared agency each is acting in pursuit of those things she wants or values in part in light of what she believes the other is doing, and where she knows the other's actions depend in part on what the other thinks she will do. Each by her lights does best given what the other does. There is in this sense a strategic equilibrium, an equilibrium in which each sees that the outcome depends in part on the actions of the other, and that those actions of the other depend in part on what the other expects one to do. And all this is public, out in the open—where to be out in the open is, in one common interpretation, to be a matter of common knowledge.[8]

What does it mean to say that all this is common knowledge? There is a large and complex literature here, involving several different approaches.[9] One standard approach appeals to cognitive hierarchies. One way to put this idea is to say that it is common knowledge among A and B that p just when (a) A knows that p, (b) B knows that p, (c) A knows that B knows that p, (d) B knows that A knows that p, (e) A is in an epistemic position to know that (d), (f) B is in an epistemic position to know that (c), and so on—where once we get past (d) the stages of the hierarchy are a matter of what A and B are in an epistemic position to know, not of what they explicitly know.[10] And an underlying idea here is that common knowledge involves some such structure of interrelated cognitive aspects of the minds of relevant individuals.

For present purposes I will mostly work with an intuitive notion of common knowledge. However, when it is useful to have a more specific model of common knowledge on hand, I will appeal to a hierarchical model along the lines just sketched. My hope, though, is that the main points I want to make are available to alternative treatments of common knowledge.

That said, let's return to the model of shared activity as a strategic equilibrium within common knowledge. And here I think there is a fundamental problem. Such mutual adjustment of each to another that is in a context of common knowledge and in strategic equilibrium—while an important phenomenon— seems not by itself to ensure the kind of sociality we are after. When two strangers walk alongside each other down a crowded Fifth Avenue without bumping into each other, their patterns of walking near each other might be in strategic equilibrium in a context of common knowledge: each is acting in pursuit of what she wants in light of her beliefs about how the other is and will be acting, where what the other does depends on his beliefs about what she will do, and all this is out in the open. Each might in this sense be acting strategically in the light of what she values, the expected actions of the other, expectations about the corresponding expectations of the other, and so on. Yet they still might not be engaged together in a shared activity of the sort we are trying to understand—they might not be, in the relevant sense, walking together.[11] There are important aspects of such shared activities that seem not to be captured by such broadly game-theoretic models; our job is to say what those aspects are and how best to understand them.

Agents who are walking together, or singing a duet together, or painting a house together, or having a conversation together, or making dinner together, or building a hut together, or planting a garden together will, we may assume, be capable of employing such strategic reasoning and arriving at such an equilibrium. My claim, though, is that we cannot adequately model the kind of shared activity in which we are here primarily interested as simply a matter of the deployment of such strategic reasoning and a resulting equilibrium, given relevant common knowledge.

Granted, there can be more complex strategic equilibria than this simple one of walking alongside a stranger. Perhaps a boy and a girl on Fifth Avenue, while strangers in the night, each walk down the avenue in a way that aims at ensuring that he or she achieves his or her personal goal of remaining close to the other.[12] Nevertheless, they still might not be engaged in what it is natural to classify as a shared intentional activity of walking together.

This does not mean that the very idea of a kind of equilibrium within common knowledge is not important for understanding sociality. Indeed, the theory I will be developing provides a model of a distinctive kind of shared practical settled-ness within common knowledge. The point is only that what we learn from this example of, as I will say, walking alongside a stranger, is that a strategic equilibrium of the game-theoretic sort just described is by itself too weak to ensure the kind of sociality at issue.

I will return to these matters later. The point now is that reflection on such cases may suggest an alternative approach to articulating what is special about walking together as a shared activity, in contrast with a case of walking alongside a stranger. This alternative approach highlights the condition that the participants in such sociality are each under obligations to the other and are entitled to hold each other accountable for their participation. The idea is that the interconnections characteristic of such sociality essentially involve mutual entitlements to hold the other accountable for playing his role in the shared activity, and mutual obligations, each to the other, that correspond to these entitlements. If we are walking together and you suddenly drop out without my permission I am, it may seem, entitled to object to you. And if we understand these entitlements and associated obligations as not essentially moral, we arrive at an idea that is central to Margaret Gilbert's understanding of shared agency.[13]

Now I agree that mutual obligations are common in cases of adult human shared agency, though I think that these will normally be familiar kinds of moral obligations—in particular, moral obligations associated with promises, assurance and reliance. But I am not convinced such obligations are present in all cases of shared agency. One example, to be discussed later, is a case of shared agency in which each of the parties explicitly insists that in participating they do not mean to be creating relevant obligations—as they say, "no obligations". This and other examples suggest that shared agency is a generic phenomenon and cases of shared agency that involve relevant mutual obligations are a special case. Further, such obligations need not ensure the basic psychological elements of shared agency, since it remains possible for the parties to have no intention to conform to these obligations. (Perhaps the assurances were insincere.) So we cannot provide a full explanation of the normal social functioning involved in human shared agency simply by appeal to such obligations. And finally, there are significant resources— conceptual, metaphysical, and normative—in the territory between these models of, on the one hand, strategic equilibrium and, on the other hand, mutual obligation. We would do well to see if there is a viable theory in that middle territory.

I will return to and try to defend these points in the discussion to follow. I now just want to note that my appeal here to the idea of the fecundity of planning structures aims to provide resources for a view in the space between these two other approaches. It seeks a plan-theoretic view of our shared agency, one that goes beyond appeal to strategic equilibrium but, while it recognizes that mutual obligations are common, does not see such interpersonal normative relations as essential.

Those, anyway, are my three interrelated aims, and my underlying conjecture. The limitation is that my focus will be primarily on the shared intentional activities of small, adult groups in the absence of asymmetric authority relations within those groups, and in which the individuals who are participants remain constant over time. Further, I will bracket complexities introduced by the inclusion of the group within a specific legal institution such as marriage, or incorporation. My interest will be primarily with duets and quartets rather than symphony orchestras with conductors, with small teams of builders rather than large and hierarchical construction companies, with small and informal neighborhood groups rather than county governments, with small group discussion rather than deliberations in the US Senate, and with friendship and love rather than legally constituted marriage. And I will assume that these small groups have a stable membership.

I do not deny that there is an important sense in which there are larger institutional agents like corporations or governments, institutions with hierarchical authority relations, with potential flux in the list of their members, and, perhaps, with an embedded distinction between those participants who are officials of the institution and those who are not.[14] Rather, I hope to gain some insight by focusing initially on the kind of small-scaled shared agency to which I have pointed. Perhaps our theory of small-scale shared agency can, with due adjustment and further additions, be extended to such larger social organizations.[15] But first things first. I will be satisfied here if we can agree on a basic approach to the indicated kind of small-scale case of shared agency—as I will say, the case of *modest sociality*—and leave to other occasions these potential extensions.

My conjecture is that the conceptual, metaphysical, and normative structures central to such modest sociality are—in a sense I aim to explain—continuous with structures of individual planning agency.[16] This is the *continuity thesis*. As we might try saying: once God created individual planning agents and placed those agents in a world in which they have relevant knowledge of each other's minds, nothing fundamentally new—conceptually, metaphysically, or normatively—needs to be added for there to be modest sociality.[17] This is because the further steps from individual planning agents who know about each other's minds, to modest sociality, while substantive and demanding steps, are nevertheless primarily applications of the conceptual, metaphysical, and normative resources already available within our theory of individual planning agency. The deep structure of at least a central form of modest sociality is constituted by elements that are continuous with those at work in the planning theory of our individual agency. So the problem of how our modest sociality is located in the natural world is primarily the problem of how our individual planning agency, in a context of knowledge of the minds of others, is located in the natural world.

Granted, once the resources for modest sociality are available they will many times, especially in the case of adult human agents, interact with norms of interpersonal morality. A full story of modest sociality will need to shed light on these interactions, and that is an issue to which I will turn in Chapters 3 and 5. But the conjecture of the continuity thesis is that the deep structure of modest sociality can be articulated without explicit appeal to such interpersonal norms of moral obligation and the like.

In saying this I am assuming that the conceptual, metaphysical, and normative resources needed to model relevant forms of common knowledge are available within our model of individual planning agency. However, since, as noted, I do not try to defend a specific theory of the nature of common knowledge, this assumption is not defended here. If it were to turn out that this assumption is incorrect—that some further, fundamental resource is needed—then we would need to qualify the continuity thesis accordingly. But such a qualified continuity thesis would still maintain what is the central point here, namely that the theory of individual planning agency puts us in a position to provide a model of modest sociality without the introduction of fundamentally new practical elements that go beyond whatever cognitive structures are involved in common knowledge.

Let me try briefly to contrast this continuity thesis—whether qualified or not—with approaches taken in the work of John Searle and Margaret Gilbert, work I will be discussing in more detail later. Gilbert, Searle, and I are in agreement that there is something very important involved in cases of modest sociality, something that goes beyond a mere strategic equilibrium within common knowledge. I aim to say what these distinctive aspects of our sociality are in a way that is broadly continuous with the resources—conceptual, metaphysical, and normative—of the planning theory of individual agency. In contrast, both of these other philosophers see the step from individual to shared agency as involving a new basic practical resource.

In Searle's view, and as we will see in more detail later, what is needed is a new attitude of "we-intention".[18] In Gilbert's view, and as we will see in more detail later, what is needed is a new relation of "joint commitment" between the participants, a relation that necessitates distinctive mutual obligations.[19] In each case the cited new element is a practical element that is not just a matter of common knowledge and is a purported new primitive element in our shared agency. And both philosophers then try to understand larger institutions in ways that draw substantially on the new element that they cite as central to small-scale shared agency.[20] My approach, in contrast, begins by distinguishing, in the individual case, between simple goal-directed agency and planning agency. Once individual planning agency is on board, the step to modest sociality need not involve a fundamental discontinuity[21]—which is not to say that all planning agents have the capacity for such sociality. But this planning approach leaves open how best to move from a theory of modest sociality to a theory of larger institutions.

2. Shared intention, individual intention

Suppose then that you and I are painting a house together. What makes this a shared intentional activity? We could imagine a contrast case in which we each intentionally go through the same motions as we do when we paint the house together, and yet there is no shared intentional activity. Perhaps we are each set only on our individual painting project and respond to each other only with an eye to avoiding collisions. While each of us acts, and acts intentionally, in a context that involves the other, ours is not a shared intentional activity: we are only painting alongside each other. Echoing Wittgenstein's question about the difference, in the individual case, between my arm's rising and my raising it,[22] we can ask: what is the difference between such a contrast case and corresponding shared intentional activity? In the case of individual intentional human action, we can see the difference from a contrast case as involving an explanatory role of relevant intentions of the individual agent.[23] As a first approximation, I propose an analogous view of the shared case: the difference in the case of shared agency involves an appropriate explanatory role of relevant *shared* intentions. Our painting together is a shared intentional activity, roughly, when we paint together because we share an intention so to act.

Granted, there are also phenomena of group or collective agency, broadly construed, within which the distinctive social organization is grounded in causal mechanisms of a very different sort than that of shared intention. A swarm of bees, or a flock of birds, may act as a unit that tracks a goal, yet ideas of intention—individual or shared—are unlikely to get at the relevant explanatory mechanisms.[24] And perhaps certain human crowds are like this. Again, and as Scott Shapiro has emphasized, there are cases of "massively shared agency" in which the mechanism of organization is, so to speak, outsourced rather than internal to the participants themselves.[25] Think of the coordinated activities of the thousands of employees around the world involved in making iPhones. Here the source of the organization is not likely to be an intention shared by the participants. Instead, the complex social coordination is externally orchestrated by a managerial group. Nevertheless, my conjecture is that in central cases of small scale human shared activity—cases naturally described as ones of shared intentional activity—the concept of shared intention does point to important, internal explanatory structures, and that it is these internal explanatory structures that are central to our answer to our social analogue of Wittgenstein's question.

What then is shared intention? And what is an appropriate explanatory relation? These questions will occupy me throughout this book. Here in this first chapter I will focus primarily on the first question about shared intention. Later, in Chapters 2 and 3, I will focus both on shared intention and on the cited explanatory relation (as I call it, the *connection condition*).

As noted, my approach to shared intention is part of an effort to forge a path between two extremes—a model of strategic equilibrium within common knowledge, and a model of distinctive interpersonal obligations and entitlements. The middle path I seek is an augmented individualism. It is an individualism that builds on a rich story of our individual planning agency, one that goes beyond the desire-belief model in philosophy[26] and the associated utility-probability model in some areas of social science. And it is an approach to shared intention that augments the model of individual planning agency by highlighting special contents of and interrelations between the plan states of such individual agents.

Such an augmented individualism is not dismissive or debunking of phenomena of modest sociality—far from it. The idea, rather, is both to highlight the significance of these social phenomena and to provide a theoretically rich structure of conceptual, metaphysical, and normative resources in terms of which we can more deeply understand these phenomena. And the conjecture is that these resources can be found broadly within our theory of our individual planning agency.

This approach takes the intentions of individuals seriously as basic and distinctive elements of individual human agency, elements that go beyond the ordinary desires and beliefs[27] characteristic of simple purposive agency. Such intentions are embedded in coordinating plans that play basic roles in the temporally extended structures that are characteristic of individual human agency. This is the planning theory of the intentions of individuals.

Later I will say more about the plan-theoretic features of intention. For now, let me emphasize a general conjecture that is in the background. The conjecture is that a theoretically fruitful strategy in the philosophy of action is to try to understand important aspects of our agency by building on the planning theory. This is the idea, noted earlier, of the fecundity of planning structures, the idea that a sufficiently rich model of the planning structures that are common in individual human agency helps illuminate important aspects of human agency. These aspects of our agency include our capacity for complex, temporally extended activity, our capacity for self-governance, and our capacity for sociality.[28] I have elsewhere explored this strategy as an approach to temporally extended agency and individual self-governance.[29] Here my primary target is modest sociality.[30] And in the background is the idea that the step from desire-belief to planning structures, while of great significance, need not introduce any new obstacles to locating our agency in the natural order.

When, in light of this strategy, I turn in particular to shared intention, I try to see it as consisting of relevant plan-embedded intentions of each of the individual participants, in a suitable context and suitably interconnected. As we might say: the *shared-ness* or *joint-ness* of shared intention consists of relevant contents of the plan states of each and relevant interconnections and interdependencies between the planning psychologies of each, all in relevant contexts. This augmented individualism depends then on a rich model of the individual agent as a planning agent whose agency is temporally extended.

The planning theory aims to understand plan states primarily in terms of their roles in the cross-temporal organization of individual human agency. As indicated, these planning structures not only help support intrapersonal organization over time, but also interpersonal social organization. This is an aspect of the fecundity of planning agency. We need not, however, see the social roles of these planning structures as undermining the claim that these plan states are, fundamentally, states of the individual planning agents that are characterized, at the most basic level, in terms of their roles in temporally extended individual agency.

Granted, much work in the philosophy of mind has argued that our ordinary ways of specifying the contents of the attitudes sometimes draw on features outside of the individual whose attitudes are at issue. These external features may include the causal context of the use of natural kind terms or of names[31] and/or relevant linguistic practices.[32] However, the kind of augmented individualism I seek is officially neutral about these debates about the nature of content. What is crucial to this augmented individualism is not whether the contents of the attitudes of the individuals involve appeal to elements outside those individuals. What is crucial, rather, is that shared intention consists primarily of relevant interrelated attitudes (especially, intentions) of these individuals, and that the contents of the attitudes that are constitutive of basic cases of shared intention need not in general essentially involve the very idea of shared intention (though on occasion they may).

3. I intend that we *J*: A first pass

In developing this plan-theoretic approach to shared agency, what we will see is that though the contents of the intentions of each that are central to shared intention need not involve the very idea of shared intention, they will nevertheless have a distinctive character. In particular, in contrast with ordinary cases of intending to act, shared intention, at least in central cases, involves intentions of the individuals whose contents appeal to the group activity. Our shared intention to paint together involves your intention that *we* paint and my intention that *we* paint. These intentions of each in favor of our painting help explain the characteristic dispositions of each in favor of taking steps in support of our painting, and eschewing options incompatible with our painting—where, in each case, our painting includes the activities of both of us.

This violates the *own-action condition* on the content of intention. According to this own-action condition it is always true that the *subject* of an intention is the *intended agent* of the intended activity. And it does seem initially plausible that intentions should respect some such constraint. Just what lies behind this initial intuition—and what its force is, on reflection—is a matter to which I will return in Chapter 3. Here I just want to acknowledge that the view I will be developing does involve rejecting this own-action condition, since it appeals to intentions of each individual participant that *they* (the group) act.

The apparent problem here is not initially a problem for talk of *our* intention to do something together. After all, when I say that *we* intend to paint together, the intention I report is *our* shared intention in favor of *our* shared action.[33] But my proposal is to understand our shared intention by appeal, *inter alia*, to *my* intention that we paint. Since that violates the own-action condition something needs to be said.[34]

One reaction to this is in the spirit of work of John Searle.[35] As noted, Searle focuses on what he calls "we-intention". What he means by this is *not* what I mean in talking about *our* intention. The fact that *we* intend to paint involves me, you, and relations between us. In contrast, Searle's we-intentions are attitudes in the head of an *individual*, though attitudes that concern the activity of a supposed "we". You could have a we-intention, in Searle's sense, if you were in fact the only person in the world, but thought there were others with whom you might act. A Searlean we-intention is, then, a candidate for the intentions of individual participants that together help constitute a shared intention, though Searle himself does not, to my knowledge, systematically discuss how the we-intentions of different participants need to be interrelated for there to be (in my sense) shared intention.

Searle's we-intentions violate the own-action condition. This may be a reason why he claims that we-intentions are not just ordinary intentions with a special *content*, a content that involves the activity of a supposed "we". We-intentions are, rather, a special intending *attitude*, to be distinguished from the ordinary attitude of intending involved in individual agency.[36] If we suppose that the ordinary attitude of intending is subject to the own-action condition, and if we countenance we-intentions, then it will be natural to see we-intentions as distinctive attitudes rather than as ordinary intentions with a special content. In this way we can be led from reflection on the conceptual resources at work in the content of the attitude to a view about the metaphysics of mind, a view that posits a distinctive attitude of we-intention and a corresponding breakdown in the continuity thesis.

An alternative approach is to emphasize the commonalities in the attitudes involved in intending to act and intending that we act, and to see the differences as deriving from differences in content and distinctive features of the first-person singular as it appears in certain of these contents. Just as I can believe that *I* will do something, I can also believe that *we* will do something—in both cases what I have is an ordinary belief. On this alternative approach the situation is similar in the case of intention. This approach allows us to draw directly on what the planning theory tells us about the nature of ordinary intention. In contrast, this is apparently blocked by Searle's strategy, since his we-intentions are not themselves ordinary intentions.

In response, might Searle insist that, though "we-intentions are a primitive phenomenon," there is a kind of isomorphism between we-intentions and the intentions described by the planning theory, an isomorphism that allows us to understand we-intentions using resources from the planning theory?[37] Could Searle say that this is why we-intentions function in ways analogous to those specified by the planning theory? Well, on the one hand, insofar as we hold onto the view that we-intentions are fundamentally different from the attitudes described by the planning theory, it is not clear what gives us the right to assume that there is an isomorphism that can play this strong theoretical role. On the other hand, suppose that we can support the idea that we-intentions function in ways that are isomorphic to the ways in which intentions function within the planning theory. But then why not say—as I am saying—that we-intentions are indeed intentions of the sort described by the planning theory, though intentions whose contents differ from ordinary intentions to perform one's own action? The distinction is not between two fundamentally different attitudes, but between two different kinds of contents of the attitude of intending, an attitude described by the planning theory.

In any case, this latter conservative resistance against positing fundamentally new and primitive attitudes will be characteristic of the approach I will be taking. My proposal will be that we locate both intending to act and intending that we act in largely similar ways within the nexus of roles and norms highlighted by the planning theory of intention (roles and norms to be discussed later). Both intending to act and intending that we act are forms of intending, as that is characterized by the planning theory—though of course they also have different contents and associated differences in role. Both intending to act and intending that we act play plan-theoretic roles and are subject to associated norms of plan rationality. And, in the end, we should judge this more conservative strategy—in contrast with Searle's appeal to a primitive phenomenon of we-intention—by seeing how it contributes to the explanation and understanding of basic forms of sociality.

That said, there remain significant concerns about this appeal to intending that we J. I will address these concerns in Chapters 2 and 3. But first I need to say more about my overall model of shared intention; and to do that I need first to return to the intentions of individuals.

4. Individual planning agency: roles and norms

Given the importance of planning structures to my approach to shared agency, I need to explain in more detail how I understand the intentions and plans of individual agents. This is what I will do in these next two sections, after which I will return to our central concern with shared agency.

According to the planning theory, intentions of individuals are plan states: they are embedded in forms of planning central to our internally organized temporally extended agency and to our associated abilities to achieve complex goals across time, especially given our cognitive limitations. One's plan states guide, coordinate, and organize one's thought and action both at a time and over time. For this to work one's plan states need to involve a view of the present and the future that is both consistent and sufficiently detailed to support effective agency. This sometimes involves being settled on one option rather than incompatible alternatives even though it also would have been sensible instead to be settled on a different alternative. Plan states play these organizing roles, both synchronically and diachronically, in part by way of a hierarchical structure: plans concerning ends embed plans concerning means and preliminary steps. And these hierarchical structures will normally involve a characteristic partiality: one's plan may favor E and yet so far not include means to E even if one knows that as time goes by one will need to settle on some such means.

Associated with this web of plan-like roles are characteristic norms of intention rationality. Primary among these norms are norms of consistency, agglomeration, means-end coherence, and stability: intentions are to be internally consistent, and consistent with one's beliefs; and it should be possible to agglomerate one's various intentions into a larger intention that is consistent in these ways. Intentions in favor of ends engage a demand, roughly, to settle, as needed and in a timely way, on means and preliminary steps. This is a demand of means-end coherence. And while intentions are subject to reconsideration and revision, they are also subject to pressures in favor of stability over time.[38]

These norms of intention rationality are associated with the characteristic roles of intention in two interrelated ways. The first is explanatory: these norms enter indirectly into a standard explanation of the normal ways in which these plan states play these roles in planning agency. In particular, we can suppose that in the case of individual planning agency the standard way in which these norms enter into such explanations is that their (at least) implicit or tacit acceptance by those planning agents helps explain how these plan states play these roles;[39] and such (at least) implicit or tacit acceptance of these norms is partly constitutive of planning agency. For example, intentions in favor of ends tend to issue in reasoning that aims at settling on means, and this is in part because the agent's associated thinking is guided by an accepted norm of means-end coherence. And intentions concerning the future tend stably to structure thought and action over time, and this is in part because of an accepted norm in favor of intention stability.

This idea of an accepted norm is tied to the idea of a disposition to see divergence from the norm as a mistake, a breakdown. If, for example, a planning agent realizes that her intention to A and her intention to B are not co-realizable, she will think she has made a mistake. A common manifestation of this will be a kind of "Darn it!" reaction. And this reaction will tend to lead to efforts to revise so as newly to come into relevant conformity with the norm.

These accepted norms focus on the agent's own psychic economy—they concern the consistency, agglomerativity, coherence, and stability of the agent's own intentions. Criticisms of violations of these norms can occur within the context of "normative discussion" among multiple participants.[40] I can criticize you for being incoherent in relevant ways. But we can recognize this potential involvement in our sociality of the individual's acceptance of these norms of intention rationality and yet still draw on the idea of such norm acceptances without thereby making an essential appeal to the very idea of shared intentional agency. Indeed, we can leave open the possibility of a planning agent— Robinson Crusoe, perhaps—whose acceptance of these norms of intention rationality guides his individual planning even in the absence of participation in social normative discussion. We can have a rich concept of the acceptance of these norms of individual intention rationality without being guilty of an unacceptable circularity when we come to use this concept in our theory of shared intentional agency.

A second way in which these norms of intention rationality are associated with the cited roles of intention involves the thought that these norms really do have normative force or significance.[41] This thought is part of an explanation of the stability under reflection of the planning system. And here the planning theory seeks to draw on substantive normative reflection in order to explain what gives these characteristic norms their distinctive force or significance. In this way the planning theory seeks to defuse the concern that it is less plausible as an explanatory theory insofar as it ascribes to us the acceptance of norms that do not pass reflective muster.[42]

As I see it, a central part of this normative story will articulate the relation between general guidance by and conformity to such norms, and reliably realizing the characteristic coordinating, organizing, and settling roles of planning. And such a normative story will go on to explain what is good about reliably realizing these roles. The idea will be that being guided by one's acceptance of these norms is an important element in how these roles are normally realized, and that it is important to us that these roles indeed be realized.

This is to begin to explain the normative significance of these norms in part by appeal to the importance to us of the general functioning their acceptance supports. We can also ask further whether there is something of distinctive and non-instrumental significance in the satisfaction of these planning norms in each particular case to which they apply. And I have elsewhere defended a version of an affirmative answer to this question, one that appeals to the role of planning attitudes in self-governance.[43] For present purposes, however, we can rest content with a pair of ideas: First, the planning theory involves both a descriptive account of the underlying, accepted norms, and an account of the normative force or significance of those norms. Second, we can understand this normative significance both by appeal to the importance of the general forms of functioning the acceptance of these norms supports, and by appeal to the distinctive, non-instrumental significance of the satisfaction of these norms in the particular case.[44]

Might the planning theory instead retreat to a "positivistic" theory that simply describes how the planning economy works, and what norms are accepted by creatures who are characterized by such a planning economy, without a concern with whether those norms do indeed have normative force? Well, since we who are theorizing about such planning agency are also ourselves planning agents, there is an instability for us in such a purely positivistic account. We ourselves, as planning agents, treat these underlying norms as having some sort of normative significance. Since our theory of planning agency is a theory of *our* planning agency, there will be pressure on our theory to ask whether that treatment of these norms makes sense, and if so why. After all, one of the lessons of recent work in social psychology is that there are patterns of thought that are quite common in human agency but which would not likely be endorsed by critical reflection.[45] Further, given an account of the normative significance of these norms we will have reason to expect that these planning structures will in general be stable under reflection by planning agents like us.[46] And, as noted, such a view about the reflective stability of these planning structures will itself be an element in our overall theory of planning agency.

The planning theory, then, will appeal to characteristic roles of plan states, to an explanatory role of norms in explaining those roles, and, in particular, to forms of norm acceptance by individual planning agents that help explain those roles. And it will try to explain the normative force or significance of those characteristic norms. In this sense, on the planning theory, the norms characteristic of planning agency have both an explanatory face and a normative face. In the case of individual planning agency, the explanatory face of these norms consists in the ways in which their acceptance by individual planning agents helps support characteristic planning roles in their temporally extended agency. An account of the normative face of these norms will appeal in part to these explanatory roles of these norms and to the importance of the functioning that they thereby help support. And such an account of the normative force of these norms promises to help explain the reflective stability of these planning structures.

5. Individual planning agency: Further ideas

The planning theory sees the intentions of individuals as plan states. Such plan states are related to but different from ordinary desires, ordinary beliefs, and ordinary evaluations. Ordinary desires are not subject to the same norms of consistency and means-end coherence. It is, after all, part of the human condition to have desires for different things that, one knows, are not co-possible. And simply desiring something does not yet put me under rational pressure to settle on means to it.

Nor are intentions merely ordinary beliefs about one's own present or future conduct. Knowing myself as I do, I might now be confident that when I am this evening faced with the temptation of a second glass of wine at dinner I will give in to that temptation, and yet I might still not now intend to drink that second glass of wine this evening. Again, simply believing that, given my social awkwardness, I will offend someone at the party does not amount to intending to offend. In particular, my belief does not pose a practical problem of settling on means to doing that. Indeed, even if I am taking steps aimed at preventing this upshot, I can still be resigned in my belief that I will nevertheless offend someone; whereas taking such preventative steps would not normally be compatible with intending. Finally, I might believe that in intentionally X-ing I will produce a certain causal upshot, Y, without intending to produce Y. (A much discussed example: A bomber intends to destroy a weapons factory in order to promote the war effort, expects thereby to destroy a nearby school, but does not intend to destroy the school. After all, he would not go back and try again if somehow the school remained intact despite the destruction of the factory.)[47]

Turn now to the relation between intention and evaluation. Intentions will normally conform to the agent's judgments about what would be best, or the agent's rankings of options from best to worst. But intentions are not to be identified with such evaluative judgments or rankings. There are many cases of intending A while judging that an alternative B is as good, or ranking B as high in one's evaluative ranking, or just being unsure about which option is best. There are cases of judging B best and yet still being undecided. And there are weak-willed intentions that are counter to what one judges best or ranks highest in one's evaluative ranking.

A key point here, as noted earlier, is that one's intentions and plans many times involve a selection of one of a number of alternatives, each of which is seen by the agent as adequately supported by relevant considerations. This can happen in Buridan's ass cases, in which one forms an intention in the face of what one sees as equally desirable options. It can happen in cases in which one sees several options as incomparable. Sartre's case of the boy who must decide between a life helping his mother and a life with the Free French is a classic example.[48] And it can happen in "Lady or the Tiger" cases in which one knows that one of several options is superior but does not know which one that is.[49]

This returns us to the conjecture that we best understand intention not as ordinary desire or belief or evaluative judgment or evaluative ranking, but rather in terms of characteristic roles and norms in our individual planning agency. In the previous section I briefly sketched a model of these roles and norms. Here let me note twelve further ideas that are part of the conjecture that intentions are plan states, ideas that will be in the background of my planning theory of modest sociality.

(1) As noted earlier, intentions help constitute coordinating plans that are normally partial. Such partiality is central for agents who, like us, have significant limits of mental resources.[50] Given this characteristic partiality, and a norm of means-end coherence, such plans will need to be filled in as time goes by. In particular, as elements of such partial, coordinating plans, intentions pose problems of means and preliminary steps, problems that

need to be solved in a timely way if one is to avoid means-end incoherence. And, given norms of agglomeration and consistency, prior intentions constrain the formation of other intentions by filtering out of deliberation options whose performance would be inconsistent with one's prior intentions, given one's beliefs. In these ways such prior intentions help provide continuity and organization over time and, if all goes well, eventually control relevant conduct.

(2) Sometimes these plan states will have a certain generality: one can have an intention to buckle up one's seat belt whenever one drives, to have only one beer at dinners, to give the correct change, to avoid deception, not to give in to anger. These general intentions are policies. Such polices, while general in their content, will frequently have implicit unless-clauses: my policy will not enjoin buckling up in an emergency situation. In this way such policies will normally exhibit a characteristic defeasibility: they will not be policies to act in cited ways no matter what. This means that in special circumstances the application of the policy to the particular case will sensibly be blocked in a way that does not entail that the agent has abandoned that policy.[51]

(3) One can also have policies about what to treat as having more or less weight in the context of certain relevant deliberation.[52] The boy in Sartre's case might arrive at a policy of giving more weight in his relevant deliberations to the political cause of the Free French, in contrast with the interests of his mother. He might arrive at such a policy in response to the need for a settled commitment, despite the apparent noncomparability of the different forms of life between which he must choose. Or he might be struck by the broad disagreement in reflective views of the relative importance of loyalty to family and loyalty to a political cause. Since he nevertheless sees the need for some sort of settled commitment, he might, out of a kind of modesty or humility of judgment, eschew a judgment of evaluative superiority but settle instead only on a relevant policy about relative weights.[53]

The idea, then, is that one might sensibly settle on a relevant policy about relative weights for certain deliberative contexts without forming a corresponding, intersubjectively accountable judgment about evaluative superiority.[54] While such policies about weights will frequently be associated with judgments of value, they need not strictly correspond to a prior evaluative or normative judgment. Such policies about weights may settle matters in response to underdetermination by such judgments; and such underdetermination may be a reflection of supposed noncomparability and/or of modesty or humility of intersubjectively accountable judgment in the face of disagreement.

(4) Given the characteristic defeasibility of policies, there is room here also for defeasibility in policies about weights. Perhaps the policy of Sartre's young man to give more weight to the political interests of the Free French is defeasible in the sense that in certain extraordinary circumstances (a direct attack on his mother's house, perhaps) the application of this policy to his practical reasoning would be blocked and he would not, in this special context, give such weight to the Free French. Nevertheless, much of his relevant practical reasoning will be shaped in characteristic ways by his (albeit, defeasible) policy to give more weight to the Free French.

(5) Intentions can exhibit a kind of reflexivity. I can intend that I do something in part because of this intention. Indeed, a number of philosophers have argued that intentions to act are quite generally reflexive.[55] But we do not need to accept this very broad claim to allow that sometimes intentions are reflexive; it is this latter, weaker idea that I will accept here.

There is such reflexivity of intention when what one intends includes the guiding role of that very intention. Sometimes this is simply a matter of intending that one's intention be effective. But sometimes one intends that one's intention be effective because one supposes that there is some distinctive value that favors that role of one's intention. And this kind of reflexivity might be exhibited by policies about weights. One may sometimes suppose that given that one has a policy of giving weight to X, there is something distinctive to be said in favor of following through and giving X such weight, since there is something distinctive to be said in favor of governing one's life by appeal to one's basic practical commitments, such as this very policy about weights.[56] So one's policy can sometimes be along these lines: give more weight to X in part because of the self-governance-related merits of giving such weight to X, merits that derive from my acceptance of this very policy.[57] Sartre's young man might then have a policy of giving more weight to the political cause of the Free French in part because of the distinctive significance of governing his life by appeal to his own basic practical commitments, including this one.[58]

(6) Return to stability. The norm of stability in part concerns the reconsideration of intentions already formed. We normally retain our prior

intentions unless we reconsider them. Reconsideration, however, takes time and uses other mental resources; and reconsideration may require, in the pursuit of coordination, rethinking various other, related courses of action on which one had earlier settled. So there is frequently reason not to reconsider, both because of the direct costs of reconsideration and because of risks of undermining coordination previously forged. This is not to say, however, that we normally deliberate about whether to reconsider. Instead, so as not to use deliberative resources inefficiently, we frequently depend on general, nondeliberative habits and strategies about when to reconsider. And given a somewhat reliable environment, habits and strategies that to some extent favor nonreconsideration will be likely, in the long run, to be conducive to the overall effectiveness of our temporally extended agency.

It is also true that once one has embarked on an intended course of action there will frequently be a snowball effect: frequently things will as a result change in ways that support further reasons to continue with what one intends.[59] One will, say, be closer to completing what one intended than one was before one began.

Once one does reconsider a prior intention, does the fact that up to now one has been so intending have its own normative significance? Well, a general habit or strategy of giving one's prior intentions a kind of default status in one's practical thinking seems likely to be broadly supportive of the temporal organization of our agency. I have also argued elsewhere—though this is controversial, and I will not try to develop the point here—that in the particular case the default stability of such a prior intention is normally an element in a kind of self-governance over time that we value.[60]

(7) We should distinguish intentions from the more general phenomenon of a goal. This is because we can have, and act on, goals that we do not see as subject to a demand for agglomeration. Perhaps my goal in filling out a certain admissions form is to gain admission to Stanford Law School. When I turn to the form from UCLA, my goal is gaining admission to UCLA Law School. But I know, let us suppose, that these law schools coordinate admissions, and so it is not possible to gain admission to both law schools, though it is possible to gain admission to each. So I, quite sensibly, do not have—and indeed reject—the goal of gaining admission to both. In this way such goals differ from intentions, since intentions are, we have said, subject to a demand of being capable of being agglomerated

without violating the consistency demand. Intentions are a special kind of goal state—namely, a plan state—and plan states are subject, in particular, to the cited demand for agglomeration and consistency.[61]

(8) If all goes well, planning structures induce cross-temporal referential connections that are both forward and backward looking. My present plan to go to Boston next week at least implicitly refers to my later, then-present-directed intention to go by getting on the airplane; and my later intention at least implicitly refers back to my earlier intention. Further, the normal stability of such intentions over time helps support a coordinated flow of activity over time. These cross-temporal constancies and referential connections help support a temporally extended structure of partial plans that can provide a background framework for further deliberation aimed at filling in these plans as need be and as time goes by. And this further deliberation is shaped in part by rational pressures in the direction of means-end coherence, intention-belief consistency, agglomeration, and stability. In these ways, a planning agent's purposive activity over time is typically embedded within interwoven structures of partial, referentially interlocking, hierarchical, and somewhat stable plan states, and in modes of further deliberation and planning that are motivated and framed by these plan states.

This idea of cross-temporally stable and referentially interlocking attitudes is familiar from the Lockean tradition of reflection on personal identity over time.[62] A central idea of that tradition is that such identity over time essentially involves overlapping strands of continuities of attitude and broadly referential connections across attitudes.[63] And what we have seen is that the standard functioning of intentions in planning agency involves such Lockean cross-temporal ties.

(9) The claim is not that the intention-like roles I have been highlighting are realized in all forms of agency, or that the associated norms on intention apply to all agents. Not all agents are planning agents. There can be purposive agents—dogs and cats, perhaps—who do not have the organizational resources of planning agency. But it seems plausible that we—adult humans—are, normally, planning agents, and that this is central to characteristic forms of cross-temporal organization in our lives. The planning theory is a theory about the nature of intentions understood as central elements in this fundamental form of human, temporally extended agency. Such intentions bring with them a complex nexus of roles and

norms that is characteristic of planning agency. And these structures go
well beyond simple, temporally local desire-belief purposive agency. So it
seems reasonable to see intentions, so understood, as distinctive elements
of the psychic economy of planning agency. This is the distinctiveness of
intention.

(10) This emphasis on planning structures may seem to point to a car-
icature of human agents as constantly planning, eschewing spontaneity,
and rigidly following through with prior plans. And I agree there is a dan-
ger here of arriving at a one-sided picture of human agency. It is a remark-
able fact about human agents that they have capacities that help to support
and to constitute deep forms of cross-temporal (and, as we will see, social)
organization. And it seems that planning capacities are central here. But of
course these planning capacities are embedded in a complex psychic
economy that also involves abilities to characterize one's plans in sche-
matic and conceptually open ways,[64] and to be spontaneous and flexible as
time goes by. A basic challenge for a theory of human agency will be to do
justice both to the centrality of planning in the constitution and support of
fundamental forms of organization, and to our important capacities for
conceptual openness, spontaneity, and flexibility. And here it will be natural to think about our agency in broadly virtue-theoretic ways, and appeal
to relevant practical virtues that are involved in well-functioning planning
agency.

(11) The planning roles I am highlighting are primarily roles of intention in temporally downstream psychic functioning, including further reasoning and action. They are downstream roles in organizing, stabilizing,
coordinating, and making effective our temporally extended activity. They
are roles that involve characteristic forms of selecting, tracking, and filtering, and in many of these temporally downstream roles prior intentions
shape further, later deliberation—as when a prior intention in favor of
E structures further reasoning about means to E. So a full story of these
downstream roles will include a story of the roles of intentions in shaping
such further deliberation.

Of course, intentions do not only shape further deliberation; they are
also typically themselves an issue of prior deliberation. So a full theory of
intention will also need to be in part a theory of the nature of the deliberation from which intentions are sometimes an issue. And indeed, I
have argued elsewhere that our precise understanding of the way in
which intention is an output of deliberation is central to our understanding of the important distinction between intending A and believing

one will A as a result of something one intends.[65] Nevertheless, in its effort to say what intentions are, and how they are distinctive, the planning theory highlights in particular the temporally downstream roles of intentions as elements in partial, coordinating plans—plans that serve, *inter alia*, as inputs to later practical reasoning. The step from simple purposive agency to planning agency is in large part a step to the capacity for attitudes that play these interrelated forward-looking temporally downstream roles in organizing our temporally extended thought and action.

(12) This planning model of these forward-looking roles is a model of what we can plausibly call "the will" in our temporally extended agency. This is a model of the complex diachronic roles that are characteristic of the will, roles that can themselves be part of the natural, causal order within which we seek to locate our agency. In this sense the planning theory is a modest and demystifying theory of the will.

6. Creature construction

We can see the step from simple, temporally local purposive agency to temporally extended planning agency, as a step in what Paul Grice calls "creature construction".[66] The aim of creature construction is to understand more complex forms of agency by building step-wise from simpler forms of agency. We build more complex structures upon a foundation of simpler structures in ways that respond to identifiable problems and issues that arise in the context of those simpler structures. And my proposal is that we build structures of planning agency on top of structures of purposive agency in response to problems of coordination and organization over time (and, as we will see, socially). We do this in a way that is responsive to our cognitive, conative, and affective limitations—where this includes limits on the time we have for reflection given the pressure for action, limits on the complexity of the contents of our thinking, and limits of knowledge about the future.[67] We do this in a way that is responsive to our need many times to choose among conflicting options in the face of underdetermination of our choice by relevant considerations. And we do this in a way that is responsive to our needs for self-control and self-management in the pursuit of organization and coordination and in the face of conflicting sources of motivation.[68]

The idea is not that this is how our planning agency actually emerged within an evolutionary, historical process.[69] The idea is only that such a hypothetical series of constructed creatures can help us understand complex elements of our actual planning agency, elements that are compatible with our limitations and build on but go beyond less complex elements in ways that respond to basic concerns with cross-temporal coordination.

When we see planning agency as such a step in creature construction, it will be natural then to see the step from individual planning agency to shared agency as yet a further step in creature construction. And that is what I will do. Further, I will argue that this step to shared agency can be conceptually, metaphysically, and normatively more conservative than the step from individual, temporally local purposive agency to individual temporally extended planning agency.

But why build shared agency on top of, in particular, individual *planning* agency? Could there not be forms of joint or collective agency whose participants were simple purposive agents and not themselves planning agents? In alluding to swarms and flocks, I have already granted that the answer to the second question is a qualified "yes". Nevertheless, my answer to the apparent challenge this poses is two-fold.

First, we are interested in *our* shared agency, and this is shared agency whose participants are, it is plausible to suppose, planning agents. Why is this so plausible? The basic answer is that this is a way of understanding and explaining the striking richness of our temporally extended and organized individual agency. And once these planning capacities are on board we should expect them to play important roles in our sociality.

Second, the ability of the theory to refer to and exploit these planning structures allows it to provide a rich model of robust forms of shared agency without introducing fundamentally new and discontinuous elements. This is an aspect of the fecundity of planning structures, and supports the thesis of continuity.

In short, planning structures are central to the kind of temporally extended individual agents we are; and the continuity thesis is the idea that once we have those structures on board they can play a central role in our sociality.

7. Social functioning and social rationality

We have available, then, a trio of guiding ideas. First, there is the general idea that we try to understand aspects of mind in terms of characteristic roles and associated norms. Second, we have available such an understanding of, in particular, the intentions of individuals as elements in partial, coordinating plans. This is the planning theory of individual agency. And third, we have available Grice's methodology of creature construction. Given this trio of ideas, how should we think about *shared* intention?

We can begin with our first, very general idea and apply it directly to shared intention. We ask: Why do we bother with shared intentions? What fundamental roles do they play in our lives, and what norms are associated with those roles? Let's focus first on roles. And here I think we should be struck by the analogues, in the shared case, of the coordinating, structuring, organizing, guiding, and settling roles of intention in the individual case. In particular, it seems plausible to suppose that the characteristic roles of a shared intention to J include interpersonal coordination of action and planning in pursuit of J, and the structuring of related bargaining and shared deliberation concerning how to J.[70] In playing these roles shared intentions help to constitute and to support basic forms of social organization.

Granted, and as noted earlier, human shared agency many times also brings with it not only coordination of thought and action but also associated practices of holding accountable. As Margaret Gilbert has emphasized, one participant may well demand that the other do her share, and hold her accountable if she does not do this. But I think it is natural to see this not as a defining role of shared intention—as what shared intention is *for*—but rather as a supporting condition that is common in adult human shared agency. The basic answer to why we bother with shared intentions and shared agency is not to hold each other accountable. The more plausible answer is to achieve forms of social coordination and organization in our relevant thought and action. And in the pursuit of such organization, practices of accountability will quite frequently come to the fore.

The roles of shared intention I have just highlighted are primarily roles in temporally downstream social functioning, including later shared reasoning and bargaining shaped by these shared intentions. This is a parallel with the planning theory's emphasis on the roles of intentions of individuals in temporally downstream functioning, including later practical reasoning. As in the individual case, we will also want a theory about the various kinds of reasoning that can intelligibly issue in such shared intentions.[71] (And, again, in many cases that reasoning will be shaped by prior intentions—individual or shared.) But the first step is to say what such shared intentions are. And here I think that, as in the case of the intentions of individuals, it is the roles in temporally downstream functioning, and their associated norms, that are central.[72]

What norms are associated with these social roles of shared intentions? Well, it seems plausible that there will be associated norms of social agglomeration and consistency, social coherence, and social stability. Roughly, it should be possible to agglomerate relevant intentions into a larger social plan that is consistent, that in a timely way adequately specifies relevant means and preliminary steps, and that is associated with appropriately stable social psychological structures. Failure to satisfy these norms will normally undermine the distinctive coordinating, guiding, structuring, and settling roles of shared intention in our social, practical thought and action.

So, as in the case of individual intention, we can expect the social roles characteristic of shared intention to be associated with characteristic norms of—in this case—social rationality. And we will want to understand both the explanatory and the normative significance of these norms of social rationality.[73]

There are three complexities here, however. The first concerns the explanatory role of norms of social rationality. In the case of individual planning agency I supposed that what constitutes the explanatory role of norms of plan rationality is primarily the explanatory role of the at-least-implicit acceptance of those norms by individual planning agents. In the case of these social norms, however, it is not immediately clear how to understand their explanatory role. Should we appeal to the acceptance of related, individualistic norms on the part of those individual participants? to the individual participants' acceptance of these social norms? to the shared acceptance of these social norms? In the view I will be developing, all three explanatory modes of social rationality are possible; but, for reasons to be discussed, the first, individualistic case has an important priority.[74]

Second, which intentions fall under these social norms? Well, at the least, whatever intentions constitute the relevant web of shared intentions. If we are singing the duet together, for example, we will have a shared intention to sing together, and perhaps also shared intentions to sing in a certain key, and in a certain style. And these will each involve intentions of each concerning the specific joint activity. But it also may be that each of us has related intentions—say, to emphasize a certain note—that concern only her own contribution to the shared activity. If there is to be relevant coordination, the social norms of agglomeration and consistency need also to apply to these intentions, not just the shared intentions, strictly speaking. Further, the social pressure for an adequate specification of relevant means to the shared end can be satisfied in part by personal intentions that are strictly only about that agent's own contributions to the shared activity. And, finally, the need for stability to achieve the social end will apply broadly to these various intentions. In this way these social norms of agglomeration, consistency, coherence, and stability have a somewhat broad scope.

But not an overly broad scope. The roles of shared intention do not require interpersonal consistency of judgment about the values at stake in the shared activity. The successful coordination of our house painting need not require that our aesthetic judgments about colors be consistent with each other, though it does require consistency in our plans about which colors to use. It is interpersonal consistency and coherence *in plan*—not in evaluative judgment—that is central to modest sociality.

Nor does shared intention require that the agents participate in the pursuit of the same goals. Perhaps you participate in our shared intention to paint the house because you do not like the present color, whereas I participate because I want to get rid of the mildew.

Must the goals for which each participates at least be consistent with each other? This returns us to the distinction, from section 5, between the generic phenomenon of a goal and the more specific goal-directed attitude of intention. In the individual case I have said that whereas an agent's intentions are subject to norms of agglomeration and consistency, this is not in general true of an agent's goals, broadly construed. In the example from section 5, I am guided by the goal of getting into UCLA Law School, and I am also guided by the goal of getting into Stanford Law School. That these goals are not co-realizable need not induce a flaw in my structure of goals (though it would induce a flaw if I were to intend to get into each law school). After all, I might pursue each of my law school application plans and let the world (or anyway, UCLA and Stanford) decide. Similarly, it seems possible for you and me to share an intention to paint the house despite the fact that it is out in the open that your goal (but not, strictly speaking, your intention) is later to sell the house at a profit and my goal (but not, strictly speaking, my intention) is later to donate it to the historical conservation society. Though this conflict of non-intention goals might turn out to thwart our efforts to act together, it need not. We might proceed with the joint house painting and leave to later a decision between the housing market and the conservation society.[75]

Modest sociality involves interpersonal coordination and organization of practical thought and action. But modest sociality is possible in the face of conflict of judgments about the right and the good, or even certain conflicts of goals. It is intentions and plans that are at the heart of the coordination and organization characteristic of modest sociality, and it is these that are the primary targets of the norms of social consistency and agglomeration. The problem posed to us by our shared intention is to find an adequate plan that is consistent and coherent and that is acceptable to each; but we need not each bring to bear the same standards of acceptability. This is an aspect of what I will call the *primacy of intention for modest sociality.*

We turn now to a third complexity concerning the relevant social rationality norms. This complexity concerns the cognitive background with respect to which relevant intentions and plans are evaluated for social consistency and social means-end coherence. We are assuming that the agents are in a position to have relevant knowledge of the minds of others. But other matters will also be in the cognitive background. In particular, these norms on intentions of consistency and coherence apply against a background that concerns, roughly, what is possible and what is effective. And the different participants in a shared intention might have differing views about these matters.

To keep my initial discussion manageable, however, I am going to assume for now, as a simplifying assumption, that the participants have the same beliefs about these matters of possibility and effectiveness, and that it is these beliefs that are in the background when we apply norms of social consistency and coherence on the relevant intentions. Later, in Chapter 7, I will revisit this complexity.

8. Constructivism about shared intention and modest sociality

So we have structures of roles and associated norms both at the level of individual intention and at the level of shared intention. Our next question is: how are these structures related? And here, as a first step, it is natural to draw on our third idea: the methodology of creature construction. We try to see the move to these social roles and associated norms as in some way building, within Gricean creature construction, on the roles and norms characteristic of individual planning agency, and in response to pressures for increased coordination and unity at the social level.

This is not to say that in the course of our actual lives we ourselves make a transition from nonsocial to social creatures. Creature construction is not a story of actual human development, and it can recognize that human lives are embedded in the social from the start—that, as Pierre Demeulenaere has put it, "the social is always already there."[76] What we are after is not a story of actual human development but an understanding of the conceptual, metaphysical, and normative deep structure of our sociality.

This Gricean picture still leaves unsettled, however, how exactly to characterize this step to modest sociality. Recall that the step from individual purposive agency to individual planning agency involves—according to the planning theory—a step to a distinctive nexus of roles and norms. According to the planning theory, this step brings with it attitudes of intending that are distinct from forms of wanting and believing characteristic of simple purposive agency—though no less embeddable in a natural causal order. Now, we have seen that a step to shared intention and shared agency involves an analogous step to a characteristic nexus of social roles and social norms. So we need to ask to what extent does this step to shared intention and shared agency involve the introduction of phenomena that are fundamentally distinct from those of individual planning agency? To what extent, in contrast, can and should this step build more conservatively on the planning theory of the intentions of individuals?

Well, let us reflect on the step from

(a) individual desire-belief purposive agency,[77]

to

(b) individual planning agency,

As I see it, this step from (a) to (b) involves the introduction of a form of psychic functioning—namely, planning—that has an independent impact on thought and action, an impact over and above the ordinary functioning of a simple desire-belief psychic economy.[78] These planning phenomena will, of course, systematically interact with ordinary beliefs and desires; but they have, according to the planning theory, their own distinctive roles in the dynamics of practical thought and action.

Now consider the step from (b) to
(c) shared intention and modest sociality.

When we go from (b) to (c) are we moving to a social phenomenon that has an independent impact on thought and action, an impact over and above the functioning of the psychic economies in (b)?

Well, we do not suppose that shared intention shapes shared action in a way that reaches its hand over the psychic functioning of the individual agents who are involved. We expect that shared intention, whatever it is, works its way through the workings of the individual psychic economies, appropriately interrelated.[79] One way to think about this would be to see shared intention as in some way consisting in relevant, interrelated intentions of the individual participants. And that suggests that we see the step from (b) to (c) as a fairly *conservative* step in creature construction.

Just how conservative this step will turn out to be will depend on how we understand the relevant, interrelated psychic functioning of the individual agents who are involved in shared agency. For now let me just sketch in broad outlines the basic picture of a conservative step from (b) to (c). The idea is to build on structures of individual planning agency primarily by characterizing certain relevant contents of the intentions of the participants, relevant contexts in which those intentions are located, and relevant interrelations among those intentions. The idea, roughly, is that the social-norm-assessable social functioning characteristic of shared intention emerges from the individual-norm-assessable and individual-norm-guided functioning of relevant structures of interrelated intentions of the individuals, as those intentions of individuals are understood by the planning theory.

We seek, that is, a construction of interconnected intentions and other related attitudes of the individuals in appropriate contexts that would, when functioning in the norm-guided ways highlighted by the planning theory of the intentions of individuals, play the roles characteristic of shared intention. And we try to see conformity to central norms of social rationality characteristic of shared intention—norms of social consistency, social agglomeration, social coherence, and social stability—as primarily emerging from guidance by norms of individual plan rationality that apply directly to the relevant interrelated structures at the individual level. If we had such a conservative construction we would have reason to say that this construction *is* shared intention, or at least one important kind of shared intention.[80] And such a conservative construction of shared agency—if it were available—would pose a challenge to a more top-down approach that begins with the shared case and posits fundamental discontinuities in the step from individual planning agency to shared agency. Such a top-down approach would have to explain the need to appeal to such discontinuities, given the (assumed) success of the more conservative construction.[81] I will return to this last point later.

In describing this approach to shared intention I am implicitly distinguishing between being assessable by a norm, being guided by a norm, being explained by a norm, and conforming to a norm. To think that relevant thought and action is *assessable* by a norm is to suppose that the norm *applies* to that thought and action. A norm *guides* relevant thought and action when its acceptance is an appropriate explanatory aspect of the actual psychological functioning. A standard way—but, as we will see, not the only way—in which a norm can help indirectly to *explain* certain psychological functioning to which it applies is by way of such acceptance of that norm by relevant individual agents. Thought and action *conform* to a norm when the norm applies to them and they do not violate it. In these senses, a norm can apply without actually guiding or in other ways explain; a norm can both apply and guide even though there is, in a particular case, a breakdown in conformity to the norm; and there can in fact be norm conformity even if the norm does not guide or in other ways explain. My aim is to provide a construction of interconnected intentions of individuals whose individual-norm-assessable, individual-norm-guided, and individual-norm-conforming functioning (according to the planning theory of individual agency) would constitute and help explain the social-norm-assessable and normally social-norm-conforming social functioning of shared intention.

I have proposed that certain social rationality norms—social norms of agglomeration, consistency, coherence, and stability—apply to shared agency, and that such shared agency will normally conform to those norms. But, as noted earlier, we need to ask who accepts and applies relevant norms. And the answer that is built into the kind of construction I seek is that in the basic case the relevant norm acceptance is that of the individual participants, and the norms accepted are, in the first instance, the rationality norms of individual planning agency. Given appropriate contents, contexts, and interrelations of the intentions of these individual participants, these phenomena then induce the social-norm-conforming social functioning of shared intention, and the applicability to that functioning of the cited social norms. And when this is the case we can say that the social norm helps explain the social functioning by way of the acceptance of associated norms of individual intention rationality by the participating individual planning agents.

The central idea is not that it is the participants in a shared intention who do this constructing. The participants in a shared intention participate in that shared intention; they need not literally construct it. Nor is the idea that there is an actual historical transition from solely individual planning agency to participation in shared intention. Rather, we the theorists seek to understand what is involved in or constitutes such a shared intention as a structure that consists in certain individualistic elements related in certain ways. We try to do this by constructing this structure of elements. And here we, the theorists, are aided by the Gricean methodology of creature construction pursued in a way that seeks a more or less conservative construction. That said, there will be cases in which it is natural to say as well that the participants themselves intentionally construct their shared intention by taking steps aimed at creating the conditions that constitute shared intention.

Call the idea that shared intention consists in a structure of relevant and suitably interrelated attitudes of the participants in a suitable context *constructivism about shared intention.*[82] We begin with the idea that shared intentions

interpersonally structure and coordinate thought and action, and that these structuring and coordinating roles involve associated social norms. We then ask: will
these social-norm-assessable social roles be grounded in the individual-norm-
assessable and individual-norm-guided functioning of appropriate attitudes of the
individual participants—attitudes with appropriate contents, in appropriate contexts, and appropriately interrelated? We seek to answer this question by constructing a structure of interrelated intentions of the individuals, and norms that apply to
and guide those intentions, that would induce the social-norm-assessable and social-
norm-conforming social roles characteristic of shared intention. We want to show
that intentions of individuals in these special contexts and with these special and
distinctive contents and interrelations would, insofar as they function properly and
in a way that is guided by the norms of individual planning agency, play the roles of
shared intention in part by issuing in thought and action that conforms to central
norms that apply to shared intention. And we want to show that in these basic cases
violations of these norms of social rationality will be constituted by violations, by one
or more participants, of associated rationality norms of individual planning agency.

Such constructivism highlights the idea that the individual participants
are assessable and guided by norms of individual planning agency, but that
given the special contents of their intentions, and their characteristic interrelations and contexts, this brings with it the applicability of, and (normally)
conformity to, corresponding social norms on shared intention. In this specific and limited sense, constructivism posits a kind of normative emergence.
When the individuals become aware of this normative emergence they may
go on explicitly to accept these social norms, and directly appeal to them in
their practical reasoning and in their relevant social interactions. And they
may do this in part because they can see the advantages that accrue to the
group's conformity to those norms, both in general and in the particular case.
Their acceptance of these social norms would then add a further element to
the explanation of conformity to those norms.

Such a step to a second explanatory mode of social rationality would still
remain within the domain of the acceptance of norms by the participating individuals. As we will see in Chapter 7, however, there is also the possibility of a
yet further step, a step to a kind of shared acceptance of these norms of social
rationality. For now the important point is that all three of these explanatory
modes of social rationality are possible, but what is at the bottom is the acceptance by the individual participants of norms of individual intention rationality.

Constructivism does not suppose that all that is important in shared
agency is fully grounded in such broadly individualistic planning structures.
Constructivism grants that our shared agency frequently draws on subtle and

frequently unarticulated commonalities of sensibility.[83] Think of our sense of conversational distance. Constructivism grants that much of our shared activity takes place within larger moral, cultural, political, and legal structures. Constructivism grants that there can be distinctive social values at stake in shared agency—for example, the value of certain forms of social unity and social governance.[84] Constructivism grants that shared agency raises distinctive issues of trust and trustworthiness, as well as issues about ordinary civility. After all, the stability of a shared intention may well depend on the extent to which the participants can reasonably trust each other. And constructivism grants that there can be complex relations between shared intention and related moral obligations of each to another, relations to which I will turn in Chapters 3 and 5. So the normative emergence posited by constructivism is only a part of the normative story.

What constructivism does say is:

(a) The characteristic functioning of shared intention is in basic cases constituted by the characteristic functioning of relevant structures of interrelated intentions of the individual participants in relevant contexts, as that functioning is understood within the planning theory.

(b) The application of central norms of social rationality to shared intention, and the conformity to those norms, emerges in these basic cases from the guidance of the individual participants by the central rationality norms of individual planning agency as those norms apply to the intentions of those individuals, given relevant and distinctive contents, contexts, and interrelations.

In this way constructivism builds on the planning theory of individual planning agency. It supposes that once we have these distinctive structures of individual planning agency on board, the further step to shared agency can be conservative. While highlighting the significance of such sociality to our lives, constructivism posits a deep continuity—conceptual, metaphysical, and normative—between individual planning agency and modest forms of sociality. That, anyway, is the conjecture.

9. Continuity, sufficiency, and Ockham's Razor

My discussion aims to contribute to a fruitful human social psychology, one that takes seriously phenomena of modest sociality. And my conjecture is that we can make progress here by exploring conceptual, metaphysical, and normative continuities between individual planning agency and modest sociality.

Of course, everything is what it is, not another thing. If there really were a deep discontinuity in the step from individual to shared agency we would not want to paper over it. But a guiding thought here is that, once we have on board the richer theory of individual agency provided by the planning theory, it may well turn out that if there is an appearance of a deep discontinuity it is misleading. And the best way to settle this issue is to try to develop a theory that satisfies this continuity constraint and see how successful it is.

This points toward a central concern with relevant *sufficient* conditions for shared intention and modest sociality. This is because appropriate sufficient conditions would be enough to establish the cited continuity. This pursuit of a conservative construction allows for the possibility of multiple constructions, each of which provides some such sufficient basis for the social roles and norms characteristic of shared intention.[85] What is crucial for this theoretical ambition is to provide at least one such structure of sufficient conditions that satisfies the continuity constraint.

In the face of several alternative constructions, each of which purports to provide sufficient conditions in a way that satisfies the continuity constraint, we would need to ask which makes better sense of the complexities of these forms of sociality in ways that also fit well the contours of individual agency. Here we might in the end give the nod to one of the purported constructions as theoretically more fruitful. But the best thing to say might turn out to be that shared intention is multiply realizable.[86] Such multiple realizability would be compatible with the kind of continuity between individual planning agency and modest sociality that I will be trying to defend.

This willingness to countenance multiple constructions, each of which satisfies the continuity constraint, does not extend to multiple constructions where one satisfies the continuity constraint and one does not. As anticipated, if we can indeed articulate sufficient conditions for modest sociality that satisfy the continuity constraint, then there will be a presumption in favor of that model of modest sociality in comparison with a proffered model that involves a basic *dis*continuity.

This is an application of Ockham's Razor. If we can get a plausible model of modest sociality without appealing to a fundamental discontinuity in the step from individual planning agency to such sociality, then there is a presumption against an appeal to such a discontinuity in our theorizing. If a conservative construction works then there is a presumption in its favor in comparison with a nonconservative model.

Now, the two main competing views that I will be discussing here—Searle's appeal to an irreducible we-intention, and Gilbert's appeal to an irreducible joint commitment—are each versions of a nonconservative, discontinuity theory. An implication of the cited application of Ockham's Razor is that a successful conservative construction of modest sociality yields a presumption against the introduction into our theory of such new, irreducible elements. And what is crucial for such a conservative construction is to provide sufficient conditions for modest sociality. Of course, it would also be good to know whether some or all of the conditions cited are necessary for modest sociality, but a concern with necessity is less pressing, for reasons noted. Further, we can also go on to ask whether conditions that are not strictly sufficient for robust forms of modest sociality may still be theoretically important in various ways.[87] Nevertheless, and for the reasons cited, my main focus will be on sufficiency for modest sociality within the constraints of the continuity conjecture.

10. Deception, coercion, shared intentional, shared cooperative

Before proceeding with this project of construction I need to note one more complexity. Sometimes human interactions involve forms of deception or coercion between the participants. And sometimes such deception or coercion blocks the claim that people are acting together in a shared activity.[88] Suppose that you and I are painting the house, but you are deceiving me about central features of how we are proceeding even though I have made it clear that these are features about which I care. For example, though it is important to me that we stay within a certain budget, and I have made it clear that I am acting on the assumption that we are indeed within budget, you know that we are very much over budget. But, in order to keep me engaged in the painting project, you intentionally deceive me about this matter. In a different case, as we proceed I begin to balk and to express a desire to stop the project. Your response is to pull out a gun and coerce me into continuing to paint, even while recognizing that my painting will now be motivated by my fear of your threatened sanction rather than an intention of mine in favor of our joint activity. In each of these cases the deception or coercion between us so infects the inner workings of our interactions that they baffle shared intentional activity. You are instead—as we say—merely using me.

Consider now somewhat different cases of deception and coercion. Suppose we are painting the house together but you lie to me about your reasons for participating. You say you are participating because you dislike the present color; but in fact you are participating to win a side bet. But suppose also that I really do not care what your reasons are for participating, so long as your reasons are not egregious and they do not get in the way of your participation. Again, suppose that you are the master and I a slave. You issue an edict, backed by a threat—we are going to build a bridge together. In response, I adopt the end of our building the bridge together and go ahead and work with you. As we proceed the threat remains in the background. I would much prefer that you not be in such a position of power over me. But I am nevertheless prepared to work with you in our joint activity, and our working together may involve various subtle forms of interaction, adjustment, and willingness to incorporate the other's intentional agency into the joint activity. In each of these cases the deception or coercion does seem to block the idea that we are each *cooperating with* the other. Nevertheless, it seems possible that the deception or coercion in these cases remains in the background and does not actually interfere with the specific ways in which we interact when we paint or build together, though of course it might. Though what we are doing seems ill-described as a cooperative activity, it may be plausible to describe it as a shared intentional activity.

I do not want to put much weight on linguistic intuitions here. What is important to note is that sometimes deception and coercion between the participants in an activity clearly block the shared-ness of the activity, but that sometimes the matter is more subtle. In these more subtle cases the deception or coercion between the parties, while it in some ways taints the sharing, need not block the specific interactions that are characteristic of shared intentional activity. About these cases I will say that there may be shared *intentional* activity but not shared *cooperative* activity. This involves a bit of linguistic legislation. But I think it is a plausible way of marking an interesting difference in the relevance of deception or coercion. On this way of thinking, the idea of cooperation brings with it a broad exclusion of deception or coercion between the relevant parties and with respect to the activity, even if that deception or coercion does not infect the specific interactions in ways that block shared intentionality.[89]

This is a sign that our concept of cooperation is to some extent a moralized notion in the sense that it incorporates certain moral prohibitions on deception and coercion. In contrast, the idea of shared intentional activity that is central here is the idea of a distinctive kind of social-psychological organization in our thinking and acting together. So it seems likely to turn out that not all shared intentional activities are shared cooperative activities.

That said, the details of our view of the relation between shared intentional and shared cooperative activity must await our overall theory, one that will focus primarily on shared intentional activity. So let us turn to our efforts to develop such a theory by way of a conservative construction of shared intention and modest sociality. Once the basic elements of our theory are on board we can return, in Chapter 4, to these issues about deception, coercion, and cooperation.

2 BUILDING BLOCKS, PART 1

We need to articulate appropriate, plan-theoretic building blocks for our construction of modest sociality. And I here I will proceed in two stages. In this and the next chapter I will focus primarily on a two-person case of modest sociality and ask about the main contours of a conservative construction of such a case. When these resources are on the table I will then turn, in Chapter 4, to an effort to formulate a conservative construction of small-scale modest sociality more generally. We will thereby arrive at a model of our modest sociality that highlights public structures of interconnected intentions, associated beliefs, interpersonal interdependence between those intentions, and mutual responsiveness in the functioning of these intentions.

Suppose, then, that in a case of modest sociality you and I share an intention to go to New York City (hereafter, NYC) together. What construction of intentions and related attitudes of each would be such that *its* norm-assessable and norm-guided functioning (as articulated by the planning theory of the intentions of individuals) constitutes the social-norm-assessable and social-norm-conforming functioning of the *shared* intention? And how does this construction of shared intention enter into a construction of shared intentional activity? To answer these questions we need to describe the building blocks for this construction. In doing this we will have our eye on forms of social functioning and social rationality that are characteristic of shared intention. And we will be looking for structures at the individual level that will help constitute or generate these forms of social functioning and social rationality.

1. I intend that we J, and circularity

Begin by noting two strategies that will not work. First, we might try to appeal simply to my intention to go to NYC given that you too so intend, as well as to your intention to go to NYC given that I too so intend. But this structure of coordinated intentions might be simply a case of strategic equilibrium, like walking alongside a stranger.

What if we appeal to the condition that we each judge that our going to NYC is the best option, or that we each rank that option highest in our own relevant evaluative ranking? Well, it seems that there could be this package of evaluative judgments or rankings even though neither party has yet decided to act in accordance with it: perhaps one or both of them is still deliberating. Further, this proposal would block shared intentions in cases of disagreement about what would be best; it would also block shared intentions that involve weakness of will on the part of one or more of the participants. But it seems that we can share an intention to go to concert C even though you think A is best and I think B is best; and a pair of weak-willed lovers might share an intention to have an affair even though each thinks this is not the best option. Here, as in the case of individual intention, we need to be careful to avoid an overly simplistic picture of the relation between intention and evaluation.

As anticipated in Chapter 1, I think that we do better by instead appealing to the condition that

(i) we each intend that we go to NYC

where the intentions alluded to in (i) are intentions of the individuals of the sort characterized by the planning theory of the intentions of individuals.[1] In particular, I am set to be guided in plan-theoretic ways by the end of *our* joint activity; and so are you.

There are two occurrences of "we" in (i). The first is what Christian List and Philip Pettit call "the distributed 'we'."[2] The appeal is to my state of intending and to your state of intending. What about the second occurrence? Well, in basic cases this use of "we" will also be distributed. But we can here also, without circularity, avail ourselves of a concept of a group. We can do this if that concept of a group does not itself bring with it the very idea of shared intentionality. I might intend, say, that those of us in this part of the park run toward the hot air balloon that has crashed. If this use of "we" (or "us") does not bring with it the very idea of shared intentionality, there need be no circle.[3]

In my understanding of (i) in a model of small-scale modest sociality I will suppose that each of us has the ability accurately to pick out the other participant and identify him as one's partner. I do not merely know of my partner as, say, the richest person in the room whosoever he or she may be. My intention is that we (that is, me and you—where I have the ability accurately to pick you out and identify you as my partner) go to NYC.[4] This assumption will make it easier to understand the more complex interrelations among the participants to which we will be led as we try to enrich the relevant building blocks. Granted, this is an assumption that would need to be relaxed if we were to try to extend the theory to larger groups. But, as I have said, I will be satisfied here if we can agree on a basic approach to small-scale cases of modest sociality; and for such cases it is plausible to make this assumption.

In appealing to (i) I am also making the simplifying assumption that in a shared intention to *J* the participants will have a common conception of *J*, that there is in this way a match in what is intended by each. This is not an assumption that the participants converge on all their beliefs and relevant preferences or evaluations about *J*. Each can intend that we *J* even if one believes certain things about what *J* would lead to and has a preference for that, while the other has instead different beliefs or preferences. Nevertheless, even this assumption of a common *J* might be weakened at some point. Perhaps we can share an intention to go to NYC if I intend that we go to the city that is the home of the Yankees and you intend that we go to the city that is the home of the Mets. But these are matters we do not need to settle here.[5]

Of course, an individual may have an intention he would express as "we will do it," and yet be mistaken that his use of "we" succeeds in referring. Perhaps he is a brain in a vat. But in that case there is no shared intention, so I put such cases aside.

A basic point is that an appeal to these intentions in (i) ensures that an intention-like commitment to *our* activity is at work in the practical thinking of *each*. Each is appropriately settled on and committed to *our* activity, where we understand such commitment on the part of each in terms of the planning theory. In particular, once *our* activity is an element in this way in *my* plans, I will face characteristic problems of means with respect to our activity—and not just my activity—given a need for means-end coherence of my plans. I face this characteristic problem about means because I *intend* our activity. In this way, and given relevant beliefs, I will normally be led from my intention concerning our activity to an intention to do something myself as a means to or element in that activity of ours, perhaps as a way of helping you play your role. In contrast, these demands of mean-end coherence of intention would not in general be engaged if each only had some desire in favor of the joint activity. Further, once our activity is an element in my plans I will be constrained by characteristic requirements of plan agglomerativity and consistency with respect to our activity. In this way I can be led to filter out intentions on my part to act in certain ways, including intentions to act in ways that would interfere with you. Again, this is because I *intend* our activity. In contrast, these demands of agglomerativity and consistency would not in general be engaged if each only had some desire in favor of the joint activity, or even had that activity merely as a goal.[6] It is, then, by appeal in particular to (i) that we can explain something we need to explain, namely: the norm-guided responsiveness of the thought and action of each to the end of the shared activity, responsiveness that is an element in the characteristic functioning of shared intention.

Might we avoid this appeal in (i) to intending that *we* act, by appealing instead to each person's intention *to* act *with* the other? Could we just appeal, say, to my intention to go to NYC with you, and your intention to go to NYC with me? This is an intriguing suggestion since it seems to bring the other into the content of the intention of each and yet retain the idea that what is intended is, at bottom, one's own action, suitably characterized by way of the with-clause.

Well, what is it to intend to go to NYC with you? When I intend to go to NYC with you, do I simply *expect* that you will be going and, given that, intend to do my part of what would turn out to be our going to NYC? Or do I *intend* that you go, as part of our going? If the latter then talk of my intending to go to NYC with you will be fairly close to my talk of intending that we go: in each case my intention extends to your role in our activity. In each case I am set to support, in plan-theoretic ways, your relevant activities. If the former—if in intending to go with you I only expect you to be going and do not intend that you go, as a part of our going—then I will not thereby have the cited dispositions of thought and action concerning social coherence and consistency, dispositions that are characteristic of shared intention. I will not, for example, thereby be disposed to track means to your going (and so to our going), or to avoid activities that are incompatible with your going (and so to our going). So I think we really do need something along the lines of (i).[7]

It is useful here to consider an objection offered by John Searle to an appeal by Raimo Tuomela and Kaarlo Miller to an intention to do one's part in a joint activity, as an element in their analysis of "we-intention."[8] Searle appeals to an example in which each of many business people pursues her own profit-making activities while knowing that that is what the others are also doing, and expects that (given the "hidden hand") this will all result in overall human happiness. But no one sees herself as cooperating with the others to achieve that overall good. If this is all that is involved in intending to do one's part in bringing about the overall good, then such an intention to do one's part is too weak to get us to shared intentionality. Searle contrasts this case with one in which each really is cooperating with the others in pursuit of that overall good. Searle supposes that in this second case each does intend to do his part in the joint activity of bringing about the overall good, in the sense that is needed for collectively intentional activity. But Searle thinks that if we appeal to this second reading we will be building the very idea of cooperation and collective intentionality into the content of each person's intention to do his part. Searle concludes that to capture the phenomenon of collective intentionality we need to appeal to an irreducible we-intention.[9]

In saying that a theory of shared intentionality needs something stronger than the first, weaker reading of intending to act with the other, I am agreeing with the spirit of the first half of Searle's critique (putting aside the question whether Searle provides an accurate reading of the Tuomela and Miller essay). And in appealing to (i) I am agreeing with Searle that what is needed here will involve some sort of reference to the joint activity. But Searle's step to the further claim—namely, that this appeal to the joint activity must itself involve the very idea of collective intentionality—is problematic. Indeed, one of the lessons of the proposals I will be defending in this book is that this further claim is unjustified. As I explain below, the appeal to the joint activity J within the content of an intention can be neutral concerning whether or not J is a shared intentional activity.[10]

Now, in his 2005 response to Searle's criticism, Tuomela indicates that on the view in his essay with Miller, to intend to go to NYC as one's part in the joint trip is not just to expect that the other will be going and, given that, intend to go oneself. Instead, Tuomela and Miller seek something roughly along the lines of the second understanding I have noted of such an intention to act with the other. And Tuomela argues that, *pace* Searle, we can get this second understanding without an unacceptable circularity.[11]

My proposal in (i) is, then, roughly in the spirit of this 2005 effort by Tuomela to get an appropriately stronger reading of intending to do one's part in the joint action. And on my view we best proceed here by appealing to an intention that we J (where, as I discuss below, J can be neutral with respect to shared intentionality), and then understanding such intentions in terms of the planning theory.[12]

But can such a view really avoid an unacceptable circularity? After all, on this approach shared intentional activity will be, in the basic case, activity suitably explainable by shared intention. But (i) is supposed to be an element in a construction of shared intention. So if the concept of our activity that is at work in (i) were the concept of shared intentional activity, there would be a problematic circularity in our construction of shared intention.[13]

This is where Searle proposes that we see the concept of shared intentionality as a primitive that enters into the contents of relevant intentions of the individuals.[14] But I propose a different tack, one broadly analogous to an approach to a corresponding issue about individual intentional action.[15]

In the individual case we try to understand intentional action primarily in terms of intentions of individuals and the right sorts of connections between those intentions and relevant behavior. But what is the content of these intentions? Well, it is common in our ordinary thought to think of what one intends as something to be done intentionally. But if the content of the cited intentions must involve appeal to the very idea of intentional action, our approach to individual intentional action seems threatened with circularity.

A first step in responding to this concern is to focus on cases in which we can appeal to a concept of activity that is itself neutral with respect to the intentionality of that activity. Examples include: falling down, shaking, giggling, opening the door, going to NYC, knocking over the table, annoying a friend, scaring those in the room, upsetting the applecart, giving away the secret, harming someone. Concerning such cases we can say, roughly, that one so acts intentionally when one intends so to act (where this act is characterized in intentionally neutral terms) and this intention appropriately explains the fact that one does so act.

That said, a person who intentionally gives away the secret may well consciously and explicitly express his intention as an intention to give it away intentionally. He certainly would not normally say he intends to give it away unintentionally. Nevertheless, given that this person does have an intention or intentions about this matter, we can ask what contents are plausibly assigned to his intentions. And here the idea is that such a person will have underlying dispositions of thought and action that are grounded in his intentions and that support the attribution of an intention-content that draws on a concept of activity that is neutral with respect to intentionality. These underlying dispositions include dispositions in thought and action to track and to adjust in support of the cited intentionally neutral activity-type, as well as dispositions of responsiveness and adjustment to conflicts between that intentionally neutral activity-type and others he is similarly set to track. There can be such dispositions of tracking, adjustment, and responsiveness to this intentionally neutral activity-type in the absence of the agent's conscious, explicit conceptualization of what he is doing in terms of this intentionally neutral activity-type. And the idea is that these intention-grounded dispositions support the attribution of the cited sort of intention-content. As we might say, an intention in favor of activity characterized in intentionally neutral terms is at least implicit in his web of intentions about this matter together with these associated, underlying dispositions of thought and action.

But what about cases of intentionally doing things for which there seems not to be a straightforwardly corresponding, intentionally neutral behavioral type; for example, praying or asserting? Here we suppose that an agent with the basic capacity to act intentionally—a capacity we specify in the indicated way—can then go on, typically in the context of a complex culture, to develop and to learn new action concepts that are, as it were, intentionally loaded. He can then go on to have intentions whose contents exploit such intentionally loaded action concepts. Nevertheless, at the bottom of these enhanced capacities for intentional agency are capacities for a basic kind of intentional agency we can understand by appeal to intentions in favor of activity characterized in intentionally neutral terms.

Granted, one lesson of the past 50 years of the philosophy of action is that it is difficult to know how to say what counts as an appropriate explanatory relation between intention and action. I am taking it for granted that this relation will be in some sense causal. But what we want is, more specifically, that the intention issues in the action in, as it is said, "the right way." And we do not yet know how to specify, without circularity, what counts as the right way. I do not try to solve this problem here. If we can solve this problem for the case of individual intentional action, we can then go on to see how we should proceed with shared intentional action. But even if we cannot solve this problem for the individual case and must grant, in the end, a kind of conceptual nonreducibility of individual intentionality of action,[16] we can still go on to see how we should proceed with shared intentional action.

And here the idea is that in at least many cases we have available a concept of *our* activity that, while it does draw on ideas of individual intentional action, is neutral with respect to *shared* intentionality.[17] We have, for example, a concept of our walking down the street that involves only the ideas that, roughly, we are each intentionally walking down the street, that our walking is alongside each other and at a comparable pace, and that we are each avoiding collisions with the other. We then use such relevantly neutral concepts in the contents of the intentions involved in our construction of initial cases of shared intention.

In saying this I am assuming that the concept of our activity at work in the contents of relevant intentions in basic cases of modest sociality (a) is neutral with respect to shared intentionality, and (b) can be articulated using the conceptual resources of the planning theory of individual intentional agency. What is crucial in response to the issue of circularity is (a). And there may be theoretical purposes for which we need concepts of our activity that satisfy (a) but need not satisfy (b). However, given our effort to defend the continuity thesis, we will primarily be interested in locating within the contents of intentions, in basic cases, concepts of our activity that satisfy both (a) and (b). (I will return to this matter in Chapter 6.)

As in the individual case, a participant in modest sociality may consciously and explicitly express her intention in terms of the very idea of shared intentionality. She may say, for example, that her intention favors our walking together, in a sense of walking together that is loaded with respect to shared intentionality. But the idea is that such a person will have underlying intention-grounded dispositions of tracking, adjustment, and responsiveness that support the attribution to her of an intention whose content draws on a concept of joint activity that is neutral with respect to shared intentionality (and is available to the planning theory of individual agency). These intention-grounded dispositions will include dispositions to adjust and compensate in one's thought and action in ways that track that shared-intention-neutral joint activity, and dispositions to be responsive to relevant conflicts with that joint activity. There can be such dispositions of tracking, adjustment, and responsiveness to this shared-intention-neutral activity-type in the absence of the agent's conscious, explicit conceptualization of what she is doing in terms of this activity-type. As we might say, this intention concerning the shared-intention-neutral joint activity is at least implicit in her web of intentions about this matter together with these associated, underlying dispositions of thought and action.

With this intention in favor of the (shared-intention-neutral) joint activity in hand, we then appeal as well to other elements of the construction (elements to be discussed later) to ensure that when these intentions connect up in the right way to the group behavior there is shared intentional activity. As in the individual case, we can then use these initial cases as bases for a conceptual ratcheting that supports intentions that involve concepts of shared intentional activity that are not neutral in this way.[18] Agents with the capacity to engage in shared activities that involve intentions with shared-intention-neutral concepts can then go on, typically in the context of a complex culture, to develop and to learn shared-intention-loaded concepts of shared activity. Examples of such shared-intention-involving concepts of joint activity might include getting married, or playing chess, or dancing a tango. And these concepts can be made available for contents of relevant intentions. In this way we seek to provide an account of shared intentional action by appealing to the appropriate roles of shared intention, but to explain what shared intention is without using, in the most basic cases, the very idea of shared intentionality in the content of the intentions of each.

I think it is plausible that our construction can in this way appeal to (i) without unacceptable circularity. Or anyway, this is at least as plausible for the case of shared intentionality as is the analogous strategy for avoiding circularity for individual intentionality. Indeed, I suspect it is more plausible. Even if it turns out that the theory of individual intentional action cannot specify the "right way" without appeal to something like the very idea of individual intentional action, we might still succeed in avoiding a corresponding circularity for the case of shared intentionality.[19] If we were to succeed we would have an important element in a model of shared intentional action that eschews appeal to a purported conceptual primitiveness of *shared* intentionality.

This response to concerns about circularity in (i) does not yet address worries about the violation of the own-action condition. I will return to these worries in Chapter 3. But first I need to add to our building blocks.

2. Interlocking and reflexive intentions

In shared intention each participant is committed to treating the other participants not merely as elements of the world that need to be taken into account (and who may in turn take into account one's reaction to them), but also as—as it is natural to say—intentional co-participants in the shared activity.[20] But what is it to treat another as an intentional co-participant?

Well, for me to treat you as an intentional co-participant I need to be able to know about and respond to relevant aspects of your mind. But this is not sufficient. I might be in a position to know about and respond to the mind of a person with whom I interact but with whom I do not engage in modest sociality at all. Think of two opposing soldiers fighting each other in wartime. Each acts on the basis of his beliefs about the other's intentions and actions, as well as his beliefs about what the other believes about him. And these beliefs about the other's beliefs about oneself can lead to what Thomas Schelling calls "the familiar spiral of reciprocal expectations."[21] But so far neither need be treating the other as an intentional co-participant in a shared activity. A theory of modest sociality needs to understand what else is involved.

It may be tempting here to turn to talk of claims or demands of each on the other, of mutual obligations of one to the other, of entitlements of each to the performance of the other. To treat you as an intentional co-participant is to see each of us as having entitlements to make relevant claims or demands on the other to perform, and to see each of us as having associated obligations to the other. The most familiar home of such claims, demands, entitlements, and obligations is commonsense morality, though, as noted earlier, Margaret Gilbert has emphasized obligations and the like that are not specifically moral.

Now, I fully agree that much of our sociality involves relations of obligation, entitlement, and associated forms of claiming and demanding. But the issue here is where these interpersonal normative phenomena best enter into our theorizing about sociality. And my conjecture is that such appeals at this very basic level to obligation and the like in our theory of modest sociality are overly hasty. If the only conceptual resources we had at the level of individual agency were the resources of the desire-belief model together with common knowledge then it might be difficult to resist this move to mutual obligation and entitlement. But the planning theory gives us more to say prior to such a move. As we will see, the planning theory provides the conceptual, metaphysical, and normative resources for a model of sociality that is stronger than straightforward desire-belief-common knowledge models, but that does not yet make an essential appeal, at the ground level, to mutual obligation and entitlement (though it does leave room for their role in many cases of modest sociality). And my conjecture is that we get a deeper understanding of our modest sociality by theorizing in detail at this intermediate level before turning to the kinds of obligations and entitlements commonly involved in our sociality.[22]

So let us consider a case in which each intends the joint activity—thereby satisfying (i)—and yet it seems that neither treats the other as an intentional co-participant. Suppose that you and I are members of competing gangs and each intends that we go to NYC by throwing the other into the trunk of the car and driving to NYC. Each might assert in, as it were, the mafia sense, that he intends that we go to NYC; and each might say to the other, somewhat ominously, "we are going to NYC." In such a mafia case (i) is satisfied,[23] yet neither is treating the other as an intentional co-participant.

Can we say what is missing without adverting to mutual obligations? Well, in intending to throw the other into the trunk each intends to bypass the other's intention. Neither intends that the joint activity of their going to NYC proceed by way of the other's intention in favor of that joint activity. This suggests that one element we need to add to our model of shared intention is the condition that each intends that they go to NYC in part by way of the intention of the other that they go to NYC. This means that the content of the intention of each includes a reference to the role of the intention of the other.[24]

So let's add to the model the idea that each intends that the joint activity go in part by way of the relevant intention of the other participant. But what should we mean here in saying that the joint activity goes in part *by way of* the intention of the other? The idea is that the joint activity both is in accord with and is in part a result of that intention of the other. But in what sense is it a result? Well, one condition is that the joint activity involves the intentional action of the other, intentional action that is guided by that person's intention in favor of the joint activity. But should we also add to the content of the relevant intentions that the way in which the intention of the other in favor of the joint activity helps lead to the joint activity is itself compatible with that joint activity being a shared intentional activity? Well, it is a natural idea that in treating the other as an intentional co-participant what each intends is that the relevant intention of the other works its way through to the joint action not in just any old way but, in particular, in a way that is compatible with shared intentionality. But the problem is that if we simply add this as an element of what each intends we seem to be back to worries about circularity. We would be saying that each intends that the other's relevant intention helps lead to the intended joint activity in a way that is compatible with the shared intentionality of that joint activity. So we would be reintroducing the idea of shared intentionality into the content of the intention of each.

In response to these conflicting philosophical pressures I propose a compromise. At some point in the theory we will need to say how the intentions of each in favor of the joint activity need to be connected to the joint action if there is to be shared intentional activity. We will need to spell out the connection condition. When we do this we will not want simply to say that the intentions of each lead to the joint action in the way involved in shared intentional activity. Instead, we will want to give an informative and noncircular account of the connection condition. So we can now anticipate this later discussion of the connection condition and say that what each intends is that the relevant intention of the other helps to lead to the joint action in a way that coheres with the connection condition, suitably explained. So long as the connection condition is explained without appeal to the very idea of shared intentionality, there is no circle.

These observations support an appeal not only to (i), but also to

(ii-initial) we each intend the following: that we go to NYC in part by way of the intention of the other that we go to NYC (and that the route from that intention of the other to our joint activity coheres with the connection condition).

There is in this way a semantic interconnection between our intentions in favor of our going to NYC: the content of my intention includes a reference to your intention and to its role in our action. And vice versa. The intentions of each semantically *interlock*.

This condition should be distinguished from a condition that says that each *believes* that the other's intention will function appropriately. In (ii-initial) it is the content of the *intentions* of each that includes a reference to the role of the other's intention.

Let me try further to clarify this idea of interlocking by considering an example offered by Seamus Miller. Miller writes:

> Suppose I have as an end that we dig a tunnel under the English Channel. You are in France and will dig from Calais, and I am in England and will dig from Dover. The tunnels will connect in the middle of the English Channel. . . . I don't care whether you have as an end that we dig the tunnel, or whether you are simply digging a tunnel from Calais to the middle of the English Channel for a bet. . . . So I don't have as an end that we dig the tunnel (even in part) because you have as an end that we dig the tunnel, though as it happens you do have as an end that we dig the tunnel. Your sentiments mirror mine.[25]

In the terms of the present discussion, what is suggested here is that each of us intends that we build the tunnel (and so the analogue of (i) is satisfied), but neither intends that we build the tunnel by way of the other person's intention that we build the tunnel (and so the analogue of (ii-initial) is not satisfied). After all, neither of us "care[s] whether the other agent has the same joint intention or end, just so long as that agent performs that agent's contributory action."[26] What to say?

Well, even though I have no preference as between a case in which you intend that we build the tunnel and a case in which instead you intend only to dig your half in order to win a bet, we can suppose that I know that in fact what you intend is that we build the tunnel. And I might well intend that this intention of yours play its relevant roles.

Suppose, to take a different example, that I have no preference as between dancing with A and dancing with B. Nevertheless, if A is now my dance partner I will intend that we dance by way of her intentions, not by way of B's intentions. I will be set specifically to help A execute her relevant intentions rather than to help B. And I will not intend to try somehow to substitute B for A. (Though I might also have no intention to resist if B were to interrupt and ask "May I have this dance?")

Similarly, and to return to Miller's example, I might well intend that we build by way of your actual intention that we build, even though I have no preference as between your so intending and instead your intending only to build your half for a bet, and even though I have no intention to resist such a switch on your part. After all, I am not on the lookout for ways to ensure that you instead participate because of an alternative intention to win a bet by digging halfway. Interlocking is a relation between our actual intentions, and is compatible with the absence of a preference that favors that intention of the other over other possible intentions that might suffice for achieving the joint activity. So Miller's example need not pose a problem for (ii-initial).[27]

Now, the idea that the content of the intentions of each includes reference to the appropriate role of the relevant intention of the other was part of our effort to capture the idea that each treats the other as an intentional co-participant in a way that contrasts with our mafia case. But in shared agency each will also treat herself as an intentional co-participant. So if each satisfies (ii-initial) with respect to the other, it will be natural to suppose that each will also satisfy an analogous condition with respect to herself. This suggests that the full statement of the condition we want here will be along the lines of

(ii) we each intend the following: that we go to NYC by way of the intentions of each that we go to NYC (and that the route from these intentions to our joint activity satisfies the connection condition).

So each intends that his own intention that we go to NYC play its appropriate role in their going to NYC. Since each person's intention that we go to NYC is built into that person's intention in (ii), a natural way to understand each person's intention in (ii) is that it is in part about an element or aspect of itself: it is a reflexive intention that we go to NYC in part by way of one's intention that we go to NYC (and also by way of the other's intention that we go to NYC).[28] So understood, the intentions of each in (ii) will be both *interlocking* and *reflexive*.

I noted in Chapter 1 that some philosophers have thought that intentions are quite generally reflexive: intending X is, quite generally, intending X by way of this intention. The present idea that reflexivity is part of a conservative construction of shared intention need not involve this idea that intentions are quite generally reflexive. The pressure for reflexivity specifically in the shared case comes from the need for interpersonal interlocking in the shared case, plus an apparent similarity in attitude toward the other and toward oneself. And this pressure is not present quite generally for all cases of intention. So the appeal to condition (ii) does not require (though it does not preclude) the general view that all intentions are reflexive.

3. Intended mesh

In cases of shared intention the agents will normally have, or be on their way to adopting, relevant sub-plans. Perhaps when we intend to paint the house together I have a sub-plan of bringing the paint, and you have a sub-plan of bringing the ladder. I now want to reflect on the attitudes of each toward such sub-plans of the participants in shared intention.

Return to our shared intention to go to NYC together. There can be cases in which each of us intends that we go to NYC in part by way of the intention of the other that we go to NYC, and yet one or both of us intends to side step or override, perhaps using deception or coercion, the sub-plans of the other. Perhaps I intend that we go in part by way of your intention that we go, but I intend to trick you into taking the Amtrak train despite your firm intention to take the New Jersey local train. Since I intend to bypass your sub-plan, I do not intend that we go to NYC by way of sub-plans of each of us that are jointly compatible. But it seems that in shared intention there will be, in contrast, a tendency to track and to conform to a norm of compatibility across the relevant sub-plans of each. This helps explain the coordinating role of shared intention and is part of what is involved in each seeing the other as an intentional co-participant.

We can express the point by appeal to a standard form of functioning of shared intention. If we share an intention to go to NYC, and if you intend that we go to NYC by taking the New Jersey local train while I intend that we go by taking the Amtrak train, we have a problem. In a case of shared intention we will normally try to resolve that problem by making adjustments in one or both of these sub-plans, perhaps by way of bargaining, in the direction of co-possibility. So we want our construction to account for this standard social-norm-responsive functioning of the shared intention.

What is needed here is the idea of sub-plans that *mesh*. The sub-plans of the participants mesh when it is possible that all of these sub-plans taken together be successfully executed. We can then use in the construction the idea that each participant not only intends the joint activity, but each also intends that this joint activity proceed by way of *meshing* sub-plans of those intentions of those participants. We appeal, that is, to the condition that

(iii) we each intend the following: that we go to NYC by way of meshing sub-plans of each of our intentions in favor of going to NYC.

In this way our construction can ensure that each is committed to, and so appropriately responsive to, the consistent, coherent, and effective interweaving of the planning agency of one another in a way that tracks the intended joint action.

Your and my sub-plans can mesh even if they do not match. Perhaps your sub-plan specifies that we not go during rush hour, whereas mine leaves that issue open; yet our sub-plans are co-realizable. Further, what is central to shared intention is that we *intend* that we proceed by way of sub-plans that mesh. This can be true even if, as we know, our sub-plans do not now mesh, so long as we each intend that in the end our activity proceed by way of a solution to this problem. Nor need we each be willing to accept just any specification of activities of each that would suffice for the intended end. There may well be, for each of us, ways of achieving the intended end that are unacceptable, and this may manifest itself in conditions that are at least implicit in the sub-plans of each. If some such condition is violated by the sub-plans of the other then there is a breakdown in mesh.

A further point is that these intentions in favor of mesh can exploit various—as Scott Shapiro calls them—"mesh-creating mechanisms."[29] Sometimes we achieve mesh by way of our common understanding of what certain types of activity involve—what it is, say, to dance a tango rather than a polka. This can bring to bear various culture-specific conceptions. Sometimes we achieve mesh in part because of the way in which some object in the world is responding to our efforts. For example, given the way in which the piano is moving as we go up the stairs with it, I intend to push a bit to the left and you intend to adjust accordingly.[30] In small-scale cases of conflict about relevant sub-plans we would normally negotiate or bargain in some way, and our commitment to mesh will be in the background of such negotiation or bargaining. But we might resort to binding arbitration.[31]

These intentions of each in favor of interpersonal mesh in sub-plans are anchored in the intentions of each in favor of the relevant joint activity—in our example, the joint activity of our going to NYC. It is sub-plans with respect to this specific, particular intended end that are to mesh. There need not be intentions in favor of overall mesh of each person's overall plans. If a participant were to give up that particular intended end—give up, in our example, the end of the joint traveling to NYC—there would no longer be a commitment to relevant mesh in sub-plans (unless there were some other, relevant, more abstract joint action—say, going somewhere or other together—that remained intended by each and with respect to which each intended mesh in sub-plans).[32]

Does (iii) add a substantive condition that goes beyond (ii), or does it only make explicit what is already implicit in (ii)?[33] Suppose, as in (ii), that I intend that we act by way of your intention that we act and my intention that we act, and by way of a route from our minds to our joint activity that satisfies the connection condition. Do I thereby intend that our joint activity proceed by way of sub-plans that mesh?

Our answer will depend on the specific account we give of the connection condition, as that is included in the content of the intentions in (ii). This is a matter to which I turn in Chapter 3. What we will see there is that given my account of the connection condition, condition (iii) is indeed implicit in condition (ii), suitably understood. Nevertheless, it will promote understanding to cite (iii) as an explicit element of the construction.

What if I plan to achieve mesh in our sub-plans by coercing you to proceed in a certain way? Suppose that we each intend that we go to NYC together by way of sub-plans that mesh. You begin by intending, more specifically, that we go by car; I begin by intending, more specifically, that we go by bus. I then threaten you that unless we go by bus I will destroy your reputation, and you acquiesce. Our resulting sub-plans now both specify that we go by bus.[34] Do our sub-plans mesh?

I think that in most cases the answer will be "No". This is because the sub-plans of most planning agents will at least implicitly include a noncoercion condition with respect to the details of those sub-plans. This is a special case of the general point, noted earlier, that the sub-plans of each may include conditions on the acceptability of ways of achieving the end. So if I insist on coercing you in this way, I evidence the absence of an intention that we proceed by way of sub-plans that mesh.

This is not to preclude all asymmetries of power. Perhaps I have significant bargaining advantages, and so am able to exert pressure in the direction of sub-plans of each that are much closer to my liking than to yours. It still may be that these sub-plans mesh, so long as neither of us includes in his sub-plan a restriction that excludes such an asymmetry of bargaining power with respect to the details of the sub-plans. So it may be that you and I satisfy a version of (iii) even though each recognizes that there is this asymmetry in bargaining power. Shared action that involves such asymmetries may not conform to certain egalitarian ideals; but condition (iii) need not preclude such asymmetries.

Finally, consider competitive activities.[35] We might be engaged in a shared intentional activity of playing chess together, even though—since we are in competition—neither intends that there be mesh of sub-plans all the way down. This limits the extent to which what we do together is a cooperative activity. It does not, however, block a shared intention to play chess together, and it allows that our chess playing is a shared intentional activity. So there will be shared intentions that involve intentions on the part of each that only favor mesh in sub-plans down to a certain level. Nevertheless, given our interest in sufficient conditions for modest sociality, I will focus on cases that involve intention-like commitments to mesh all the way down.[36]

4. Intending, expecting, and a disposition to help

Suppose that I intend that we go to NYC in part by way of your intention that we go and meshing sub-plans, and in ways that cohere with the connection condition. My intention engages norms of means-end coherence and consistency. This puts rational pressure on me both to track necessary means to this intended end and to filter further intentions accordingly.

Now, sometimes we intend something given a certain precondition but do not intend that precondition. I might, for example, intend to respond to your threat, but not intend your threat. However, my cited intention that we go to NYC does not see your contribution to our joint activity as merely an expected precondition of our going to NYC, a precondition to which I am, as Nicholas Bardsley puts it, simply "adding-on" and "providing the finishing touch."[37] Your contribution to our going to NYC is, rather, a part of what I intend. In satisfying my side of (i)–(iii), part of what I intend is that we both go, where that involves your going in part by way of your intention that we go.

This means that the demands of means-end coherence and of consistency apply to my intention in favor of, *inter alia*, your playing your role in our joint activity: I am under rational pressure in favor of necessary means to that, and in favor of filtering out options incompatible with that. I am under rational pressure in the direction of steps needed as means if you are to play your role in our joint activity. And I am under rational pressure not to take steps that would thwart your playing your role. This mean that, insofar as I am rational, I will be to some extent disposed to help you play your role in our going to NYC if my help were to be needed.

Granted, I can intend our going, and so your role in our going, and still be willing to bear only a limited cost in helping you. Perhaps I am set to give up my intention if helping you unexpectedly becomes too onerous. (Though if these limits on my willingness to help were public, our shared intention might be less stable.) But if I intend our going then I am under rational pressure to be willing to some extent to help you if need be. This is in part because I need to be set not to thwart you; and so I need to be set to help you at least to the extent of refraining from thwarting you. But, further, if I intend our going, and do not just intend to go given that, as I expect, you will go, I will be under rational pressure to be willing to some extent to provide some (perhaps limited) positive support for your role in our going. And I am under such rational pressure even if I expect that you will in fact not need such help.[38]

5. Out in the open

Analogues of (i)–(iii) will be basic building blocks in our construction. Given the planning theory, these intentions of each will help ensure modes of norm-guided functioning that are characteristic of shared intention. These modes of functioning will include intention-like responsiveness of each to the end of the shared action, the pursuit of coherent and effective interweaving of sub-plans, and at least minimal dispositions to help.

The next point is that in shared intention the fact of the shared intention will normally be out in the open: there will be public access to the fact of shared intention. Such public access to the shared intention will normally be involved in further thought that is characteristic of shared intention, as when we plan together how to carry out our shared intention. Since such shared planning about how to carry out our shared intention is part of the normal functioning of that shared intention, we need an element in our construction of shared intention whose functioning supports some such thinking of each about our shared intention.

It is here that something like a common knowledge condition seems apt, at least given our primary interest in sufficient conditions. As noted in Chapter 1, there are different approaches to common knowledge, and my hope is provide a theoretical framework for thinking about modest sociality that is available to different approaches. To fix ideas, however, we can here think of common knowledge as consisting in a hierarchy of cognitive aspects of the relevant individuals: it is common knowledge among A and B that p just when (a) A knows that p, (b) B knows that p, (c) A knows that B knows that p, (d) B knows that A knows that p, (e) A is in an epistemic position to know that (d), (f) B is in an epistemic position to know that (c), and so on. And what we want is that a constituent of our shared intention to J is a form of such common knowledge of that very intention.[39] But we do not want to reintroduce problems about circularity by explicitly including in the content of the individual attitudes that are involved in the common knowledge the very idea of shared intention: we do not want simply to say, for example, that each knows that they share the intention. This suggests that we appeal to common knowledge whose content is, more precisely, that the cited multiple components of the shared intention are in place. And we can do this by adding as a further building block:

(vii) [40] there is common knowledge among the participants of the conditions cited in this construction.

It is important that such knowledge is primarily about intention and belief, and not about each person's "vasty deep."[41] If shared agency were generally to require a depth-psychological knowledge of the minds of the participants, shared agency would be much more difficult and much less common than it is. But knowledge of relevant intentions and beliefs seems less problematic and more within ordinary human cognitive limits.

On the assumption that the required common knowledge involves the relevant knowledge of each participant, condition (vii) induces a tight connection between shared intention and each participant's knowledge that the conditions obtain that constitute the shared intention. How does this connection compare to the connection between intention and knowledge in the case of an individual agent? Suppose that I intend to go shopping on Tuesday. Normally, I will know that I so intend. And my knowledge will have two features. First, it will normally not be based primarily on the kind of evidence I usually need to arrive at knowledge of another person's intentions. I normally have some sort of special standing with respect to, or epistemic access to, my own intentions—though exactly how to fill in this idea is a matter of controversy. Further, when I think "I intend to go shopping on Tuesday" I normally seem to be, as Sydney Shoemaker says, "immune to error through misidentification" of *whose* intention is at issue.[42]

I do not say that whenever I intend *A* I know that I so intend. It seems possible, for example, that while I think I intend to shop on Tuesday, I am being absent-minded and what I actually intend is to shop on Monday.[43] Nevertheless, I will normally know what I intend, and my knowledge will normally have the cited pair of features.

Now, in the case of shared intention, my knowledge of the conditions that constitute our shared intention will involve my knowledge about relevant intentions of the *others*. And this knowledge will be importantly different from my normal knowledge of my own intention. My belief that *you* intend that we *J*, if it is to be justified, will normally need to draw substantially on standard sorts of evidence. And there is here no immunity to errors of misidentification of the others. So my knowledge of the conditions that constitute our *shared* intention will normally draw substantially on ordinary sources of evidence, and is in a context in which certain kinds of "error through misidentification" remain possible. In these two important respects, the participants' knowledge of conditions that help constitute a shared intention, knowledge that is itself a constituent of that shared intention, differs from the kind of knowledge an individual normally has of his own intentions.

Conditions (i)–(iii) and (vii) provide basic building blocks for our construction. But now we need to return, as promised, to our rejection of the own-action condition. This will lead us to reflect on important forms of interdependence between the intentions of the participants in a shared intention.

3 BUILDING BLOCKS, PART 2

1. I intend that we J, and the own-action condition

In Chapter 2 I argued in favor of including in our building blocks for our shared intention to go together to New York City (NYC) the following four conditions:

(i) we each intend that we go to NYC

(ii) we each intend the following: that we go to NYC by way of the intentions of each that we go to NYC (and that the route from these intentions to our joint activity satisfies the connection condition).

(iii) we each intend the following: that we go to NYC by way of meshing sub-plans of each of our intentions in favor of going to NYC.

(vii) there is common knowledge among the participants of the conditions cited in this construction.

Let's focus for now on the intentions cited in (i). These intentions violate the own-action condition. It is time to see whether this grounds an objection.[1]

What might lead a theorist to accept the own-action condition as a condition on intention? Granted, if we use only the infinitive construction—intending *to*—then it will seem that we are indeed limited in this way. But we also have the idea of intending *that*.[2] We seem, for example, to be at home with talk of a parent's intention that his son clean up his room, or a teacher's intention that the class discussion have a certain character, or a composer's intention that the performance of the finale be grand, or your intentions concerning how the executor of your will is to distribute your assets.[3] We seem to be at home with the idea that my intention can sometimes concern and more or less ensure or settle a complex that involves the intentional activity of others. This suggests that we should take seriously the idea of intending that, as well as the idea of intending to.

Once we take seriously the idea of intending that, it will be no defense of the own-action condition simply to say that in intending X one believes or supposes one's intention will (likely) lead to or ensure X. After all, I can believe that my intention that my son clean up his room will lead to his cleaning the room; and you can believe that your intention will lead to appropriate actions on the part of the executor of your will. If there are persuasive grounds for the own-action condition on intending, they will require some further articulation and development.

Perhaps in the background here there is a general skepticism about the very idea of intentions that are plan states that are not identified with intentional actions.[4] And perhaps one can try to argue that if one's intention is itself one's own intentional activity, what is intended is always, at bottom, one's own activity. But a major lesson of the planning theory is that appeal to plan states that need not themselves be intentional actions provides important resources for understanding the diachronic structure of our agency. So, though there are large issues that I will not try to settle here, I think that a persuasive defense of the own-action condition cannot rest simply on a flat-out skepticism about such plan states. So let us try to understand what further basis for the own-action condition on intending there might be. We can then try to respond to these concerns.

Without claiming to exhaust the field, I will discuss two lines of thought that may seem to support the own-action condition on intention. My argument will be that in neither case do we have good reason to accept that condition on intention. I will then turn, in the next section, to a different but related objection, one that appeals not to the own-action condition but rather to what I will be calling the settle condition on intention, and/or to a related control condition.

The first idea in purported support of the own-action condition comes from Frederick Stoutland, who writes:

> An agent cannot intend to A if she is not prepared to take full responsibility for having done A intentionally . . .
>
> This condition can be met only if the agent who intends the action *is* the agent whose action fulfills it.[5]

I take it that Stoutland aims to be offering an argument for the own-action condition that does not simply presuppose, without argument, that all intending is intending *to*. Rather, Stoutland aims to provide an argument for the own-action condition that appeals to a connection between intending and taking full responsibility. I am, however, skeptical about both elements in this argument.

Begin with the idea that to intend X I need to be prepared to "take full responsibility" for X. Now, I agree that adult humans normally should be prepared to take full responsibility for an intended X, in the sense of being prepared to be held accountable for X. And we normally take a person's speech act of expressing her intention as a way of indicating that she is indeed taking responsibility in this sense. But I do not see this as essential to intending, though it may well be central to the normal social functioning of adult human beings who are intenders. Intending, as I see it, is to be understood in terms of its roles in planning agency. Its role in practices of accountability seems to me, while obviously of the first importance, not essential to what intending is—though such practices of accountability would make less sense if intending did not play something like the roles highlighted here. It seems to me that you can be a planning agent while being reticent to take responsibility for what you plan to do. Indeed, someone can be a planning agent and yet refuse to treat himself as accountable at all. Perhaps a certain kind of sociopath is like this. Such an agent would be cut off from important aspects of our social world; but such an agent might still be a (scary) planning agent. To deny that such a sociopath could be a planning agent would be to moralize[6] the very idea of intending in ways that seem to me not plausible.

Both for individual and for shared intention there may be a temptation to see a connection to accountability—or anyway, to believed or accepted accountability—as an essential feature. Stoutland's idea here is a version of such a view. But I think that we get a better understanding of these most basic elements in our psychic economy by seeing the connection to (believed or accepted) accountability as grounded in more basic roles in thought and action, rather than as definitive of the very phenomenon of intending.

By the way, I do not recommend this strategy for all talk of intentionality. In earlier work I conjectured, drawing on work of Gilbert Harman, that our commonsense idea of acting intentionally is indeed tied to judgments about accountability. In the case of individual intentional action I saw this as one reason to be wary of an overly tight connection between intending and intentional action, and so to be wary of what I called the "simple view."[7] That is why I talked of "two faces of intention," one—as in the case of the verb 'to intend'—tied to psychological explanation and understanding, and one—as in the case of the adverb 'intentionally'—to some extent responsive to concerns with accountability. And there may well be similar complexities in our concepts of shared intentional and shared cooperative activity. But here my focus is specifically on intending and its roles in the individual's practical thinking and action, roles that help explain our agency, both individual and shared.

In any case, I am skeptical also of Stoutland's second idea, which is that I can be prepared to take full responsibility for *X* only if *X* is my action. Perhaps I will be prepared to take *sole* responsibility for *X* only if *X* is my action (though even this is not obvious—why cannot *X* sometimes be a non-action state of affairs that I cause?). But I do not see why I can be prepared to take *full* responsibility for *X* only if *X* is my action. If you and I conspire to rob a bank together, I can be prepared to take full responsibility for this joint robbery— and so can you, though neither of us should think he is *solely* responsible.[8]

I think, then, that appeals to the relation between intending and taking responsibility should not lead us to endorse the own-action condition on intending. So let me turn to a second potential ground for this own-action condition. This potential ground derives from the thought that intending involves an anticipation of the experience of acting. We can express the thought this way: when I intend to *A* I am normally in a position to "anticipate experiencing,"[9] from the perspective of he who is acting, the performance of *A*. In violating the own-action condition a purported intention that *we J* fails to involve this connection between intending X and being in a position to anticipate experiencing, from the perspective of he who is acting, the performance of X. This is because I am not in a position to anticipate experiencing, from the perspective of he who is acting, *our* performance of *J*. And this is because there is not something which is a group's experience of acting. But this connection to anticipating experiencing, from the perspective of he who is acting, the execution of an intention, is a basic feature of intention. So it is a mistake to appeal to my intending that we *J*. Or so it is claimed.

I think, however, that this objection overgeneralizes.[10] It may be that to intend *to* A I need to be in a position to anticipate experiencing, from the perspective of he who is acting, the performance of A. But this is not essential to intending *that*—as when I intend that my son clean up his room. We can still see intending *that* as intending, though of course differences in content between intending *that* and intending *to* will be important. We can see intending that as intending because we can expect that intending that will be suitably embedded in the relevant, plan-theoretic nexus of roles and norms. Intending that will respond to a demand for means-end coherence by posing problems for means-end reasoning; it will respond to demands for agglomeration and consistency by filtering incompatible options; it will normally involve associated tracking and associated guidance of thought and action; it will be subject to norms of stability; and so on. And it is by virtue of being embedded in this nexus of roles and norms that an attitude qualifies as one of intending—in contrast with, for example, ordinary desire or belief.[11] It is intending *that* we J—not intending to—that is needed in condition (i) of our theory of shared intention; and in intending that we J I need not anticipate experiencing, from the perspective of he who is acting, our J-ing.

I conclude that condition (i) is not challenged by an acceptable own-action condition. Since my grounds for saying this are that we do not have good reason to accept such a condition on intention, we can also conclude that conditions (ii) and (iii) are not blocked by an acceptable own-action condition.

This is compatible with the point that if I intend that we J and I am rational then I will intend my (known) part in our J-ing.[12] If I rationally intend that we J I will intend to help bring it about that we J by performing my part in our J-ing.[13] And that latter intention does satisfy the own-action condition. But it does not follow that I do not, as well, intend that we J; and my intention that we J will normally play important roles in my relevant thought and action.[14]

2. The settle condition, and persistence interdependence

I now turn, as promised, to an objection that does not insist that intentions must satisfy the own-action condition, but appeals rather to the idea of an intention settling or controlling what is intended. As before, I will begin by focusing on the intentions cited in condition (i), and then return to conditions (ii) and (iii) at the end of this section.

J. David Velleman poses the challenge in a clear and forceful way.[15] He writes:

> Your intentions . . . are attitudes that resolve deliberative questions, thereby settling issues that are up to you.[16]

Suppose then—to focus on the general case—that I intend that we J. So my intention settles the issue of whether we J. But then how can you too intend that we J? For you to intend that we J *your* intention must settle whether we J. But if I have settled this issue, how can you settle it, too? We can put this as a concern about how I can see my intention that we J:

> How can I frame the intention that "we" are going to act, if I simultaneously regard the matter as being partly up to you? And how can I continue to regard the matter as partly up to you, if I have already

decided that we really *are* going to act? The model seems to require the exercise of more discretion than there is to go around.[17]

The model of shared intention that I am proposing requires that each of us intends that we *J*. But then it seems that each of us needs to believe that his intention really does settle whether we *J*. Call this the *settle condition* on intention. And the concern is that it is difficult to see how we could *both* be right.

Now, whereas I have argued that it is a mistake to treat the own-action condition as a condition on intention, I agree that something like this settle condition is a plausible constraint on the intention that we *J*. Indeed, I built a related idea into my initial description of the characteristic roles of plan states, when I included in that description the settling role of intention. I will argue, however, that both of the intentions cited in condition (i) can sensibly satisfy this constraint;[18] and understanding why will help us articulate important building blocks of shared intention.

A basic step in response to this challenge is to appeal to an appropriate kind of interdependence between each person's intention that we *J*. This interdependence can help explain how it can be true that the intention of *each* of the participants settles whether they *J*. To see this, begin with

(a) we each intend that we *J*.

And now suppose that these intentions of each are interdependent: other things equal,[19] each will continue so to intend if, but only if, the other continues so to intend. Suppose, more precisely, that there is this interdependence because each will know whether or not the other continues so to intend, and each will adjust to this knowledge in a way that involves responsiveness to norms of individual plan-theoretic rationality.[20] Call this *persistence interdependence*. And suppose that

(b) there is persistence interdependence between the intentions of each in (a).

Finally, let us suppose that these intentions in (a) would together be appropriately effective. That is:

(c) if we do both intend as in (a), then we will *J* by way of those intentions (and in accordance with the connection condition).[21]

And now a basic point is that if we are in the conditions specified in (a)–(c) then each of our intentions in (a) will settle whether we J in part by way of its support of the intention of the other. In such a situation my intention that we J (in (a)) supports (by way of (b)) the persistence of your correspond-ing intention, and these intentions of each of us in favor of our J-ing to-gether lead appropriately to our J-ing (as in (c)). My intention that we J leads to our J-ing, in part by way of its support of your intention that we J, and vice versa. The control my intention has over our J-ing goes in part by way of its support of your intention that we J. And vice versa. So my intention in (a) settles that we J, in part by way of its support of your intention that we J; and vice versa.[22] So given (b) and (c), the intentions in (a) *each* settle whether we will J.

Suppose then that (a)–(c) are true and this is known by each of us. In knowing (a)–(c), each knows that *his* intention that we J will appropriately lead to *our* J-ing in part by way of its support of the other's intention that we J (and thereby of the other's relevant actions). Each knows this while also knowing that the corresponding intention of the other participant also appropriately leads to the joint J-ing, in part by way of its support (as in (b)) for his own relevant intention. Each knows that he would give up his intention that we J if, in conditions of common knowledge, the other were to change her mind in relevant ways. And each knows that the other's intention that we J is similarly dependent on his own intention that we J.[23] So each can see her own intention that we J as settling whether we J, while also recognizing that the other's in-tention also settles that. So each can intend that we J and also, as Velleman says, "simultaneously regard the matter as being partly up to" the other. So in shared intention both can coherently intend that we J, where these intentions satisfy the settle condition. And this can be true even though these intentions violate the own-action condition.[24]

This also explains why each person's intention that we J will, given these conditions, satisfy an analogous control condition:[25] each will sensi-bly see her intention that we J as controlling (though not as the sole control of) whether they together J, where this control goes by way of the other agent's intention, one that is itself supported by her own intention given persistence interdependence. So while each person's intention that we J fails the own-action condition—a condition I have argued against—each can in this way satisfy plausible versions of a settle condition and a control condition.

What about the more complex intentions cited in (ii) and (iii)? The con-tents of these intentions spell out how it is that the agents intend that the intentions in (i) will lead to the joint activity. And the basic answer is that the resources to which we appealed in explaining how the intentions in (i) can satisfy an appropriate settle condition (and so an appropriate control condition) can be used for a similar defense of (ii) and (iii).

We can simplify our discussion by focusing on the settle condition, and by anticipating a result from section 7. There I argue that in intending conformity to the connection condition one intends relevant meshing of sub-plans. This means that we can focus on the intentions in (ii), since they will bring in their wake the intentions in (iii). So, to consider a generalized version of (ii), suppose that each knows that

(d) we each intend the following: that we *J* by way of the intentions of each that we *J* and in a way that satisfies the connection condition

To articulate an analogue of (c), let us also suppose that each knows that

(e) if we do both intend as in (d), then we will *J* by way of those intentions (and in accordance with the connection condition).

And, as before, each also knows that

(b) there is persistence interdependence between the intentions of each in (a).

Now, the intentions of each in (a) are each aspects of the intentions of each in (d). So if each knows that (b) then each is in a position to know that her intention in (d) supports and is supported by the other's intention in (d), by way of the interdependence in (b). So if each knows that (b), (d), and (e), then each is in a position to know that her intention in (d) will appropriately lead to the joint *J*-ing in part by way of its support (by way of (b)) of the other's intention in (d). And each is in a position to know that the intention of the other in (d) also will appropriately lead to the joint *J*-ing in part by way of its support (by way of (b)) for her own intention in (d). So each can acknowledge both that her intention in (d) settles the joint *J*-ing in accordance with the connection condition (where this goes by way of support for the other's intention in (a), and thereby for the other's intention in (d)), and that the other's intention in (d) has a similar settling role. So each can intend as in (d) and yet "simultaneously regard the matter as being partly up to" the other. So, in particular, the intentions of each in (ii) can each satisfy an appropriate settle condition.

3. Persistence interdependence and overdetermination

Let me now reflect further on the very idea of persistence interdependence. Suppose that, as in (b), there is persistence interdependence between each of our intentions in favor of the joint activity. My recognition of your persisting intention helps support the persistence of my intention in a way that involves the rational functioning of my own psychic economy. And similarly for you. The idea is not that the support that each intention that we J provides for the other must be a matter of leading the other to a *new* intention that we J. It is possible that the onset of one intention triggers the onset of the other; though such dependence would be asymmetrical. What is needed, however, is not *onset* interdependence, which would be a puzzling idea, but rather that the *persistence* of one's intention that we J supports the *continued persistence* of the other's intention that we J, and vice versa. Think of two boards independently placed in a vertical position immediately next to but not touching each other. Each continues standing only if the other does. But for each board the etiology of the fact that it is standing does not involve the other board. The dependencies in (b) can be like this.[26]

For example, at the end of a wonderful concert each of us might intend that we applaud together. That this was a wonderful concert is, among us, what Robert Stalnaker calls a "manifest event": it is an event "that, when it occurs, is mutually recognized to have occurred."[27] This supports my confidence, given our common knowledge about the kind of people who attend such concerts, that you also intend that we applaud together. And similarly for you. Each of us arrives at his intention that we applaud primarily in response to the performance and its manifest quality, together with relevant prior common knowledge about the kind of person who attends such concerts. Neither assures or promises the other in the run-up to the shared applause. Nevertheless, if I were to give up my intention that we applaud you would recognize this and, let's suppose, as a result give up your intention that we applaud (though you might put in its place simply an intention to applaud on your own); and this would be a matter of your own rational functioning.[28] And, let's suppose, vice versa. So the persistence of each of our intentions that we applaud is rationally dependent on the persistence of the other's corresponding intention, even though the onset of each person's intention that we applaud is due primarily to some external event (the wonderful concert) together with relevant, background common knowledge, not to some prior causal influence of an intention of the other that we applaud, or an intentional effort by the other to assure.

The dependence here is a form of counterfactual dependence: I intend that we *J*; you intend that we *J*; if but only if you were to cease so intending then, other things equal, so would I; and vice versa.[29] In understanding this interdependence, however, we need to be careful about possible forms of over-determination.

Suppose that if you were to cease intending that we *J* you would intend something else, and suppose that this would be enough for you to make your contribution to our *J*-ing. And suppose that this would suffice for me to retain my intention that we *J*. (Though in this counterfactual situation we would no longer have a *shared* intention to *J* since you would no longer intend that we *J*.) In such a case it might not be true in our actual situation that if you were to cease intending that we *J* then I would also cease intending that we *J*. Nevertheless, in such a case what you in fact intend is that we *J*, and this is the intention that I recognize as supporting our *J*-ing; and, further, I would indeed give up my intention that we *J* if you gave up yours and it was not replaced by a different intention that would suffice for your part in our *J*-ing. In this sense my intention that we *J* is counterfactually dependent on your intention that we *J*, *other things equal*—where those other things include the absence of such a substitute intention on your part. And we will want to interpret the dependence in (b) as such a counterfactual dependence—other things equal, one that allows for such forms of overdetermination.

Return to our shared intention to applaud. Suppose that if you were to give up your intention that we applaud you would put in its place an intention to applaud on your own. And suppose that if I knew you had made this substitution I would still intend that we applaud in the light of my knowledge that your intention to applaud, together with my intention that we applaud, would lead to our applauding. (Though in this counterfactual case in which you do not intend that we applaud, but only intend to applaud, we do not share an intention to applaud.) It can remain true that my intention that we applaud is counterfactually dependent on your intention that we applaud, other things equal—where those other things include the absence of such a substitute intention on your part.[30]

Return to Seamus Miller's example of the two tunnel builders.[31] Perhaps what is true in Miller's example is that I intend that we build the tunnel, and so do you; but if you were to replace your intention that we build the tunnel with an intention simply to dig halfway, I would still intend that we build the tunnel.[32] In this counterfactual situation we would not share an intention to build the tunnel together, since in this counterfactual situation (in contrast with the actual situation) you would not intend that we build it. But the question now is whether this indicates that in our actual situation my intention that we build the tunnel is not appropriately dependent on your intention that we build the tunnel. And the answer is: No. In such a case my intention that we build the tunnel remains counterfactually dependent on your intention that we build the tunnel, other things equal. After all, I would abandon my intention that we build the tunnel if you abandoned yours and did not put in its place some such intention to dig halfway.

This takes us to a final complication.[33] Suppose that we each intend that we *J*. Suppose that in a counterfactual circumstance in which you were to abandon your intention that we *J* and not put a relevant substitute in its place, I would be confident that—perhaps by way of my own persuasive powers— you will, in a sufficiently timely way, return to the fold and come again to intend that we *J*. And suppose that, given that confidence, I would throughout retain my intention that we *J*. In this counterfactual situation, then, I would retain my intention that we *J* even while you no longer so intend. Still, my intention that we *J* does depend on my expectation of the timely return of your intention that we *J*. So, in the actual situation, my intention that we *J* remains appropriately dependent on your intention that we *J*.

4. Three forms of persistence interdependence

The persistence interdependence between my intention that we *J* and your intention that we *J* involves mutual rational support. My intention that we *J* will be rationally sensible given that I know that you intend that we *J*; and my intention that we *J* would cease to be rationally sensible if I came to know that you no longer so intend.[34] And vice versa.[35] It is this abstractly characterized interrelation between the participants to which we have appealed in defending the ability of each of the intentions in favor of our *J*-ing to satisfy an appropriate settle condition. And we will be appealing to this abstractly characterized interrelation when we turn in section 6 in this chapter to further building blocks for our construction. Nevertheless, it is important to note that this abstractly characterized interrelation can be realized in several different (though potentially overlapping) ways.

Suppose that we each intend that we *J*. And assume for simplicity that there is symmetry in the type of dependence of each on each. The persistence interdependence between these intentions of each might be grounded in the judgment of each that so long as each continues so to intend, this intended joint activity would be desirable, but if either of us stopped so intending then that joint activity would no longer be desirable.

Romeo, for example, might see Juliet's intention that they flee together as necessary for the desirability of their fleeing together. As Romeo sees it, their fleeing together would be desirable if and only if each of them so intends; and, in particular, it would not be desirable if instead Juliet only intended to flee (to avoid the tax collector, perhaps). And, let's suppose, vice versa. Given the assumption that each will retain her or his intention so long as she or he continues to judge that the joint activity would be desirable, and given that all this is out in the open, each will know that the other will continue so to intend just in case she herself continues so to intend. And that is a kind of known persistence interdependence that can explain how the intention of each in favor of the joint activity can satisfy the settle condition. Call this *desirability-based interdependence*.

In a second kind of case, the persistence interdependence between these intentions of each is grounded in the knowledge of each that the joint *J*-ing would be realistically possible, other things equal, just in case both intend that joint *J*-ing. Consider, for example, two gang members, Alex and Ben. Each thinks that their going together to NYC would be desirable, and each intends that they do indeed go together to NYC. Each recognizes that given the complexities, and given the limits on the power of each, this joint activity is not going to happen, other things equal, unless both of them so intend,[36] though it will indeed happen if each does so intend. But neither sees the other's intention as contributing to the desirability of their joint travelling to NYC. Perhaps each would get a reward so long as there is the joint travelling. Each sees the other's intention as only a feasibility condition—and not a desirability condition—for what he intends, namely that the two of them go to NYC together.[37] Nevertheless, rationally to intend X one must not believe that X is not realistically possible. So these known relations of feasibility can support a known persistence interdependence, one that can explain how the intention of each in favor of the joint activity can satisfy the settle condition. Call this *feasibility-based* interdependence.

In a case of solely feasibility-based interdependence, each has a kind of opportunistic attitude toward the other: each is prepared to take advantage of the fact that the other has the needed intention even though, as he sees it, that intention does not contribute to the desirability of the joint activity. This contrasts with the joint activities of lovers or friends. And many joint activities will be in this respect like that of lovers or friends: they will be joint activities in which each sees the intention of the other in favor of the joint activity as significantly contributing to the desirability of that joint activity. Still, not all sharing is the sharing of lovers or of friends; and such opportunistic attitudes need not baffle shared intention so long as the other conditions for shared intention are satisfied. Modest sociality can be opportunistic sociality.[38]

Such modest but opportunistic sociality is not merely a matter of strategic interaction. Each still *intends* that the joint activity proceed appropriately by way of the relevant intention of the other. Even if Alex knows that the dependence of his intention on Ben's is only a feasibility-based dependence, he can still intend that their going together to NYC involve the effective role of Ben's intention. Alex can be disposed to help Ben play his role if that help is needed. And Alex can be set to filter options with an eye to consistency with the role of Ben's intention in the joint action. After all, even if Alex does not see Ben's intention as contributing to the desirability of the joint activity, he does see that Ben's intention and its effectiveness is, in the circumstances, needed for the feasibility of the joint activity. And that can be a reason for Alex to intend that Ben's intention be effective in the joint activity, and not merely to expect that Ben will act in accordance with what he intends.

Turn now to a third kind of case of persistence interdependence. Sometimes the relevant mutual support will involve the recognition by each of mutual moral obligations in which earlier interactions have issued. Suppose, for example, that each has promised the other that she will stick with the joint project so long as the other also sticks with it. And suppose that as a result each has an associated obligation to stick with her intention in favor of the joint project so long as the other does. Suppose further that each cares enough about such obligations that she will retain her intention so long as she continues to have this obligation to retain it. If all this is out in the open, each will know that they will both continue to intend the joint project just in case she herself continues so to intend. And that is a kind of known persistence interdependence that can explain how the intention of each in favor of the joint activity can satisfy the settle condition. Call this *obligation-based interdependence*. There can be desirability-based and/or feasibility-based interdependence that does not depend on such obligation-based interdependence, though a shared intention that involves such desirability-based and/or feasibility-based interdependence might issue in downstream interactions that induce, in addition, obligation-based interdependence.

We have, then, at least these three forms of persistence interdependence. A particular case may involve various combinations of these three forms of interdependence. That said, and as noted, it is the abstractly characterized, generic interrelation of persistence interdependence that will figure as a basic building block in our theory.

When there is such persistence interdependence, the stability of each participant's intention that we *J* will tend to make the other's intention that we *J* stable. And we have seen that, according to the planning theory, there are distinctive rational pressures in favor of stability of intention.[39] Given persistence interdependence, these plan-theoretic pressures for the stability of the relevant intention of one of the participants induce corresponding pressures for the stability of the corresponding intention of the other participant, and vice versa.[40]

5. Persistence interdependence, etiology, and temporal asymmetry

Recall conditions (a)–(c):

(a) we each intend that we *J*,
(b) there is persistence interdependence between the intentions of each in (a),
(c) if we do both intend as in (a), then we will *J* by way of those intentions (and in accordance with the connection condition).

I have argued that when these conditions are known, both intentions that we *J* can satisfy the settle condition even though neither agent unilaterally determines what happens. But (b) concerns the *persistence* of each person's intention that we *J*. So we can ask: how exactly do we each *arrive at* those intentions? Given the interdependence in (b), it may seem that I cannot form my intention that we *J* until you do, but also that you cannot form your intention that we *J* until I do. So how could we ever get started?[41]

Well, sometimes there is an element in our common environment that sensibly induces the structures in (a)–(c). This is what happens in the case—discussed in section 3—of shared applause in response to the wonderful concert we have all just heard. Here the public wonderfulness of the concert is a kind of catalyst, given our prior common knowledge about who attends such concerts and their dispositions in the direction of intending that the group applaud in response to such a concert. This catalyst publically makes sense of group applause as an appropriate response; and it thereby publically helps make sense of intentions in favor of the group applause, and thereby helps induce intentions of each in favor of the group applause. Granted, each of these intentions in favor of the group's applause is formed on the assumption that the others also so intend, an assumption grounded in common knowledge of the kind of person who attends such concerts. And that is in part why there is persistence interdependence. But non-conditional intentions are commonly formed against a background of certain assumptions about the world.

I do not say that in such a circumstance the formation by each of an intention in favor of the group applause is a uniquely rational outcome. There need be no rational breakdown if some are more cautious and only form a conditional intention that favors the group applause if (but only if) others intend that the group applaud. This might set the stage for the kind of interaction I describe later. Nevertheless, there also need be no rational breakdown if each member of the audience simply arrives at a nonconditional intention that the group applaud, given their confidence, grounded in relevant common knowledge, that this is what the others will do—though the persistence of these nononditional intentions of each can still depend on the persistence of these nonconditional intentions of the others.

Here is another example.[42] You and I are the only people sitting on the beach, and we are watching our friend swimming. Nearby is a rescue boat whose operation requires two people. All this is out in the open. Suddenly our friend yells for help. Given our common knowledge both of our situation and of relevant dispositions of each, we each respond by forming an intention that we together use the boat to save him. Each intention is formed on the assumption that the other also so intends, an assumption grounded in relevant common knowledge. And that is in part why there is persistence interdependence. In particular, there is feasibility-interdependence, since it is common knowledge that the use of the boat requires both of us. (This can be true even though, were you to drop out, I would turn to another, personal plan for saving our friend—say, to call 911.)

Again, while this is a sensible and intelligible outcome, it need not be the uniquely rational outcome. Perhaps you only conditionally intend that we use the boat together if I intend that we use it. I then make manifest my nonconditional intention that we use it. And so you too arrive at a nonconditional intention that we use it.

Sometimes, then, the route to our interdependent intentions in favor of our joint activity is grounded primarily in a catalyst in our common environment: a wonderful concert, say, or an emergency. But sometimes this route centrally involves a characteristic kind of interaction over time.

In one such interaction over time I simply indicate to you my nonconditional intention in favor of the joint activity, given my confidence that you will thereby be led also to that nonconditional intention. After all, though I know that you are a free agent, I can still many times reliably predict how you would freely respond in various circumstances. In particular, given my knowledge of the kind of person you are—what you care about, how you feel about me, how you see our present circumstances, and so on—I can many times reliably predict that if I were to intend that we *J* and make that manifest, then your knowledge of my intention would lead you also to intend that we *J*. I can reliably predict this without supposing I have any special authority to tell you what to do, any more than I need to suppose I have such authority when I reliably predict you will voluntarily tell me the time when I ask for it. So in many cases I can form the intention that we *J* fully confident that you will thereby then be led also to intend that we *J*. (This interaction need not be explicitly linguistic, by the way. Perhaps I just start singing the tenor part of a duet we know well; as I expect, you thereby recognize my intention that we sing the duet together; and so, as I predict, you too intend that we sing and so come in with the alto part.)

Some such interactions may also involve a prior stage-setting. You might set the stage by forming and announcing a conditional intention that we *J* if I nonconditionally intend that we *J*. And I might recognize this and so form and announce my nonconditional intention that we *J*, fully confident that this will lead you also to such a nonconditional intention. In this way we might be led to interdependent, nonconditional intentions in favor of our *J*-ing.

In some versions of these interactions there is a kind of assurance or promise that potentially grounds relevant moral obligations. Perhaps you promise that if I intend that we *J* then so will you. And so I go ahead and form and announce the intention that we *J*. In such cases we can thereby be led to promissory obligations of a sort involved in obligation-based persistence interdependence. I will return to such cases in Chapter 5.

When the persistence interdependence arises by way of such interactions (whether or not these lead to obligation-based interdependence) there will be symmetry in the resulting persistence dependence of each person's intention on the other, even though the etiology of those intentions involves a temporal asymmetry. When there is such an asymmetry in etiology, there will be a period during which I intend that we *J* but you do not (yet)—a period during which there is not yet a shared intention to *J*. Nevertheless, even during this preliminary period I will believe that you will (shortly) come to intend that we *J*, in part by way of your recognition of my intention. And that is enough for me sensibly to believe, even during this time lag, that my intention that we *J* will be effective, in part by way of its support of your corresponding intention.

6. Further building blocks

In defending the coherence of both your and my intention that we *J*, given a plausible settle condition, I have appealed to cases in which we each know that

(a) we each intend that we *J*,
(b) there is persistence interdependence between the intentions of each in (a), and
(c) if we do both intend as in (a), then we will *J* by way of those intentions (and in accordance with the connection condition).

In the light of this appeal, what further building blocks should we explicitly introduce into our construction of shared intention and modest sociality?[43]

A preliminary point is that we already have on board a common knowledge condition. So we can suppose that both conditions (i)-(iii) and whatever further building blocks we introduce will fall within the scope of this common knowledge.

So let us return to our shared intention to go to NYC. Here, in light of the appeal to (c) in our defense of the coherence of each in intending that we *J*, and in light of the common knowledge of (i), it seems that we will at least want to add to our construction associated beliefs on the part of each:

(iv) we each believe the following: if each of us continues to intend that we go to NYC, then we will go to NYC by way of those intentions (and in accordance with the connection condition).

In this way we build into the construction a condition that helps ensure the coherence of the intentions cited in conditions (i)–(iii). Granted, in order to make the case as strong as possible in defending the coherence of each participant's intention that we *J*, I earlier appealed to *knowledge* of condition (c). But now we can observe that if (assuming other relevant conditions in the background) those intentions that we *J* are coherent in a case in which each knows (c), they will be coherent if each believes (c).[44] So for the purpose of ensuring the coherence of relevant intentions in the construction we can just add (iv) to the construction.[45]

A complication is that, as I see it, it is too strong to say, quite generally, that in order to intend X one must believe that if one continues so to intend then it will be that X.[46] But our primary concern now is with sufficient conditions for robust forms of shared intention and modest sociality. So we can reasonably include among these conditions somewhat strong beliefs about success, as described in (iv).

Should we also include the condition that these beliefs in (iv) are true? No. We want to allow for the possibility of a shared intention that fails.

Turn now to (b). Here again it seems that in light of our appeal to knowledge of (b) to support the coherence of each intending the joint action, and in light of the common knowledge of (i), we will at least want to add to our construction relevant beliefs about interdependence:

(v) we each believe that our intentions in (i) are persistence interdependent.[47]

Should we also include the condition that these beliefs in (v) are true? Well, I do not think we need to assume that they are true in order to guarantee the coherence of the intentions on the part of each that we go to NYC. If, as I have argued, those intentions are each coherent (assuming other relevant conditions in the background) in a case in which each knows (b), they will each be coherent if each believes (b). Nevertheless, it does seem that at least in central cases of shared intention and modest sociality the participants will not be in error in having these beliefs about interdependence: modest sociality will normally not be built on such an illusion on the part of the participants about how they are interconnected. Granted, even in the face of such mutual misunderstanding there could be aspects of modest sociality, especially if the absence of interdependence was not manifest. Nevertheless, given that we are aiming at sufficient conditions for robust forms of modest sociality, it seems reasonable to add a condition that blocks such a significant self-misunderstanding on the part of the participants.[48] So let us add to our construction:

(vi) The intentions in (i) are persistence interdependent.

The proposal, then, is to add versions of (iv)–(vi) to our construction of shared intention. (iv) and (v) appeal to beliefs that are needed to support the ability of the intentions of each in (i)–(iii) to satisfy an appropriate settle condition.[49] (vi) appeals to an actual interdependence between intentions of each in (i). This actual interdependence is not itself a necessary condition of the very coherence of each intending that we *J*; but it is, plausibly, a central element in robust cases of shared intention and modest sociality.

Now, we already have the idea in (ii) that the intentions of each interlock. This is a kind of semantic interdependence, since the success of the reference in the content of the intention of each to the intention of the other requires that the other does in fact so intend. We are now appealing, in (vi), to a different form of interdependence between the intentions in favor of the joint activity.

These two forms of interdependence can come apart. Suppose, on the one hand, that you and I each intend that we go to NYC. The persistence of these intentions might be interdependent even if these intentions do not interlock. Perhaps each intends that they go to NYC, and would continue so to intend if, but only if the other so intends. (Perhaps each person's intention is in part a response to the opportunity provided by the other's intention.) Yet neither intends that the joint action go by way of the intention of the other.

On the other hand, suppose that our intentions that we go to NYC interlock, as in (ii). So if you cease to intend that we go to NYC then, assuming all is out in the open, I will no longer intend that we go to NYC in part by way of your intention that we go to NYC (since I will know that you no longer so intend). But even if you cease to intend that we go to NYC I might continue to intend that we go to NYC. So there might not be persistence interdependence between our intentions that we go to NYC, since my intention that we go would persist even if you gave up your intention that we go. So interlocking does not guarantee persistence interdependence of the intentions in favor of the joint activity.

7. The connection condition and mutual responsiveness

In shared intentional activity, joint action is appropriately explained by a relevant shared intention. I have called the condition that specifies the nature of this explanatory relation the *connection condition*. Appeal to this connection condition is built into the contents of the intentions cited in (ii) and the beliefs cited in (iv). And this connection condition is itself part of the metaphysics of shared intentional activity. We need to say more about what this connection condition involves.

Suppose, then, that there is a shared intention that issues in corresponding joint action. What can we say about the connection between that shared intention and the joint action when this joint action is thereby a shared intentional action?

My conjecture is that the standard route from our shared intention to our joint action, in a case of shared intentionality, involves an appropriate form of mutual responsiveness of each to each. What form of mutual responsiveness? Well, the basic idea is that each is responsive, in her relevant intentions and actions, to the relevant intentions and actions of the other, in a way that keeps track of, and guides in the direction of, her intended end of their joint action—where all this is out in the open. Borrowing, and adjusting, a term from Robert Nozick, let's say that when someone keeps track of and guides her intention and action in the direction of E, she *tracks* E.[50] So the basic idea is that what is central to the connection condition is that each is responsive to the intentions and actions of the other in ways that track the intended end of the joint action—where all this is out in the open.

This public mutual responsiveness will involve responsiveness of each to each in relevant subsidiary intentions concerning means and preliminary steps. This is responsiveness in intentions that are elements in subplans concerning the intended joint action; and a tendency toward this is supported by the interlocking intentions in favor of the joint activity. There will, further, be responsiveness of each to each in relevant actions in pursuit of the joint activity; and a tendency toward this is also supported by the interlocking intentions in favor of the joint activity. This is responsiveness in action. Responsiveness in action is largely, though perhaps not entirely, shaped by responsiveness in sub-intentions. However, in appealing not only to responsiveness in sub-intentions but also to responsiveness in action we are making it explicit that the relevant responsiveness goes all the way to action.[51]

Such public mutual responsiveness involves practical thinking on the part of each that is responsive to the other in ways that track the intended end of the joint activity. This practical thinking on the part of each is shaped by that person's intention in favor of the joint activity. It is also shaped by her beliefs or expectations about the other's intentions and actions. Since the other's intentions and actions are themselves shaped by her analogous beliefs or expectations, there can be versions of Schelling's "familiar spiral of reciprocal expectations."[52]

As noted, this mutual responsiveness in intention and in action will be explained in part by the relevant interlocking intentions of each, interlocking intentions that partly constitute the shared intention. And this points to a further complexity. As we have seen, in this central case of shared intention what each intends is not just the joint activity. Each intends the complex end of joint-activity-by-way-of relevant-intentions-of-each. (Recall that we appealed to such interlocking of intentions in the light of the mafia example in Chapter 2 section 2.) But then we can expect that in the connection from shared intention to shared intentional action the mutual responsiveness will track not just the joint activity but, more specifically, the joint-activity-by-way-of-relevant-intentions-of-each. So let us build this more complex, intended end into our model of the mutual responsiveness that is central to the connection condition. The idea, then, is that what is central to the connection condition is public responsiveness, in intention and in action, of each to each, in a way that tracks the end, intended by each, of the joint-activity-by-way-of-relevant-intentions-of-each.[53]

This mutual responsiveness is in the space between two extremes. On one extreme there is on the part of each a very general responsiveness to and support of the aims of the other. In contrast, the mutual responsiveness that is involved in the connection condition is specifically limited to the particular joint activity that is intended (though of course it does not preclude a more general responsiveness). On the other extreme is a mutual responsiveness in which each is trying to thwart the guiding end of the other. This is the mutual responsiveness of two soldiers who are enemies and are fighting each other to the death. In contrast, the mutual responsiveness that is involved in the connection condition tracks an end that is intended by both, namely the joint-activity-by-way-of-relevant-intentions-of-each. In this way this mutual responsiveness is in the space between a very general responsiveness of each to the ends of the other, and forms of responsiveness in which each seeks to thwart the guiding end of the other.

In appealing in this way to mutual responsiveness, I am supposing that the connections between your intentions to act and your actions are appropriate for the individual intentionality of your actions, and similarly concerning the individual intentionality of my actions. My question is: in shared intentional action what is normally present, in the connection between our intentions and our joint action, that goes beyond these basic connections between each person's thought and that person's individual intentional actions? And my answer is: public responsiveness of each to each, both in sub-intention and in action; responsiveness that is relativized to and tracks the end intended by both of the joint-activity-by-way-of-relevant-intentions-of-each.

There can be such mutual responsiveness even if in fact no actual adjustment takes place since none is called for. However, if there is such mutual responsiveness then each is at least set to adjust sub-plans and actions appropriately if need be, and each has some sort of cognitive access to possible conditions that would call for adjustment.

Return to our duet singing. The idea is that if our singing the duet is a shared intentional activity that is grounded in our corresponding shared intention, then (at least in a central case) my sub-intention about, say, when to come in with my own part, and my associated actions, will be responsive to your sub-intention about your own part, and your associated actions, in ways that track what each of us intends, namely our joint duet singing by way of each of our intentions in favor of that. And vice versa.

This may seem overstated. After all, there will not be such mutual responsiveness in action if we decide in advance on our respective roles and then simply proceed to act individually in a prepackaged way that does not involve even the possibility of mutual adjustment of each to each. Two explorers might set out in different directions with a prior shared plan about what each will do, knowing that there is no possibility of contact once they begin (there are no cell phones), and so no possibility of mutual adjustment and responsiveness once they begin. Or two divers in a synchronized high diving routine might achieve complex coordination solely by way of prior planning and training, since (in contrast with dancing a tango together) it is not realistically possible for there to be mutual responsiveness during the very brief period of the actual joint dive. So we need to ask whether our condition of mutual responsiveness is overly demanding.

Well, such cases of prepackaging are an analogue, in the shared case, of a kind of ballistic action in the individual case. Individual intentional action normally involves responsiveness of action to the world, responsiveness that tracks what is intended. If I intend to guide the boat into the harbor I will normally be set to adjust in response to the various currents, and in a way that keeps track of the harbor and other boats. Such responsiveness seems a normal feature of the connection between intention and action, a feature that is characteristic of individual intentional action. But there can be cases of intentional action in which one simply exerts an immediate, one-off effort, and there is no further room for responsiveness: one acts and then the rest is up to the world. Perhaps I get to push the boat just this once, and the rest is up to the currents—just as I throw a bowling ball down the alley, aiming at the top pin. Prepackaged shared action is a shared analogue of such ballistic action. In both cases we have intentional action—individual or shared—but we do not have the cited forms of downstream responsiveness.

That said, we do have a more robust phenomenon of shared intentionality when there is the cited kind of mutual responsiveness in sub-intention and action. And our basic concern is with whether we can get robust shared intentionality without retreating, in the end, either to a doctrine of the conceptual primitiveness of shared intentionality or to a doctrine of a deep metaphysical and/or normative discontinuity between individual and shared agency. So there is reason to build the stronger condition of mutual responsiveness in sub-intention and action into our construction while acknowledging the possibility of (and in some cases the importance of) attenuated forms of shared intentionality in the absence of such mutual responsiveness.

I will proceed, then, on the assumption that the connection condition can be modeled in terms of such public mutual responsiveness in sub-intention and action, even though I grant that there can be attenuated forms of shared agency of the prepackaged variety. Insofar as intentions and beliefs of the participants appeal in their contents to this connection condition—as they do in conditions (ii) and (iv)—we can understand this as an appeal to such public mutual responsiveness. Since we have explained this condition of mutual responsiveness without an irreducible appeal to the very idea of shared intentionality, we can include this appeal to mutual responsiveness in these contents without an unacceptable circularity in our account of shared intentionality. And that is what we wanted to do.

So we arrive at a final condition:

(viii) there is public mutual responsiveness in sub-intention and action, mutual responsiveness that tracks the end, intended by each, that there be the joint activity in (i) by way of the intentions of each in (i).

This mutual responsiveness is a form of interconnection in functioning between the intentions and actions of the participants. This interconnected functioning across the intentions and actions of each is central to the standard connection between social thought and social action. And this interconnected functioning is explained in large part by the relevant intentions of those participants. In contrast, the persistence interdependence cited in (vi) need not be explained by appeal to the intentions of each, though in some cases it may.

This last point about condition (vi) may seem to be in tension with our understanding of condition (ii). That condition (as we are now understanding it) says that each intends that the joint activity proceed by way of the relevant intention of each other and relevant mutual responsiveness of sub-intention and in action. Does this entail that each intends that the intentions of each in favor of the joint activity are persistence interdependent in the sense of condition (vi)? No, it does not. The intended mutual responsiveness cited in

(ii) (as we are now understanding the appeal in that condition to the connection condition) concerns each participant's relevant *sub*-intentions: it is responsiveness in each participant's sub-plans with respect to the intended joint activity by way of relevant intentions. One can (as in (ii)) intend that things go by way of such responsiveness in sub-plan without intending that (as in (vi)) the intentions in favor of the end of the joint activity themselves be interdependent (though belief in this interdependence plays the indicated role in defending the coherence of the intentions of each of the participants in (i)).

We can now return to a question that was raised earlier about the relation between (ii) and (iii).[54] Suppose that one has the intention cited in (ii). Does it follow that one intends that the joint activity proceed by way of meshing sub-plans? Now that we have an account of the connection condition that is cited in (ii), an account that appeals to relevant mutual responsiveness, we can answer this question.

Suppose, as in (ii), that I intend that we act by way of your intention that we act and my intention that we act, and by way of a route from our intentions to our joint activity that satisfies the connection condition. As we are now understanding it, this is an intention that we act by way of relevant mutual responsiveness in sub-intention and action. This intended mutual responsiveness includes mutual responsiveness in the sub-intentions that constitute the relevant sub-plans of each. So the intention in (ii) involves an intention that these relevant sub-plans be mutually responsive to each other. And that involves an intention that these sub-plans mesh (which is not an intention that they match). The intention that the activity proceeds by way of sub-plans that mesh is, then, one aspect of the intention that that activity proceed by way of relevant mutual responsiveness: intending that there be relevant mutual responsiveness in sub-intention involves intending that there be mesh in sub-plans.

So when we have a full understanding of condition (ii)—one that draws on our substantive account of the connection condition—we can see that, as we anticipated earlier, (iii) is indeed implicit in (ii). So we can see (ii), suitably understood, as in part the condition that each intends the joint activity by way of the intention of each, relevant mutual responsiveness, *and so* meshing sub-plans. And this helps clarify the significance of the intention in favor of mesh in sub-plans. However, though (iii) is implicit in (ii), there remain good reasons for explicitly highlighting (iii) as a condition of modest sociality, given its prominent role in our construction. So that is what I will do.

8. Taking stock

We have now articulated eight interrelated building blocks for our construction:

(i) we each intend that we go to NYC.

(ii) we each intend the following: that we go to NYC by way of the intentions of each that we go to NYC (and that the route from these intentions to our joint activity satisfies the connection condition).

(iii) we each intend the following: that we go to NYC by way of sub-plans of each of our intentions in favor of going to NYC that mesh with each other.

(iv) we each believe the following: if each of us continues to intend that we go to NYC, then we will go to NYC by way of those intentions (and in accordance with the connection condition).

(v) we each believe that our intentions in (i) are persistence interdependent.

(vi) our intentions in (i) are persistence interdependent.

(vii) common knowledge among us of conditions (i)–(vii).

(viii) public mutual responsiveness in sub-intention and action, mutual responsiveness that tracks the end, intended by each, that we go to NYC by way of the intentions of each that we go.

We have understood the connection condition in terms of (viii). And we can now read this understanding of the connection condition back into the contents of the attitudes cited in (ii) and (iv).

These resources in hand, let's try to formulate a general, conservative construction of modest sociality.

4 A CONSTRUCTION OF MODEST SOCIALITY

1. The basic thesis

In pursuit of a conservative construction of modest sociality, the first idea will be to see generalized and adjusted versions of (i)–(vii)[1] as together constituting shared intention (or, anyway, an important form of shared intention). And the second idea will be to see modest sociality (or, anyway, an important form of modest sociality) as joint activity that is appropriately explained—in part by way of relevant mutual responsiveness, as in (viii)—by such shared intention.

In proceeding in this way I am supposing that we can plausibly scale up from the two-person case of our going to NYC together—the case on which we have primarily focused in formulating (i)–(viii)—to somewhat larger cases of modest sociality. We can scale up from, as it were, duets to quartets or sextets or octets. (It is important, though, that we continue to put aside asymmetric authority relations.) Granted, as we move from duets to quartets and beyond, analogues of (i)–(viii) will be more complex.[2] But so long as we keep in mind our focus on sufficient conditions for robust, modest sociality, we can acknowledge this without allowing it to block our strategy.

So let us consider shared intention. Using **boldface** to indicate adjusted generalizations of the conditions cited earlier, the idea is that shared intention, at least in a basic case, involves

  (i) intentions on the part of each in favor of the joint activity,
 (ii) intentions on the part of each in favor of the joint activity by way of the intentions of each in **(i)** and by way of relevant mutual responsiveness in sub-intention and action,
(iii) intentions on the part of each in favor of the joint activity by way of meshing sub-plans of the intentions of each in **(i)**,
 (iv) beliefs of each that, if the intentions of each in **(i)** persist, the participants will perform the joint activity by way of those intentions and relevant mutual responsiveness in sub-intention and action,

(v) beliefs of each that the intentions of each in (i) are persistence interdependent

(vi) the intentions of each in (i) are persistence interdependent, and

(vii) common knowledge of (i)–(vii).

Finally, the connection between shared intention and joint action satisfies the *connection condition* just in case:

(viii) the connection between the shared intention (as in (i)–(vii)) and the joint action involves public mutual responsiveness in sub-intention and action that tracks the end intended by each of the joint activity by way of the intentions of each (in (i)) in favor of that joint activity.

And (viii) specifies what counts as *relevant* mutual responsiveness in (ii) and (iv).

In articulating these conditions I have not put a great deal of weight on appeals to our ordinary talk about shared intention, shared intentionality, shared cooperation and the like. Indeed, one of my reasons for introducing the term "modest sociality" has been to help us focus on the actual phenomena, not primarily on ordinary language. I do think that the model I am sketching broadly coheres with pre-analytic talk of shared intention and of shared intentional and shared cooperative activities. And such pre-analytic talk can be a useful, if defeasible, guide. But my primary concern is not with our pre-analytic talk but with shared intention as a central element in the *explanation* of the activities involved in (what I am calling) modest sociality. I take it that in the case of individual intentional agency, intentions are central to the explanation of the agent's relevant practical thought and action. And I seek a model of shared intention that helps us get at a phenomenon that plays an analogous explanatory role in the case of modest sociality. In each case I suppose that a fundamental kind of human activity—temporally extended activity, on the one hand, and, on the other hand, shared intentional activity—essentially involves a distinctive explanatory role of relevant aspects of mind. And in each case my conjecture is that this explanatory role involves capacities of planning agency.

Returning to conditions (i)–(vii), the central claim is that these public, interconnected intentions and associated beliefs of the individual participants will, in responding to the rational pressures specified by the planning theory of individual agency, function together in ways characteristic of shared intention. This structure will, when functioning properly, normally support and guide coordinated social action and planning, and frame relevant bargaining and shared deliberation, in support of the intended shared activity. Conformity to social rationality norms that are central to shared intention—norms of social agglomeration, social consistency, social coherence, and social stability—will emerge from the norm-guided functioning of these interrelated attitudes of the individuals. Violation of such social norms will normally consist of a violation of associated norms of individual planning agency. And when such structures of shared intention explain our activity by way of the connection condition—condition **(viii)**—our activity is a shared intentional activity and a candidate for shared cooperative activity.

Call the conjunction of these claims about shared intention and modest sociality *the basic thesis*. The thesis is that shared intention and modest sociality consist, at least in central cases, in appropriately interrelated public structures of individual planning agency. These interrelated planning structures go beyond the merely cognitive interrelations involved in knowledge of each other's minds and present in standard forms of merely strategic interaction. But these structures go beyond these merely cognitive interrelations in ways whose understanding involves the application of conceptual, metaphysical and normative resources that are available within the theory of individual planning agency.[3] Such shared intention consists of a complex state of affairs that involves relevant, public interconnected attitudes of individual planning agents. And modest sociality consists in the proper functioning of such shared intentions. Such modest sociality is interconnected planning agency; and we have characterized the relevant interconnections without an essential appeal either to mutual obligations or to judgments of the participants about such mutual obligations (though we have left room for such obligations to play important roles in certain cases).

The basic thesis provides a model of the social glue that ties together the participants in modest sociality.[4] According to this model, this social glue is not solely a cognitive glue of common knowledge, though it does involve a form of common knowledge. This social glue also includes the forms of intentional interconnection and interpersonal support specified in **(i)**–**(iii)**, beliefs about success and interdependence cited in **(iv)** and **(v)**, the actual interdependence cited in **(vi)**, the mutual responsiveness in sub-intention and action cited in **(viii)**, and the normative pressures of social rationality that emerge from these structures given relevant norms of individual plan rationality. The forms of intentional interconnection cited in **(ii)**–**(iii)** involve semantic interrelations across the intentions of the different participants, semantic interrelations analogous to those we have observed to be characteristic across the plan states of an individual at different times in her temporally extended planning agency. These interrelated intentions in favor of the joint activity help support mutual responsiveness in sub-intention and action of the sort cited in **(viii)**. And a failure to play one's part will normally involve a violation of the emergent pressures of social rationality.

2. The emergence of modest sociality

Suppose then that there is the public structure of interrelated intentions and beliefs cited in **(i)–(vii)**. And suppose these attitudes of the individuals function properly in the sense spelled out by the theory of individual, rational planning agency. Given the contents of these intentions there will tend to be the mutual responsiveness cited in **(viii)**. And when all this works its way out, without interference or breakdown, there will be the rational social functioning that is characteristic of modest sociality. Let us see in more detail why this is so.

Condition **(i)** helps ensure that each participant rationally tracks not only her own actions but also the joint activity—where this will include associated dispositions to help the others if needed. And condition **(i)** also helps ensure that each participant rationally filters options for deliberation with an eye on compatibility with the joint activity. Conditions **(ii)** and **(iii)** help articulate in a more fine-grained way what each participant tracks. And they thereby help to explain characteristic ways in which each tends to support the role of the other. They thereby go beyond merely cognitive links among the participants to capture an important way in which each is treated by the others as an intentional co-participant.

Conditions **(iv)** and **(v)** ensure that the participants see themselves as both interdependent and, together, practically effective. These conditions thereby help explain how the intentions of each in favor of the joint activity satisfy plausible settle or control conditions on intention. Condition **(vi)** captures an actual interdependence among the agents, thereby ensuring that the beliefs in **(v)** are not in error. The common knowledge condition—condition **(vii)**—helps ensure that the construction of shared intention will itself support a standard form of functioning associated with modest sociality, namely, thinking (including thinking together) about what to do given that we share this intention. This common knowledge condition also helps support—by ensuring that the basic intentions of each are out in the open—the interdependence in **(vi)**. The mutual responsiveness in condition **(viii)** captures the connection between social thought and social action that is characteristic of modest sociality, a connection that is supported by the interconnected intentions cited in **(i)**–**(iii)**. And since this mutual responsiveness is out in the open, the participants are in a position to reason together concerning their on-going shared activity.

Consider then my intention that we *J* in part by way of your intention that we *J*, and by way of mutual responsiveness and so meshing sub-plans. This complex content of my intention connects it with your intentions and thereby imposes rational pressure on me, as time goes by, to fill in my sub-plans in ways that, in particular, fit with and support yours as you fill in your sub-plans. This pressure derives from the rational demand on me to make my own plans means-end coherent and consistent, given the ways in which your intentions enter into the content of my intentions. By requiring that my intention both interlocks with yours, and involves a commitment to respond to and mesh with yours, the theory ensures that rational pressures on me to be responsive to and to coordinate with *you*—rational pressures characteristic of shared intention—are built right into my *own* plans, given their special content and given demands of consistency and coherence directly on my own plans. And similarly with you. So there will normally be the kind of mutual, rational responsiveness in intention—in the direction of social agglomeration, social consistency, and social coherence—that is characteristic of modest sociality.

Suppose, for example, that I intend that we paint together in part by way of your intention that we paint and by way of mutual responsiveness and so meshing sub-plans. Given the way reference to your intention, and to responsiveness and mesh, appears in the content of my own intention, I am committed to filling in my sub-plans in a way that responds to how you fill in yours; and I am committed to being responsive to what is needed for your intentions to be effective and for our intentions together to be effective. And similarly with you, assuming you too intend that we paint in part by way of my intention that we paint and by way of mutual responsiveness and so meshing sub-plans. So what emerges from these intentions, given guidance by central norms of individual planning agency, are forms of mutual responsiveness characteristic of modest sociality.

The basic thesis works, in part, by building appropriate reference to the other into the contents of the intentions of each. While it acknowledges the potential roles of various unarticulated commonalities of sensibility, it does not just appeal to "a Background sense of the other as a candidate for cooperative agency".[5] It seeks to generate relevant rational normativity, and corresponding functioning, at the social level out of the individualistic normativity, and corresponding functioning, that is tied to the contents of the intentions of each. The basic thesis seeks contents of the intentions of each that ensure, given rational demands on those intentions of each (demands rooted in the planning theory of individual agency), responsiveness to central social rationality demands. In this way, the basic thesis sees the social norms of consistency, agglomerativity and coherence, and corresponding social functioning as emerging from associated individualistic norms and corresponding functioning.

What about the social norm of diachronic stability? Well, there will frequently be a social version of the snowball effect: once we are embarked on our shared activity, there will frequently be as a result new reasons to continue. But, as we noted in Chapter 3 section 4, there will many times also be a kind of stability of shared intention that derives from the interaction of the interdependence between each person's intention in favor of the joint activity and the individual stability of the intentions of each. Given this interdependence, the plan-theoretic pressures for stability on your intention will tend to make my intention more stable. And vice versa. So there will be a kind of interdependent stabilization of the intentions of each in favor of J.[6]

These are primary ways in which the basic thesis explains the emergence of these social norms of intention rationality within structures of individual planning agency with appropriate contents and interrelations. As noted earlier, the participants may each also go on directly to accept these social norms. And in Chapter 7 I will discuss yet a further possible form of support for these social norms, one that derives from certain shared policies in favor of these social norms (where such shared policies will themselves be understood by way of the basic thesis).

Consider now the way in which a shared intention can frame bargaining about means. Return to our shared intention to paint together. Given this shared intention we might, for example, bargain about what color to use, and about who is to scrape and who is to paint; and this bargaining will be framed by our shared intention. How does this work? Well, on the theory, we each intend the shared activity in part by way of the relevant intention of the other and by way of mutual responsiveness and so meshing sub-plans. Each intends that the other's intention be effective by way of sub-plans that mesh interpersonally. So we are each under rational pressure to seek to ensure that our sub-plans, agglomerated together, both are adequate to the shared task and do indeed mesh interpersonally. And that is why, in the absence so far of adequate and meshing sub-plans, our shared intention is in a position to structure our bargaining in the pursuit of such sub-plans. Of course, the shared intention, by itself, ensures neither that there will be such bargaining nor that such bargaining will be successful in arriving at meshing sub-plans.[7] Nevertheless, the shared intention is a source of rational pressure to try to arrive at such mesh. And we explain that rational pressure as emerging from the rational pressures on individual planning agency, given these distinctive contents of relevant intentions.

The sharing of intention need not involve commonality in each agent's reasons for participating in the sharing. You and I can have a shared intention to paint the house together, even though I participate because I want to change the color whereas you participate because you want to remove the mildew. Or you and I can have a conversation together even though I participate because I want to learn more about the subject of our conversation, whereas you participate because you want to impress me.[8] In each case, though we participate for different reasons, our shared intention nevertheless establishes a shared framework of commitments; and this can happen even if these differences in our reasons are out in the open. Granted, extreme divergence in background reasons might undermine the shared intention. Things might fall apart. Nevertheless, much of our sociality is *partial* in the sense that it involves sharing in the face of—in some cases, public—divergence of background reasons for the sharing.

Indeed, I think that versions of such social partiality are endemic to our modest sociality. It is an important fact about our sociality that we manage to share intentions and act together in the face of substantial differences of reasons for which we participate. We work together, we play together, and we engage in conversations together even given substantial background differences in our reasons for participation and our reasons for various sub-plans. This is especially characteristic of a pluralistic, liberal culture. This is the *pervasiveness of partiality in our sociality*. It is a virtue of the basic thesis that it makes room, in a theoretically natural way, for this pervasiveness of partiality.[9]

Shared intentions coordinate planning and action and frame relevant bargaining, all this in ways that tend to conform to characteristic norms of social rationality. And the claim is that this social functioning and social rationality will emerge from the individualistic structures described by the basic thesis.[10] As noted, the claim is not that the step from individual planning agency to modest sociality is simple or undemanding. Indeed, the basic thesis seeks to articulate the complexity and psychological richness of this step. You could be a planning agent and yet still not be capable of these further complexities. The basic thesis offers an articulated model of what is involved, at least in a central case, in being not only a planning agent whose agency is temporally extended in characteristic ways, but also a participant in modest sociality. And according to this model, the further developments of the psychic economy of planning agency that provide the bridge to modest sociality are themselves applications of conceptual, metaphysical, and normative resources already available within the theory of individual planning agency.[11] This is the conservatism of our construction of modest sociality. And this is the sense in which, as anticipated, our capacity for planning agency is a foundation for our capacities for distinctive forms both of temporally extended and of social agency.

3. Modest sociality and strategic interaction

A central thought of this discussion is that modest sociality, while consisting in appropriate forms of interconnected planning agency, is not merely strategic interaction within a context of common knowledge. It is time to see how this thought is supported by the basic thesis.

Suppose you are walking alongside a stranger, and you are each acting in ways that are in strategic equilibrium in a context of common knowledge. Each knows what the other intends to do and does; each pursues what he wants or values in the light of this knowledge of the other, knowing that the other is reasoning in a parallel fashion; each knows that if both so act there will be a coordinated concatenation of their walking actions; and all this is out in the open. And now the important point is that such public strategic interaction need not satisfy the conditions of the basic thesis.

First, though each believes that there will be the cited coordinated concatenation of walking actions, it does not follow that each *intends* that. To intend the coordinated concatenation each would need to be disposed to take that complex of activities both as an end for his own means-end reasoning and to be guided in action by this end; and each would need to be disposed to filter potential options for deliberation with an eye to their compatibility with this end. But it may be that none of this is true of you or the stranger. Perhaps the stranger does not *intend* (though he does expect) that you will act in these ways, and has no disposition to help you if you need it. Indeed, perhaps he is looking for ways to thwart your progress down the street without physical violence, even though he sees that you are indeed progressing down the street and he is doing what he thinks best given that you are. This stranger does not *intend* that the two of you walk together down the street. Given what he knows to be the limits on his powers, he does *expect* that you will in fact walk in the way you are walking. And he intends to respond to that, and so expects that there will in fact be a coordinated concatenation of the walking actions of each. But this is not yet to intend that coordinated concatenation.

Again, perhaps the stranger expects that your walking will be the issue of your relevant intentions and yet does not *intend* that. Perhaps he is keeping his eyes open for a preferred mechanism that would issue in your walking in a way that bypasses those intentions of yours.[12] Being a realist and not especially strong, however, he does not believe that this is what will happen; he expects that you will walk by way of your relevant intention, and he does what he sees as best given that. But he does not intend that your intention be efficacious, and is set to thwart this if an appropriate opportunity should arise. So his intention does not appropriately interlock with yours.

It follows that this case of walking alongside a stranger does not satisfy the conditions set out in the basic thesis. So the basic thesis can say this is a case of strategic interaction that is not a case of modest sociality. And that is what we wanted.

This result depends on taking seriously the idea that the basic thesis requires that what is intended (and not merely expected) by each participant includes the joint action where that includes the other's role in it. If all that were required were that each expects the other to intend and act in relevant ways and then intends his own actions in the light of that expectation, the account would be too weak: we would not thereby have ensured relevant dispositions to track and support and not to thwart the other's role in the joint activity, to filter options with respect to that joint activity, to help the other if need be, and so on.[13] But it is fundamental that the basic thesis requires that each *intends* the joint action, where this joint action includes the roles of each. And intention differs from ordinary expectation.

Granted, you and I might share an intention to walk together even if you are indifferent as between walking with me and walking with my nearby twin. Still, what you intend is that we—you and I—walk, not that you and my twin walk. And what you intend is that this walking be in part the issue of my intention, not some intention of my twin. So you are set to support my role in our walking in standard plan-theoretic ways. (Though you may have no intention to resist if my twin were to interrupt and ask "may I have this walk?") And, we can suppose, similarly with me.

Consider now an objection from Bjorn Petersson:

Suppose I want the window smashed. When I note your presence on the street, I think that if you act in a certain way, the window can be smashed as a result of both our acts, and I form an intention accordingly. What I intend in that case is merely to get the window smashed, while predicting that your actions will be components in the process leading to that result. This prediction may rest upon my knowledge that your intentions are similar to mine, and that our subplans are likely to mesh in a way that enables me to reach my goal. There is mutuality and interdependence, in line with Bratman's requirements. Still, I would say, nothing in this picture captures "sharedness" or "collectivity" in any sense distinct from what we can construe in terms of standard individualistic theory of action.[14]

Petersson thinks that a theory like mine will be led to say that the case he describes is a case of "sharedness"; and Petersson thinks (correctly, in my view) that this would be a mistake. What to say?

Note first that this case, as described, seems so far not to satisfy the conditions cited in the basic thesis. This is in part because Petersson's description appeals at crucial moments to *prediction* when what is required by the basic thesis is *intention*; and it is a central theme of the planning theory that these attitudes differ in systematic ways. Though in Petersson's example I expect that you will act in ways that promote the smashing of the window, it is not clear from the description of the example that I *intend* that. Perhaps I have no disposition at all to help you if you need it,[15] or to reason about means to supporting you in your role, or to filter options incompatible with your playing your role. And though I expect your intention to be effective it is not clear in the example that I intend that. So it is not clear in Petersson's example that I *intend* our joint window smashing in part by way of your intention. So in the case as described by Petersson I may not satisfy my side of a shared intention, as that is understood by the basic thesis. And similarly with you. So I agree with Peterson that there is neither shared intention nor "sharedness" in his case, as his case is naturally understood; but I do not see that this is an objection to the basic thesis.

Nevertheless, Petersson may think that even once it is made explicit that these conditions of the basic thesis are indeed satisfied by (an upgraded version of) his example, we will still not have "sharedness". But at this point much of our discussion comes into play. Conformity to the basic thesis—and the distinctive intentions and forms of interrelation across intentions that it highlights—ensures standard forms of rational functioning of shared intention in linking us together and organizing our thought and action. There is here, in the satisfaction of the conditions cited in the basic thesis, a significant social glue.

Does this suffice for "sharedness"? Perhaps we can capture one of the intuitions behind Petersson's concern by returning to the distinction between desirability-based, obligation-based, and feasibility-based interdependence.[16] In the kind of (upgraded) case toward which Petersson points, each treats the other's intention opportunistically as a condition of the feasibility of the joint activity. Neither sees the other's intention as contributing to the desirability of the joint activity, and neither supposes that there are relevant mutual obligations. If there is interdependence it is only feasibility-based. Nevertheless, for this to pose a problem for the basic thesis we must go on to suppose that the various conditions of that thesis are nevertheless satisfied: each intends the joint activity and that it proceed by way of each other's intentions, mutual responsiveness, and so meshing sub-plans; each is appropriately responsive to the other; each is set not to thwart the other and is at least minimally disposed to help the other if needed; there is (feasibility-based) persistence interdependence in relevant intention; there is, as a result of all this, rational pressure in the direction of social rationality; each expects all of this to issue in the joint action each intends; and all this is out in the open. Once this is all made explicit, it seems to me plausible that this is a version of the kind of "sharedness" in which we are interested, though I grant that such a case differs from the desirability-based interdependence characteristic of Romeo and Juliet (as commonly understood), or a case of interdependence grounded in mutual obligation.

Natalie Gold and Robert Sugden explore a similar worry. They consider a hawk-dove game characterized by the following payoff matrix for two agents:[17]

	dove	hawk
dove	2,2	0,3
hawk	3,0	−5,−5

Here the first number in each box represents the "payoff" for the first player, the player who is choosing between the two different rows; the second number represents the payoff for the second player, the player who is choosing between the two different columns. In two plays of this game—namely (dove, hawk) and (hawk, dove)—each agent's response is the best response (as measured by his payoff) to the other's response. Neither agent can improve his payoff by unilaterally changing what he chooses, holding fixed what the other chooses. Each play involves, in this sense, a Nash equilibrium. Suppose then that the players arrive at (dove, hawk) in a context of common knowledge. Must the basic thesis say that there is then a shared intention in favor of (dove, hawk)? If so, the basic thesis would be too weak, for it would have failed "to differentiate collective intentions from the mutually consistent individual intentions that lie behind Nash equilibrium behavior in games."[18] What to say?

Well, when these players arrive at (dove, hawk) in a context of common knowledge, each knows what the other intends to do and does; each knows that the upshot is (dove, hawk); and each knows that this outcome is a Nash equilibrium. But to know need not be to intend. And it does not follow that each *intends* that the other act in the way specified in (dove, hawk). After all, neither is likely to be prepared to help the other play her role if need be, or to filter options incompatible with her playing her role. Indeed, on a natural understanding of the case, were the first player in the (dove, hawk) scenario to see a way of tricking the other into playing "dove," he would. Nor does it follow that there is any intention on the part of each that, were there to be a need for sub-plans (a potential need that is not represented in the cited payoff matrix), these sub-plans are to mesh.

As in the case of Petersson's objection, then, a clear view of the difference between *expecting* the other to intend and act in a certain way, and *intending* both the joint action and that the other's relevant intention be successful, blocks the present worry that the basic thesis does not adequately capture "collective" or shared intentions. So I think that Gold and Sugden may not be sufficiently attentive to the difference between intending and believing or expecting.[19]

We have, then, a trio of cases of strategic equilibrium within common knowledge: walking alongside a stranger, the initial (non-upgraded) version of Petersson's window-smashing case, and Gold and Sugden's hawk-dove case. In each case we have seen how a defender of the basic thesis can plausibly claim that the conditions cited by that thesis are not satisfied. And in each case this reply depends on taking seriously the idea that the basic thesis requires that what is intended (and not merely expected) by each participant includes the joint action (where that includes the relevant activity of the other) and the role of the other's intention in that joint action.

To be sure, in each of these cases of strategic interaction, the participants intend to act in certain ways given that, as they expect, the other will act in certain ways. But in each case we should resist the inference from S intends *A, given that (as she expects) the other will B,* to S intends *(the joint activity of A and B).* After all, S may intend *A, given that (as she expects) the other will B* without any disposition to filter out options incompatible with the other's performance of *B* or to take the other's performance of *B* as an end for her means-end reasoning or to act in order to support the other's performance of *B.* And when we resist this inference, and insist on the distinction between intending and expecting, we are in a position, in the words of Gold and Sugden, "to differentiate collective intentions from the mutually consistent individual intentions that lie behind Nash equilibrium behavior."

4. Quasi-Lockean social ties

In its understanding of modest sociality, the basic thesis appeals not only to planning attitudes in the heads of each of the individuals but also to interrelations among those attitudes of the different participants. It sees modest sociality as a special form of interconnected planning agency. This contrasts with John Searle's apparent assumption that what is essential to shared intentional agency is exhausted by certain attitudes in the heads of the participants.[20] However, though the basic thesis makes essential appeal to interrelations across the participants, it aims to characterize these interrelations without an essential appeal either to distinctive kinds of interpersonal obligation or to special forms of asymmetric authority.

Return now to the point, from Chapter 1, that the normal functioning of a planning system in temporally extended individual agency systematically involves cross-temporally stable and referentially interconnected plan states. We noted there that such stability and interconnection involves cross-temporal ties that are, on a broadly Lockean view, aspects of the persistence of one and the same person over time. What we have now seen is that the basic thesis highlights referential interlocking of the intentions of the different participants in modest sociality and commonality of content of their relevant intentions. In this limited respect, then, the basic thesis sees a parallel between the social glue characteristic of modest sociality and the cited Lockean structure of individual planning agency over time. So we can say that, according to the basic thesis, these social ties are *quasi-Lockean*.

However, we need to understand this idea with care. The parallel is that in both the case of a person over time and in the case of modest sociality there are interconnections and commonalities. These interconnections and commonalities in the shared case help support the claim that there is an important kind of *shared* agency, not just a concatenation of the agency of each. But of course there are also important differences. These ties in modest sociality will normally be quite limited both in their extent and in their duration: you and I might push the piano up the stairway just for a couple of minutes and then go our separate ways; and even while we are pushing we might each be independently doing various other things—rehearsing a different poem in each of our heads, perhaps. In contrast, the ties that are characteristic of the persistence of one and the same person over time will normally involve a rich overlay both at each time and over time. Further, in modest sociality these ties will normally cross-cut. I might be walking with you while I am having a conversation with someone else on my cell phone; and in such a case there are, so to speak, two "we's," not one.

Yet a further limitation to the parallel concerns the role of consciousness. Locke famously claimed that what is central to being a person is that a person "can consider it self as it self, the same thinking thing, in different times and places; which it does only by that consciousness, which is inseparable from thinking, and as it seems to me essential to it . . ."[21] Following J. David Velleman, we can express a central aspect of this remark as the idea that there are certain experiences in the future that "we can anticipate first-personally",[22] and certain experiences in the past that we "can think of reflexively, in the first-person."[23] In each case one has a special kind of first-personal experiential access to the point of view of a past or future subject of experience. One aspect of a Lockean view of personal identity over time will be that the relevant cross-temporal ties include such first-personal experiential access to the point of view of a past or future subject of experience. And this first-personal experiential access goes beyond the causal, semantic and epistemic connections highlighted by the parallel we have noted between the intra-and inter-personal cases. I can anticipate, or remember certain experiences of mine "first-personally"; but in acting together with you I do not thereby come to be able to anticipate or remember "first-personally" relevant events in *your* life.

So while it is an important fact that the ties characteristic of modest sociality are quasi-Lockean, there are also important dis-analogies between these ties and the Lockean ties characteristic of personal identity. I will return to this point in Chapter 6, when I reflect on the idea of a group subject of a shared intention.

5. Social networks

The basic thesis highlights interlocking and interdependent intentions of the different participants in modest sociality, intentions with a common social content. In this way, as noted, the basic thesis sees the social glue characteristic of modest sociality as quasi-Lockean, since these interpersonal ties are to some extent analogous to the cross-temporal Lockean ties characteristic of individual planning agency over time. In the previous section I noted some of the limits to this parallel between interpersonal and diachronic, personal ties. I now want to note a theoretical benefit of this parallel. By appealing to such quasi-Lockean social ties we can model a phenomenon that lies in the territory between a mere concatenation of distinct instances of modest sociality, on the one hand, and on the other hand the shared intention and modest sociality of a larger group.

Consider a structure of overlapping strands of the quasi-Lockean ties involved in instances of small-scale modest sociality. A and B, let us say, are engaged in shared activity J_1, where this involves their shared intention that they perform J_1. So there are ties of interlocking and interdependent intentions, with common social contents, between A and B. B and C, let us suppose, are engaged in a shared activity J_2, which involves an associated shared intention in favor of J_2. So there are ties of interlocking and interdependent intentions, with common social contents, between B and C. C and D, let us suppose, are engaged in J_3 . . . And so on, all the way to Y and Z. There is a chain of overlapping quasi-Lockean interpersonal strands connecting A with Z, even if there are no direct ties of interlocking and interdependent intentions between A and Z. The relation between A and Z is in this respect parallel to the relation between the child and the senile general in Anthony Quinton's defense of a Lockean view of personal identity in response to Reid's famous example.[24]

There can be such overlapping strands of modest sociality in the absence of a shared intention on the part of the overall group. And many times the different J_i's in such overlapping strands will have only an accidental relation to each other; though we can nevertheless investigate how such overlapping social strands might propagate various kinds of social influences. (Certain kinds of crowds might be like this.) But there will also be cases in which the J_i's are related in ways that are theoretically important. Perhaps each of many overlapping pairs of agents is a lobbying group trying to exert influence on a specific issue, though there is no overall lobbying issue on which all are working. Or perhaps each of many overlapping pairs of agents is a small business group that is trying to maximize the profit of that very group, though no one is trying to maximize the overall profit of the overall group.

So consider a structure of overlapping strands of modest sociality where the act-types that are the target of the involved shared intentions on the part of the relevant small groups stand in an appropriate (so far, unspecified) relation. Using a currently popular way of talking, we might call this phenomenon a social network. Assuming the involved joint act types are indeed appropriately related, the group consisting of the members of all of the cited overlapping small-scale lobbying groups, or of all the cited overlapping small business groups is, in this sense, a social network.

There may be no overarching shared intention in such social networks. And an absence of an overarching shared intention will induce important limits given the central role of shared intentions in framing bargaining and, as we will see, shared deliberation. Nevertheless, a social network in this sense involves social interconnections that go beyond those involved in a mere concatenation of multiple, distinct instances of modest sociality on the part of different small groups.

Another kind of example involves overlapping strands of modest sociality over time. On natural assumptions, this is what can happen in certain temporally extended, large-scale scientific research projects or—to use an example from Seamus Miller—the construction of a certain cathedral over several hundred years.[25] The various agents in the temporally extended research project or the construction of the cathedral over those many years may have participated in a temporally extended social network.[26]

I will not try to say generally what relation is needed between the J_is for there to be a social network. Different ways of specifying the needed relations will give us different ideas of a social network, and it will depend on our theoretical interests how we will want further to specify this idea. The point here is only that the basic thesis gives us resources to develop theories about such social networks of overlapping interconnections across multiple, local instances of modest sociality. It gives us these resources while highlighting both that such cases need bring with them no overall shared intention on the part of the overall group, and that the absence of such a shared intention will involve important limitations on shared reasoning.[27]

6. Treating as a means?

According to the basic thesis, a central case of our sharing an intention to J involves my intention that we J in part by way of your intention that we J, and vice versa. This interlocking of our intentions is, according to the theory, an important aspect of the interconnections between us that are characteristic of shared intentionality. But, as Christine Korsgaard has emphasized (in correspondence and conversation), this can seem puzzling. In intending that your intention be effective in the pursuit of our joint activity, I may seem to be seeing your intention and your agency as, at bottom, a means to what I intend—namely, our joint activity. But is it plausible that at the heart of shared agency is an intention to treat the other as a means?

Well, in intending that we J in part by way of your intention that we J, I am indeed intending that your intention play its role in guiding your activity as part of our activity. Recall, however, that I also intend that my own intention that we J function in a standard way. So I am not only intending that your intention function in the connection between your thought and your and our action; I am also intending that my intention function in the connection between my thought and our action. In this sense my intention supports the agency of each of us. In so intending, then, if there is a sense in which I treat you as a means, it is a sense in which my intention also involves treating myself as a means. Since treating myself as a means in this special sense is, I take it, compatible with full-blown individual intentional agency, I infer that the sense in which I also treat you as a means (if there is such a sense) is compatible with full-blown shared intentional agency.[28]

7. Deception and coercion revisited

Another advantage of the basic thesis is that it supports a plausible view of the interaction between coercion, deception, shared intentionality, and cooperation. To explain, allow me to return to examples and ideas initially broached in Chapter 1 section 10.

The first point is that the basic thesis helps us see the ways in which many forms of deception or coercion involve attitudes that baffle shared intentionality. If you are deceiving me about the finances of our house painting, despite my expressed intention that we stay within a certain budget, then you are thereby failing to be committed to our acting by way of sub-plans that mesh. After all, you are willing for us to paint together in a way that, as you know, violates my sub-plan that we stay within the budget. Further, we can suppose that I intend that in pursuing the joint activity I act on the basis of beliefs about means and the like that are accurate. And you are not committed to mesh with that part of my sub-plan. Again, when you threaten me with your gun and tell me to keep painting, you may well be failing to intend that we paint by way of an intention of mine in favor of our painting together. What you intend, instead, is that I paint out of fear.

Many kinds of deception or coercion will, then, involve attitudes that straightforwardly violate one of the conditions cited by the basic thesis as central to shared intentionality. However, the basic thesis also helps us see how in some cases deception or coercion may fail to block shared intentionality, since they may fail to block these central conditions. Suppose you deceive me about some of your reasons for participating in our painting. Perhaps these reasons are a bit embarrassing. But suppose, as you know, I don't care why you are participating (within certain limits): nothing about this gets into my relevant sub-plans. And suppose that if I did care about this, in a way that was built into my relevant sub-plans, and if you came to know about this, you would adjust in some way. If this were true then it may be that, despite your deception, you are in fact committed to our painting by way of sub-plans that mesh.

Again, the master's coercive power might be exercised with the aim of getting the slaves to intend the joint activity with the master, rather than with the aim of shaping the specific interactions and sub-plans. An example, due to Daniel Markovits and Gideon Yaffe, is the joint building of the bridge on the River Kwai, as portrayed in the movie of that name. The Japanese troops in charge of the prisoner-of-war camp have coercive power over the British prisoners. And perhaps because of this coercive power both the Japanese troops and the British prisoners come to intend the joint bridge building. Perhaps they thereby also come to intend that their sub-plans for their building the bridge mesh, and that their joint activity of building of the bridge proceed by way of each of their intentions in favor of their building it. If so, there might be the forms of shared-end-tracking coordination, mutual responsiveness, and bargaining between the Japanese and British troops concerning their bridge building that are characteristic of modest sociality.

It seems to me plausible to say that in some versions of these last two cases of, respectively, deception and coercion, there can be shared intentional activity. This can be so even if deception and coercion quite generally block *cooperative* interaction—where we understand cooperation in a way that is, as discussed earlier, to some extent moralized. So there can be shared intentional activity that is not shared cooperative activity.[29]

The basic thesis helps us understand ways in which deception and coercion block, and ways in which they may not block, shared intentionality. Deception and coercion block shared intentionality of the sort highlighted by the basic thesis, when they do block it, not primarily because they violate some moral ideal of human interaction (though they do violate such an ideal), but because they involve attitudes that violate the specific social-psychological conditions highlighted by that thesis. And these conditions are highlighted by the basic thesis not primarily because of some background moral ideal of human interaction, though a defender of the basic thesis may, of course, also defend some such ideal. These conditions are highlighted, rather, because they are elements of a social-psychological, rational economy that realizes the main features of modest sociality.[30]

8. The compressed basic thesis

We can now express the basic thesis in a somewhat compressed form. We see conditions **(i)–(iii)** as articulating a complex intention condition, and conditions **(iv)–(v)** as specifying beliefs that support the coherence of the cited intentions. We see condition **(vi)** as ensuring an important accuracy of view of the participants concerning their interdependence. We see the mutual responsiveness in **(viii)** as central to the connection condition (and so to the contents of the attitudes in the intention and belief conditions). And, as in **(vii)**, we see these conditions as out in the open. We are thereby led to the following somewhat compressed sufficient conditions for our shared intention to *J*:

A. *Intention condition*: We each have intentions that we *J*; and we each intend that we *J* by way of each of our intentions that we *J* (so there is interlocking and reflexivity) and by way of relevant mutual responsiveness in sub-plan and action, and so by way of sub-plans that mesh.

B. *Belief condition*: We each believe that if the intentions of each in favor of our *J*-ing persist, we will *J* by way of those intentions and relevant mutual responsiveness in sub-plan and action; and we each believe that there is interdependence in persistence of those intentions of each in favor of our *J*-ing.

C. *Interdependence condition*: There is interdependence in persistence of the intentions of each in favor of our J-ing.

D. *Common knowledge condition*: It is common knowledge that A-D.

And we can then go on to say that what is needed for shared intentional activity, and so for modest sociality, is that this shared intention to *J* lead to our *J*-ing in accordance with the following connection condition:

E. *Mutual responsiveness condition*: our shared intention to *J* leads to our *J*-ing by way of public mutual responsiveness in sub-intention and action that tracks the end intended by each of the joint activity by way of the intentions of each in favor of that joint activity.

And **E** specifies what counts, in **A** and **B**, as relevant mutual responsiveness.

The *compressed basic thesis* is the claim that conditions **A-E** provide sufficient conditions for shared intention and modest sociality. At the heart of the theory, then, is a quintet of conditions: the participants have an interlocking and reflexive structure of *intentions* in favor of the joint activity by way of relevant mutual responsiveness and so mesh; the participants have relevant *beliefs* about efficacy and persistence interdependence; there is *interdependence* in persistence of relevant intentions; there is *common knowledge*; and there is relevant *mutual responsiveness*. When we step back to see the basic outlines of the theory it will be this quintet that will be in view, though in many cases it will be important to keep track of details that are more easily accessed by appeal to the noncompressed version of the thesis.

9. Too demanding?

Is our model of modest sociality too demanding?[31] Consider, in particular, the intention condition in the compressed basic thesis. This condition requires intentions that are interlocking, reflexive, and favor the joint *J*-ing by way of relevant mutual responsiveness, and so by way of meshing sub-plans. But, one might object, couldn't there be agents—four-year-old humans, perhaps— who engage in a form of modest sociality but for whom such complexity is not yet psychologically available?

In response, the first thing to say is that it is unclear that this concern with psychological demandingness applies more forcefully to the basic thesis than it does to proposals that appeal instead to we-intentions or to joint commitments. After all, given their purportedly primitive status, it is difficult to know how psychologically demanding we-intentions or joint commitments are.

Further, the level of psychological complexity available to a four-year-old human, or indeed to a normal adult human, is a difficult empirical issue.[32] Indeed, we might in the end see the capacity of young humans for modest sociality (if such there be) as itself evidence of the sort of psychological complexity at issue in the basic thesis.

Finally, we need to understand this concern about psychological demandingness within the context of three important features of the basic thesis. The first is that the complex content of the intentions cited in the intention condition may be only tacit or implicit. The agents need to have relevant intentions that ground associated dispositions of tracking, support, adjustment, and responsiveness in thought and action; and this web of intentions and associated dispositions needs to support the attribution of intentions with the complex content cited in the intention condition. But this need not involve explicit conscious awareness of this complex content. Further, we can also allow that the intentions cited by the basic thesis need not be actual causes of relevant behavior but function only as what Philip Pettit calls "standby factors" that exercise "virtual" rather than "active" control.[33] So the conditions cited in the intention condition are not as psychologically demanding as they may at first seem.

Second, the modest sociality modeled by the basic thesis can involve forms of interpersonal responsiveness that are not reflected in the contents of relevant intentions. Consider the subtle, interpersonal adjustments involved in establishing conversational distance, or dancing a tango. Our shared intention to converse, or to dance a tango, can frame such subtle interpersonal adjustments without the details of these adjustments appearing in the contents of our intentions.[34]

The third point returns to the central theoretical aim of the (compressed) basic thesis. This thesis aims to show how a robust form of modest sociality can be constituted by structures that have their home in the planning theory of individual agency, and it aims to show that the distinctive, rational normativity of modest sociality will emerge from those individualistic structures. In this way it aims to show that there need not be a deep conceptual or metaphysical or normative discontinuity between individual planning agency and modest sociality. That is why its fundamental concern is with sufficient conditions for modest sociality.

If the basic thesis succeeds in these efforts it will thereby have defended the continuity thesis. And this would be an important result. We would then be at liberty to go on to investigate whether certain less demanding social psychological phenomena might in certain cases to some extent functionally substitute for these more demanding attitudes of each.[35] Such an investigation could exploit the multifaceted model of shared agency provided by the basic thesis. That model provides us with a web of resources—a kind of theoretical toolbox—that includes intentions concerning joint action, interlocking intentions, intended and actual mutual responsiveness and mesh, interdependence, and the idea of being out in the open. So we can ask whether certain forms of shared agency involve versions of some but not all of these elements: say, mutual responsiveness and interdependence in the absence of interlocking.[36] Some such less-demanding structures might, perhaps, turn out to be common in the sociality of younger human children.[37] This more fine-grained theorizing would raise developmental issues concerning the later transition to modest sociality of the more demanding sort modeled here. Nevertheless, all this is compatible with the claim that the (compressed) basic thesis articulates the structure of a fundamental and robust form of modest sociality, and that this structure is continuous—conceptually, metaphysically, and normatively—with structures at work in individual planning agency.

Now, the worry that the basic thesis is too demanding is, so far, a worry about the psychological complexity and demandingness involved in realizing the structures described by that thesis. But there is also a related, though different, worry about theoretical parsimony. A version of this worry returns us to Searle's appeal to a new attitude of we-intention. Do considerations of theoretical parsimony argue in favor of Searle's approach?

It is useful here to turn to David Lewis's distinction between qualitative and quantitative parsimony. As Lewis says:

> A doctrine is qualitatively parsimonious if it keeps down the number of fundamentally different *kinds* of entity. . . . A doctrine is quantitatively parsimonious if it keeps down the number of instances of the kinds it posits.[38]

Now, the basic thesis is qualitatively parsimonious in appealing only to psychological kinds that are already needed for individual planning agency. But the basic thesis does appeal to a complex web of instances of such attitudes, and is in this sense less quantitatively parsimonious.[39] Searle's proposal, in contrast, is qualitatively nonparsimonious in appealing to a new phenomenon of we-intention, but this may perhaps allow for a kind of quantitative parsimony in avoiding some of the complexities of the basic thesis.

However, without trying to defend this here, it does seem to me that from the point of view of a concern with theoretical parsimony it is qualitative parsimony that most matters. Here I am agreeing with Lewis:

> I subscribe to the general view that qualitative parsimony is good in philosophical or empirical hypotheses; but I recognize no presumption whatever in favor of quantitative parsimony.[40]

If this is right then there is not an argument of theoretical parsimony that favors Searle's view over the basic thesis. Indeed, concerns about qualitative theoretical parsimony favor the basic thesis over the introduction by Searle, as well as by Gilbert, of a new "fundamentally different *kind*" of practical element.

5 MODEST SOCIALITY AND MUTUAL OBLIGATION

It may seem that if you and I share an intention to paint the house together then there are distinctive, corresponding obligations of each to the other, obligations that include obligations to play one's part unless one has been given permission by the other to opt out. And it may seem that these obligations are essential to and partly constitutive of the shared intention. As noted, this idea is central to the work of Margaret Gilbert.[1] And the objection we now need to consider is that the basic thesis does not adequately provide for this feature of shared intention.

In the background is the combined thought that

(a) the participants in modest sociality are tied together in distinctive ways that go beyond common knowledge, and

(b) it is an essential feature of these ties that they involve distinctive obligations.

As noted, the basic thesis subscribes to (a). But it purports to characterize these social ties by appeal to the cited structures of interconnected planning agency. The idea is that these social-psychological structures constitute sufficient conditions for modest sociality. And these structures, and their basic explanatory roles, need not make an essential appeal to the obligations cited in (b).

Nevertheless, the basic thesis can and should grant that shared intentions of the sort it characterizes are, at least for adult human agents, commonly, even if not universally, supported by associated mutual obligations, given plausible principles of obligation. First, a shared intention, once formed, may issue in downstream assurances or the like, and these may induce relevant obligations that then help support the functioning of the shared intention, in part by supporting its stability or reinforcing preexisting interdependence. Second, and as noted in Chapter 3, one form of persistence interdependence itself involves relevant mutual obligations. The question we now face is how best to understand these connections between shared intention and mutual obligation within the planning theory of modest sociality.

A first step is to review and to some extent supplement our discussion so far of how the basic thesis understands the explanatory roles of shared intention.

1. Shared intention, social explanation

The basic thesis highlights structures of interconnected attitudes of individual planning agents, and it sees these structures as helping to explain significant aspects of modest sociality. Suppose, for example, that our walking together satisfies the various conditions of the basic thesis. So I intend that we walk in part by way of your intention that we walk, my intention that we walk, mutual responsiveness, and so meshing sub-plans. This complex content of my intention connects it with your intentions and thereby imposes rational pressure on me, as time goes by, to fill in my sub-plans in ways that fit with and support yours as you fill in your sub-plans. This pressure derives from the rational demand on me to make my own plans coherent and consistent, taken together with the ways in which reference to your intentions enters into the content of my intentions. Rational pressures on me to be responsive to and to coordinate with *you* are built into my *own* plans, given their special content and given demands of consistency and coherence directly on my own plans (demands that are a part of the planning theory of individual agency). And similarly with you. Given that each of us is a planning agent who is to some extent guided by such rational pressures, and given assumptions of common knowledge, we have an explanation of various forms of social responsiveness that are characteristic of modest sociality. We have, for example, an intention-based explanation of why each seeks to coordinate relevant sub-plans with the other and to keep pace with the other. And if one or both of us fails to be appropriately responsive to the other, while continuing to be participants in the shared intention, we have an explanation of the sense in which there has thereby been a rational breakdown.

Again, the model provides an explanation of the way in which shared intentions frame bargaining and/or shared deliberation about means and the like. In shared intention of the sort described by the basic thesis, we each intend the shared activity in part by way of the intention of the other and by way of mutual responsiveness and so meshing sub-plans. So we are each under rational pressure to seek to ensure that our sub-plans, taken together, both are adequate to the shared task and do indeed mesh. And that is why, in the absence so far of adequate and meshing sub-plans, our shared intention will tend rationally to motivate, to structure, and to constrain bargaining and/ or shared deliberation in the pursuit of such sub-plans.

Further, the basic thesis helps explain a kind of rational stability of shared intention, given that the intentions of each of the participants are themselves subject to characteristic rational pressures for stability. There will be a kind of mutual stabilization, given the interaction between plan-theoretic pressures for stability of the intentions of each and characteristic forms of persistence interdependence.[2]

Finally, this model can provide for these explanations even if there are significant differences in each agent's reasons for participating in the sharing. Though we participate for different reasons, our shared intention nevertheless establishes a shared framework that can explain downstream thought and action.

These explanations suppose that the functioning of the planning agency of the individual participants will be guided by basic norms of individual intention rationality—where these include norms of consistency, agglomeration, coherence, and stability. Failures of such guidance will be rational breakdowns. And, as we have seen, associated norms of social rationality emerge from such individualistic rationality. The appeal, at the ground level, is to the relevant, public, interrelated intentions of the participants, and to relevant norms of individual intention rationality. And the claim is that these interrelated intentions, in these contexts and guided by these norms of intention rationality, provide a basic structure for explaining the main contours of socially rational shared intentional activity, including coordinated action and planning in the pursuit of a common end, and associated bargaining and shared deliberation.

Consider the practical reasoning of the participants in such a shared intention. If you and I share an intention to paint the house, I am in a position to reason roughly as follows: "I intend this joint activity, and so do you; these intentions are interdependent in their persistence; and we both intend that this proceed by way of these intentions of each, mutual responsiveness, and sub-plans that mesh. I can promote what I intend by settling on my buying the paint, given my belief that if I do that you will go ahead and bring the paint brushes and so our sub-plans will both be adequate and mesh with each other. And if you were knowingly to fail to coordinate with me in this way I could point out to you that this would be out of sync with what you (and we) intend, and so a kind of rational breakdown on your part. So, I hereby intend to buy the paint as my part in our joint project." When you also reason in similar fashion, and thereby arrive at an intention to bring the brushes, we thereby proceed with our joint project.

2. Shared intention, persistence interdependence, and mutual obligation

So we have a model of shared intention as an explanatory structure of interconnected attitudes of planning agents. In presenting this model in the previous section I made no essential appeal either to mutual obligations or to beliefs about such obligations. But now we need to reflect further on the place of such mutual obligations within our planning theory of modest sociality.

Return to our discussion in Chapter 3 of persistence interdependence between the intentions of each in favor of the joint activity. There is such persistence interdependence when, other things equal, each will continue so to intend if but only if the other does as well. This will involve mutual rational support: other things equal, each participant's intention in favor of the joint activity will be rationally sensible, in conditions of common knowledge, if and only if the other continues so to intend. And we have noted three separable (though potentially overlapping) kinds of persistence interdependence: desirability-based, feasibility-based, and obligation-based.

We have also noted different kinds of etiologies of persistence interdependence. First there can be cases in which these interdependent structures of intentions of each are induced by an element in the common environment. This is what we supposed might happen in the case of shared applause in response to a wonderful concert, or shared reaction to a manifest emergency. Second, there can be cases involving characteristic, temporally extended interactions between the participants. One participant might indicate her intention in favor the joint action in full confidence that the other will, in response, follow suit, and that there will ensue a structure of interdependent intentions of each in favor of the joint action. And sometimes this confidence that the other will respond in this way may be grounded in a prior, stage-setting indication by the other of a conditional intention in favor of the joint activity if the others intend that joint activity.

Such temporally extended interactions among the participants—at least those that take place among adult human beings—frequently engage familiar norms of moral obligation. After all, in many such interactions each of the participants will have, in effect, assured the other that she will intend the joint activity, and/or intentionally encouraged the other to rely on this and/or intentionally reinforced the other's reliance on this.[3] Though the details are a complex issue in moral theory, it seems that such forms of assurance and/or intentionally induced or reinforced reliance will frequently issue in moral obligations of each to each to continue so to intend. And in such cases, the participants' recognition of these mutual moral obligations will frequently help explain why there is persistence interdependence. It is because each recognizes these mutual obligations, in a context of common knowledge, that each is set, other things equal, to retain her intention so long as the other does. And so the resulting interdependence will be obligation-based (though it may also be desirability-based and/or feasibility-based).

I do not say that such interactions in support of interdependence always issue in such moral obligations. After all—and to return to an earlier example—while indicating the cited intentions, each might also explicitly indicate that she reserves the right to change her mind: "no obligations," each might say.[4] Even if this caveat on the part of each blocks relevant obligations, it need not block relevant predictability of each to each; and so it need not block the kind of mutual rational support that lies behind persistence interdependence.[5]

Indeed, there is here a range of hard questions in moral philosophy about precisely when such interactions do indeed ground mutual obligations. What if the targeted activity is trivial and short lived, as when two people accidentally meet while walking down 5th Avenue and walk together for a block before one of them peels away?[6] What if the shared activity is itself immoral, as when two people engage in a shared activity of torture? What if there is a background of coercion, as there is in the case, discussed earlier, of the British prisoners of war and their Japanese guards together building the bridge on the River Kwai? What if there is a background of deception? These are hard questions in moral philosophy. But we do not need here to provide detailed answers: the basic thesis need not settle these debates in moral philosophy. We can simply note that sometimes a temporally extended etiology of persistence interdependence induces mutual moral obligations whose recognition by the participants is part of the explanation of that persistence interdependence. And we can leave it to substantive moral theory to articulate and defend detailed principles concerning such moral obligations.[7]

Relevant persistence interdependence is one of our building blocks in our construction of shared intention and of modest sociality. We have seen that there can be different cases of persistence interdependence; and one important case involves recognized moral obligations that are the issue of prior interactions. Not all persistence interdependence depends on such mutual obligations. There can be desirability-based and/or feasibility-based interdependence that does not depend on the presence of relevant mutual obligations. The trigger of such forms of interdependence might be merely a catalyst in the common environment. And even when the etiology involves the cited kinds of interactions, it is a complex issue in moral theory when these interactions induce relevant obligations. Nevertheless, obligation-based persistence interdependence is an important species of the generic interdependence characteristic of shared intention.

The idea is not that such recognized mutual moral obligations themselves ensure shared intention. That seems false. After all, there can be recognized mutual moral obligations even if one or both of the participants intends not to comply with those obligations. You and I might each insincerely promise the other that he will help plow the commons. Since we have each promised—albeit, insincerely—we each have a moral obligation to the other to plow. (Here I bracket issues about special circumstances that can block such obligations.) Nevertheless, each of us intends *not* to plow, even though, we can suppose, we each know of our obligation to plow. In such a case there is known mutual obligation without shared intention. We do not have a shared intention to plow together because we are not in a state that is set to explain our plowing. Rather, we are each in a state—intending not to plow—that is set to explain why we do *not* plow together. Since, despite our (insincere) promises, we are not in a state that is set to explain our plowing together, ours is not a case of shared intention. So not only are such mutual obligations not necessary for the relevant explanatory structures; they are also not, in general, sufficient. Nevertheless, one species of the persistence interdependence that is, according to the basic thesis, an element in shared intention is obligation-based interdependence.

The persistence interdependence that is, according to the basic thesis, an element in shared intention can then be realized by different kinds of interpersonal structures. We have, in particular, distinguished three (potentially overlapping) cases: desirability-based, feasibility-based, and obligation-based. The appeal to persistence interdependence by the basic thesis is an appeal to the generic interrelation captured by our abstract characterization of such interdependence. It is this generic interrelation appeal to which is motivated in part by reflection on the settle condition. And the basic thesis can appeal to this generic condition of interdependence without making an essential appeal to the special case in which this interdependence is based on mutual obligations. Nevertheless, the basic thesis can acknowledge that at least for adult human agents one common form of such persistence interdependence is obligation-based interdependence. As we might say: for us, persistence inter-dependence is *contingently morally realizable.*[8]

This way of understanding the relation between shared intention and mu-tual obligation has three theoretical advantages. First, it allows for an attractive division of philosophical labor: we can defend the basic thesis while leaving for further normative inquiry the precise principles of relevant moral obliga-tion. Second, it acknowledges the important role that morality can sometimes play in our modest sociality without making obligations essential to modest sociality. So we can ask, for example, whether the great apes, or young chil-dren, are capable of modest sociality, and so capable of relevant interdepen-dence, without presupposing that an affirmative answer entails that the great apes, or young children, thereby stand in relations to each other of mutual obligation, or that they think that they do.

The third advantage is that this understanding allows us to retain a model of modest sociality that is broadly continuous with the planning theory of in-dividual agency while making room for the possible role of distinctive inter-personal norms of moral obligation. The structure of modest sociality articulated in the basic thesis does not make an essential appeal to such inter-personal norms of obligation. In particular, it makes no such appeal in its characterization of relevant persistence interdependence. But we can never-theless see how, once such forms of interpersonal moral obligation are avail-able to us, they can be put to work in the creation of a form of the persistence interdependence that is an element of our modest sociality. This is the possi-bility that is reflected in the contingent moral realizability of persistence inter-dependence. And this possibility of a kind of persistence interdependence that involves mutual moral obligations does not block the claim that the norms essentially involved in the basic thesis itself, and its purported suffi-cient conditions for modest sociality, are continuous with the norms of indi-vidual planning agency.

3. Gilbert on joint commitment

It is time to focus more carefully on work of a philosopher who proposes a tighter connection between shared intention and mutual obligation, Margaret Gilbert.

As Gilbert sees it, the move from individual to shared agency involves a move to a "joint commitment".[9] Gilbert does not try to provide an analysis of this idea of a joint commitment. She sees it as a basic, nonreducible idea, one that is the analogue in the case of shared agency to the idea of an individual, personal commitment—as when an individual reaches an individual decision—in individual agency. Whereas the basic thesis tries to provide a broadly reductive, multifaceted theory of that in which "joint-ness" or "shared-ness" consists, the idea that a Gilbertian joint commitment is *joint* is, in effect, a primitive, nonreducible idea for Gilbert. Granted, Gilbert does in a way try to explain this idea further. For example, she says that "a typical context for the formation of a joint commitment of two people involves the parties in face-to-face contact mutually expressing their readiness to be jointly committed, in conditions of common knowledge."[10] But it is clear that this is no analysis, since the very idea of being jointly committed is appealed to in this remark.

It is worth pausing to appreciate this point. The approach I am developing aims to provide a substantive account of that in which the *shared-ness* of shared intention and shared intentional action consists (at least in a central case). This shared-ness of shared intention consists, roughly, in public planning attitudes of each that interlock and are interdependent and that favor the joint activity and the mutually responsive, meshing roles of both. In contrast, if we were to ask Gilbert what makes a commitment a *joint* commitment—in what does the *joint-ness* of the commitment consist—the answer would be that this joint-ness is a primitive, nonreducible phenomenon.[11]

However, even given the nonreducibility of joint commitment, one can try to make certain substantive claims about such commitments. And that is what Gilbert aims to do. Gilbert proposes, first, that when—and only when—there is such a joint commitment is there a "plural subject".[12] I will return in Chapter 6 to this idea, and to the question whether it adds anything of substance to the theory of joint commitment.[13] For now what is central is a second claim Gilbert makes, namely that "*obligations with corresponding entitlements inhere in any joint commitment.*"[14] According to Gilbert, then, the step from individual to shared intention involves the introduction of this fundamental new phenomenon of "joint commitment", and thereby of obligations that "inhere" in, and so are an essential constituent of, such joint commitments. And this contrasts with the effort of the basic thesis to provide substantive, sufficient conditions for shared intention without an essential appeal to mutual obligations, while recognizing the possibility of a contingently moral realization of the interdependence cited by the basic thesis.

Gilbert's basic claim here is not that in modest sociality the participants *believe* that they have such obligations and entitlements. Her basic claim here is rather that in modest sociality there *are* these obligations and entitlements. Gilbertian joint commitments are an interrelation between the participants; they are not just a matter of the beliefs of the participants about

those relations. And there is an aspect of this idea with which the basic thesis agrees. Like Gilbert, the basic thesis sees modest sociality as essentiality
involving certain interpersonal interrelations: both theories reject the idea—
an idea that, as noted earlier, seems to be endorsed by John Searle—that
what is essential to modest sociality is, at bottom, solely certain special attitudes of each of the participants. The relevant difference between Gilbert's
view and the basic thesis lies in the understanding of these interrelations. In
Gilbert's view, but not according to the basic thesis, what is fundamental and
essential includes mutual obligations and entitlements that "inhere" in the
joint commitment.

The basic thesis seeks to characterize forms of interconnected planning
agency that can constitute modest sociality. The basic thesis grants that an aspect
of the basic structure of modest sociality—namely, relevant interdependence—
can be realized by certain recognized mutual moral obligations. But the basic
thesis also allows for relevant forms of interdependence that do not depend on
such mutual obligations. Bracketing the point that the obligations to which Gilbert appeals are not understood by her as specifically moral obligations, we can
say, roughly, that what the basic thesis sees as one species of shared intention
Gilbert identifies with shared intention.

A further contrast concerns explanatory resources. The basic thesis provides a broad range of resources for explaining the social interactions characteristic of modest sociality. These resources include intentions in favor of the
joint activity, interlocking of intentions, intended mutual responsiveness and
mesh, and persistence interdependence. In contrast, Gilbert's view does not
give us a way of characterizing the social functioning central to modest sociality without appeal to joint commitments that essentially involve interpersonal obligations.[15] The basic thesis offers a multifaceted structure of
explanatory resources rather than such a single-faceted appeal to joint commitment (and the obligations that "inhere" in a joint commitment).

Let me try to advance the discussion by considering Gilbert's recent essay,
"Shared Intention and Personal Intentions," where she offers the following
quartet of ideas:[16]

a. "Intuitively an appropriate *agreement* between the parties is sufficient to
   bring a shared intention into being."
b. "an adequate account of shared intention is such that it is not necessarily
   the case that for every shared intention, on that account, there be correlative personal intentions of the individual parties." [Gilbert sees the intentions of the participants that are cited in the planning model of shared

intention as "correlative personal intentions".] Gilbert calls this "the disjunction condition".

c. The disjunction condition is defended by way of an example in which Olive
reports "Our plan was to hike to the top of the hill. We . . . started up. As he
told me later, Ned realized early on that it would be too much for him to go
all the way to the top, and decided that he would only go half way. Though
he no longer had any intention of hiking to the top . . . he had as yet said
nothing about this to me . . . [Before halfway] we encountered Pam who
asked me how far we intended to go. I said that our intention was to hike to
the top . . . as indeed it was." Gilbert thinks Olive speaks truly in saying "as
indeed it was", and that this supports the disjunction condition.

d. "an adequate account of shared intention will entail that, absent special
background understandings, the concurrence of all parties is required in
order that a given shared intention be changed or rescinded . . ." Gilbert
calls this "the concurrence condition" (and she also supports this with an
example).

In reply, I do not accept any of these claims (as naturally interpreted). In particular, it seems to me that the plausibility of the purported disjunction and
concurrence conditions on shared intention comes from not sufficiently distinguishing shared intention and mutual obligation.

Begin with a., the claim that "an appropriate *agreement* between the
parties is sufficient to bring a shared intention into being." Perhaps this
claim has some intuitive support. But if we are really talking about shared
intention of a sort that is set appropriately to explain joint activity, the claim
seems to me false as a general claim. This is because—as noted earlier—
people can insincerely agree to, say, plow the fields together, even though
each participant fully intends not to act in accord with that agreement. In
such cases of insincere agreement there normally is, to be sure, a normative
structure of obligations and entitlements. So we may agree that "intuitively
an appropriate *agreement* between the parties is sufficient to bring a [*mutual
obligation*] into being." But, given the possibility of insincerity, an agreement
seems not to ensure that there is a shared intention of a sort that explains
joint action.[17] And a problem with an appeal to intuitions here is that intuitions can mislead, by not keeping track of the distinction between shared
intention and mutual obligation.[18]

Could Gilbert insist that agreements—even when insincere—do ensure
shared intention since, after all, they do ensure mutual obligation? Well, you can
use the words "shared intention" here if you want. But then we should be clear

that shared intentions, so understood, do not ensure the intention-based motivational basis of modest sociality, since they do not ensure relevant intentions to act. Granted, we may suppose that the recognition of such an obligation on the part of each of the insincere parties will many times to some extent motivate.[19] But in these cases of insincere agreements and the absence of "correlative personal intentions", it seems that whatever motivation is supplied by the recognition of the obligation is not going to be adequate to motivate conformity to that obligation. This means that in the absence of an individual-intention-based motivational basis we do not yet have a phenomenon that can play the basic *explanatory* role that, as I have been supposing, shared intention is to play.

Turn now to b. and the disjunction condition. It is clear that the planning model of shared intention, as articulated in the basic thesis, would not agree with the disjunction condition, since that planning model sees shared intention as consisting of what Gilbert calls "personal intentions". (Though these are "personal intentions" with special social contents and interrelations.) So what is the argument for the disjunction condition? Well, the basic argument is the example in c. But it seems to me that insofar as we are willing to agree with Olive, what we are thinking is that even after Ned changes his mind, Olive and Ned have a *mutual obligation* to climb the hill to the top. As I see it, once Ned has changed his mind they no longer have a *shared intention* to climb to the top, one that is set to explain their climbing to the top. After all, at that point Ned no longer intends to climb to the top, or that they together climb to the top, and instead fully intends *not* to climb to the top; and what is now going to need to be explained is not their climbing to the top, but rather their *failure* to climb to the top. Granted, Olive's belief that they have a shared intention to climb to the top might have remained epistemically justified after Ned changed his mind but before Ned had told her of this change of mind. But it can be justified and yet not true.

A similar point can be made concerning d., the claim that "the concurrence of all parties is required in order that a given shared intention be changed or rescinded". It seems to me that at most what is true here is that concurrence is needed in order to cancel the mutual obligations. Though Ned cannot unilaterally cancel relevant obligations, it is nevertheless true that once Ned no longer intends to climb to the top and fully intends not to climb to the top, he and Olive no longer have a shared intention to climb to the top, in a sense of shared intention that gets at the basic explanatory phenomenon.

So I think that while the concurrence condition and the disjunction condition are plausible conditions on mutual obligation, they are not plausible conditions on shared intention, understood as a basic explanatory factor.

Gilbert sees mutual obligations as basic building blocks of modest sociality, and seeks to explain the social functioning of modest sociality by appeal to those obligations. But we have seen reason to doubt that such obligations will be, in general, either necessary or sufficient for such explanations of relevant social functioning. And this supports a contrasting view. We first characterize the social-psychological structures that provide basic explanations of the social functioning involved in modest sociality. On the theory I am proposing, these will be social-psychological structures that are broadly continuous with the psychology of planning agency, a psychology we have independent reason to highlight as central to our temporally extended lives. We characterize these social-psychological structures without essential appeal to mutual obligations. But we also allow that, at least in cases involving adult human beings, certain aspects of those social structures can sometimes be realized by or supported by relevant, recognized mutual moral obligations.

4. Normativity, sociality, and Ockham's Razor

Though the basic thesis does not make an essential appeal to mutual obligations, it would not be accurate to say that the basic thesis eschews essential appeal to the normative. After all, it is central to the planning theory that there are norms of individual intention rationality. It is, further, an important claim of the basic thesis that within relevant structures of interconnected planning agency these norms induce associated norms of social rationality. What the basic thesis claims is that these forms of rational normativity, individual and social, suffice for the normative elements of basic forms of modest sociality, though they can be supplemented by further moral obligations. The issue between the basic thesis and Gilbert's theory, then, concerns whether our theory of shared intention must advert, at the ground level, not only to the cited norms of intention rationality, both individual and social, but also to the distinctive mutual obligations highlighted by Gilbert as essential to shared intention.

Why might one think that such mutual obligations must come in at the ground level? Well, return to cases of mere concatenation of activities with mutual adjustment. We can suppose that such cases take place within a context of common knowledge. It is, for example, common knowledge, between me and the stranger, that we are walking near each other and in the same direction and at roughly the same pace down the street. And that is why we keep an eye out to avoid collisions. But ours is not a case of shared intentional activity. Why not? It is not a matter of the absence of knowledge of each about each. Instead, there is in the case of shared intentional activity a distinctive practical tie, one that is not ensured by our knowledge. But what could this practical tie be? And here, as I have noted before, it is tempting to say these are, at least in part, ties of *obligation* of each to each.

This last step supposes that if the practical ties are not merely a matter of common knowledge then they are, at least in part, ties of mutual obligation. But we have seen that our philosophical options are richer than this. Once we have on board the planning theory of individual agency, we have the resources—conceptual, metaphysical, and normative—to characterize, without appeal to mutual obligations (and so without appeal to Gilbertian joint commitment), both intentions with distinctive contents and distinctive practical ties of interlocking, intended mesh, interdependence, and mutual responsiveness. Granted, the recognition of relevant mutual, moral obligations will sometimes ground relevant interdependence. And there will be cases in which the prior concerns of the participants diverge in ways that make a stable shared intention unlikely without the support of such mutual obligations. In such cases we will frequently have good reason, in support of our joint activity, to try to arrive at relevant obligation-creating mutual assurances, agreements, or promises. Nevertheless, the conjecture of the basic thesis is that, given its resources, we can characterize the fundamental practical ties without essential appeal to such mutual obligations (or, indeed, to beliefs on the part of the participants that there are such obligations). We can do this while recognizing that in certain cases the interdependencies highlighted by the basic thesis are grounded in familiar forms of obligation.

This is to grant that there is an important species of modest sociality in which the agents are indeed tied together in their pursuit of a common end by relevant mutual moral obligations. But this is not to identify that species with the genus, modest sociality. Nor is it to grant that our theory should appeal to Gilbert-type joint commitments. After all, joint commitment is supposed to be a distinct and unanalyzable phenomenon, not just a familiar kind of moral obligation. So we need to know if we really do need to appeal to this further practical primitive, over and above both morality and the modest sociality characterized by the basic thesis. And here Ockham's Razor counsels caution.[20] We need to know why we need to appeal in our theory to this yet further practical primitive. And my argument has been that we do not find grounds for the introduction of this further practical primitive in the consideration of garden-variety modest sociality. We can understand such sociality along the lines of the basic thesis; and we can then go on to explore the different ways in which cases of modest sociality can involve relevant moral obligations.

This Ockham's Razor argument generalizes. Once we have available the resources of the planning theory, we can construct an explanatorily rich model of modest sociality along the lines of the basic thesis. This model provides resources to understand and explain complex forms of social functioning and social rationality involved in modest sociality. We can then go on to recognize that these structures of modest sociality can interact in complex ways with relevant norms of moral obligation. A theorist who replies to this (as do, in different ways, Gilbert and Searle) that we still need a further, new practical primitive, needs to argue that we have so far still failed to capture important forms of small-scale sociality. At this point, the burden of argument seems to me to be on such a theorist.[21]

6 GROUP AGENTS WITHOUT GROUP SUBJECTS

In modest sociality, according to the basic thesis, the participants are interconnected planning agents. Given appropriate planning attitudes, and interconnections across those attitudes, it will be true that, say, *we* intend to paint the house together, and, if all goes well, that *we* do indeed paint the house together as a shared intentional— and perhaps a shared cooperative—activity. In expressing each of these claims, 'we' functions as a grammatical subject. Should we also think that in such cases 'we' refers to a group *agent* who paints? to a group *subject* who intends to paint?

1. Group agents and the basic thesis

Begin by returning to Petersson's essay. In Chapter 4 I discussed Petersson's argument that my account did not provide a strong enough model of modest sociality. I concluded that Petersson's objection, as well as a similar objection from Gold and Sugden, did not succeed, as we could see once we fully appreciated the distinctiveness of intention. Nevertheless, we can learn from reflecting on the amendment to my account that Petersson goes on to offer.

Petersson asserts that our theory of, as I call it, modest sociality needs a notion of collective activity that does not involve shared or collective intention but that does conceive of the group as itself a "causal agent."[1] To think of the group as a causal agent, in Petersson's sense, one need not see it as the subject of intentions or the like. Talk of "agent" here is not intended to go beyond the idea of an internally structured locus of causal powers and of the causal attribution of effects to that locus. As Petersson says, "this way of speaking simply places the object in a certain causal role, and refers to an effect for which internal features of the object is a condition."[2] To see a group as a causal agent, in the relevant sense, one need only see it as having sufficient internal organization such that, because of that internal organization, we can reasonably attribute to

that group "causal powers or dispositions,"[3] and can reasonably attribute certain upshots to it as something it, the group, causes.[4] For example, we may see
a swarm of bees as such a group causal agent:

> We may . . . watch the swarm as one causal agent and think about what
> it might do, wonder what makes it fly this way rather than that, think
> that some of its acts seem unexpected, and so on. . . . What makes you
> regard the swarm as the unit of causal agency need not be any specific
> knowledge about its internal structure, but just that its behavior gives
> you reason to think there is some such structure.[5]

This idea in hand, Petersson goes on to propose that this "weak notion of
collective activity [involving a weak idea of a group causal agent] *must* figure
in the content of the intentions of the parties to a collective action."[6] And here
he sees himself as going beyond the account of these contents that I have
provided.

It is central to Petersson's proposal that these ideas of collective activity
and group causal agency can appear in the contents of the intentions of each
participant, in the account of shared intention, without that account falling
prey to a circularity objection. This is because the cited idea of a group causal
agent does not involve the idea of shared intentionality. After all, swarms can
be group causal agents in Petersson's sense, as can, I take it, flocks, or certain
human mobs or crowds in the absence of a shared intention. In this respect,
Petersson and I have similar theoretical ambitions: we each seek an account
of the contents of the intentions of the individuals that help constitute the
shared intention, an account that does not fall prey to an unacceptable circularity. However, Petersson's concept of collective activity with a group causal
agent is somewhat stronger than the one I have used for this purpose at the
most basic level of my construction. This is because Petersson's concept explicitly brings with it the idea of the group as causal agent, whereas, roughly
speaking, mine makes do with, as Petersson puts it, "the notion of a mere set
of intertwined acts."[7] Petersson says that his claim is

> stronger than Bratman's initial proposal that it is sufficient that the act
> description, as it figures in the content of the agent's intention, merely
> satisfies the behavioral conditions for a joint activity. Such a descrip-
> tion would be neutral with respect to causal agency . . . My additional
> requirement is that the notion of the team as the causal agent *must*
> enter that content.[8]

Now, I take it that in appealing to the idea of a group causal agent (in the absence of group intentions or the like) the thought is not that this form of causation is metaphysically distinct from the underlying causal processes involving the organized elements of the group. The thought is, rather, that it can be true in this weak sense that the group is a causal agent, but when this is true this truth consists in facts about the relevant underlying structure of interrelated individuals (the bees in the swarm, for example) and casual processes that are shaped by that organizing structure. This is a metaphysically modest idea of a group causal agent, one that is compatible with an underlying metaphysics of interrelated individual agents. Nevertheless, we can see Petersson's proposal as an independent—albeit, limited—challenge to the *conceptual* adequacy of my account of the intentions of the participants: does my account of modest sociality need to include within the contents of those intentions an idea of the group as a causal agent, an idea that goes somewhat beyond the conceptual resources of the planning theory of individual agency?[9]

I think not. I agree with Petersson that when there is, as I have called it, modest sociality, we can plausibly see the participants as together constituting a group that, because of its internal organization, is a bearer of causal powers and something to which certain effects can be causally attributed. So we can see them as constituting a group causal agent in Petersson's (weak) sense. That the house is now painted can, for example, be causally attributed to *us*. But this does not show that we need, in the foundations of the theory of modest sociality, a concept of a group causal agent that goes beyond the conceptual resources already provided by the planning theory of individual agency and that "must" appear in the relevant intention-contents.

Consider what Petersson says about what it is to think of the group as a causal agent:

> In regarding the group as the causal agent, we imply that there is some glue—there is something about the intrinsic features of the group and about the participants' role in the base of the group's causal powers, which distinguishes members from nonmembers—although we refrain from specifying this glue.[10]

Petersson supposes that if one does believe that there is some internal organization that provides the appropriate sort of "glue" then one regards the set of participants as constituting a causal agent.

Now, according to the basic thesis, what glues together the individual participants in central cases of modest sociality—in contrast with swarms or flocks or certain kinds of crowds—are the cited social-psychological ties. It is, in a basic case, this social-psychological structure that explains the organization of their activity. Given this social-psychological structure and this organized activity, we can then go on to talk of the group as a causal agent that is constituted by its participants, organized in these social-psychological ways. This talk of the group as causal agent is built on our appeal to this social-psychological structure. As I see it, however, we do not need this idea of a group causal agent to articulate this structure in the first place.

This is not to deny that there is a concept of a group causal agent that can be explained independently of explicit appeal to the particular social-psychological structures highlighted in the basic thesis. We can follow Petersson and introduce a higher-order notion that involves existential quantification over potential forms of relevant glue: to say that there is a group causal agent is to say that *there is* a form of internal organization that appropriately explains relevant causal upshots; and we can say this without specifying exactly what that internal organization is and, in particular, without referring specifically to the social-psychological structures highlighted in the basic thesis. Examples like those of swarms of bees, or flocks, suggest that such a concept would be theoretically useful. Since this weak concept of a group agent involves existential quantification over forms of social organization, it does, strictly speaking, go somewhat beyond the conceptual resources of the planning theory of individual agency (though, as emphasized, it remains neutral with respect to shared intentionality). What I doubt, however, is that it is necessary to include this concept within the contents of relevant intentions of individuals in order to specify the basic social-psychological ties at issue in modest sociality. After all, the argument in Chapter 4 that the basic thesis provides sufficient conditions for modest sociality did not depend on including this concept of a group agent in the relevant intention contents.

Of course, if the participants have the attitudes and interrelations cited by the basic thesis, then it follows "that *something* glues [the relevant] components together."[11] On the assumption that Petersson has given us sufficient conditions for regarding a "set of objects as one causal agent,"[12] it follows that the participants who satisfy the conditions of the basic thesis are in a position to see their group as a causal agent in Petersson's (weak) sense. And they are each in a position to see that if their intentions are realized there will be a joint activity of which the group is a causal agent. But it does not follow that the contents of their intentions in the basic case must include a further, primitive idea of a group causal agent.

Granted, it is Petersson's view that if these contents do not include this further idea of a group causal agent then the theory will not be able to distinguish (what I call) modest sociality from mere strategic interaction. This is the challenge that I considered in Chapter 4. But, as I argued in that chapter, once we recognize the distinctiveness of intention and the interrelations cited by the basic thesis, we can see that this challenge fails.

This is to reject Petersson's challenge to the conceptual underpinnings of the basic thesis, but to endorse the idea that the metaphysics of modest sociality may include group causal agents (in the cited, weak sense of causal agent). However, this appeal to group causal agents is to be understood in a sense that identifies these groups with a structured complex of the participants, and identifies their causal role, in any particular case, with relevant causal roles of those participants suitably interrelated. And the basic thesis provides a model of the distinctive glue that is characteristic of those cases of group causal agency that are, in particular, cases of modest sociality.

According to the basic thesis, in modest sociality the contents of the intentions of each do involve the concept of "we." In basic cases this is either simply the distributed "we," or a concept of "we" (such as "those in this room"), that picks out a group of people in ways that do not involve an appeal to the very idea of shared intentionality. However, if all the conditions of the basic thesis are satisfied, it will follow that these several, distributed participants are interconnected—social-psychologically glued together—in a way that makes it true that they together constitute a group causal agent, one to which various effects can be causally attributed. Further, they are tied together in ways characteristic of, in particular, shared intentionality. Though the concept of "we" involved in the contents of the intentions of each need not, in the most basic cases, invoke the very idea of a group causal agent, the basic thesis describes a world in which there are (in the cited, weak sense) group causal agents involved in modest sociality. These group causal agents are not mere collections of the several, distributed participants, though they do consist in those participants organized and interlinked in the ways highlighted by the basic thesis. In this sense, while the basic thesis is *conceptually conservative* about the concepts that need to be employed in the contents of the intentions central to our basic construction of modest sociality, it is *metaphysically accommodating* concerning the group agents (in the cited weak sense) that are causally involved in modest sociality. It can say that the agent of, say, the duet singing is the group, and it is the structure of the participants that is characterized by the basic thesis that constitutes the group that is that agent. Since such group agents are identified with appropriately interconnected structures of individual agents—where these are plan-theoretic interconnections—this is a form of metaphysical accommodation that is compatible with the continuity thesis.

Once we see this we can allow that the parties to a shared intention may themselves go on to conceptualize what they intend in a way that involves the idea of a group causal agent. This is compatible with the claim that the concept of "we" at work in the contents of intentions in the basic cases of modest sociality need not itself involve the very idea of a group causal agent.

2. Group subjects?[13]

The basic thesis provides a model of shared intention as consisting in a complex state of affairs, one that involves interconnected attitudes of the participating planning agents. Now, when there is an intention of an individual agent there is an individual subject who so intends. So we need to ask: when there is a shared intention, is there a group subject who so intends?

Consider Jones who, alluding to her partner Smith, says:

1. We are singing the duet together as a shared intentional activity,

and

2. We intend to sing the duet together.

According to the basic thesis, 1. and 2. are true if there is an appropriate social-psychological web, and this web connects up in the right way to action.

Now, again according to the basic thesis, the contents of the intentions of the participants that help make 1. and 2. true might only involve a distributed notion of "we." Still, following Petersson, I argued in the previous section that if 1. and 2. are true in the way envisaged by the basic thesis then there will in fact be a group causal agent that is not merely a concatenation of the individual agents, but is a structured complex of those individuals. There will be an interconnected collection of the individuals that, because of its internal organization, will count as a group causal agent (in the cited weak sense) of the action reported. So, if 1. is true in the way envisaged by the basic thesis, then there is this group causal agent.

Further, this group will be the agent of, in particular, a shared intentional activity: this is not like the agency of a swarm of bees or a panicky crowd. And what makes this a shared intentional action is in large part the shared intention reported in 2. Should we say then that the group agent of the shared intentional action is the *subject* of this intention?

I think that this is not in general true: in modest sociality there need not be a group subject who has the shared intention. To talk of a *subject* who intends is to see that subject as a center of a more or less coherent mental web of, at the least, intentions and cognitions. The idea of a subject who intends X but has few other intentional attitudes—who intends X in the absence of a mental web of that subject in which this intention is located—seems a mistake. This moderate holism of a subject is a lesson we can learn from Donald Davidson's work on the holism of the mental.[14] But in cases of modest sociality the sharing will typically be partial and limited: Jones and Smith might have no other shared projects before them, and might significantly diverge in the reasons for which they participate in this shared project and in their relevant judgments of the right and the good. The sharing can also be transitory: this might be a short duet. And the sharing can cross-cut: Jones might sing this duet with Smith while playing chess with Brown.[15] These features of the sharing need not block the idea of an internally organized group causal agent of a shared intentional activity, an agent that is limited in its causal impacts and, perhaps, quite temporary. But the moderate holism of subject-hood distinguishes this idea of a *causal agent of a shared intentional activity* from the idea of a *subject of a shared intention.*

In modest sociality it seems plausible that the group—a structured collection of individuals—is, in a weak sense, the agent of the shared intentional activity. And shared intentional activity involves shared intention. But when we turn to the idea of the *subject* of the shared intention we should not expect that in modest sociality there will in general be a sufficiently robust, coherent web of relevant shared attitudes to support the claim that the group is that subject. In this way, being the agent of the shared action can come apart from being the subject of the shared intention, even given that the shared action is organized by the shared intention.

This is not to deny that there may be special cases in which it is plausible to talk of a Davidsonian group subject.[16] The claim is only that there can be shared intentional agency, and associated shared intention, in the absence of a social subject of that shared intention, and that this is indeed the normal case of small-scale modest sociality.

If 1. is true in the way envisaged by the basic thesis, then there is an internally organized group causal agent of the shared intentional activity, an agent whose structure is articulated by that thesis. That agent is a causal source of the shared intentional activity (which, as we have seen, is not to say that the participants must include this idea of a group agent in the content of their relevant intentions). If 2. is true in the way envisaged by the basic thesis, then there is an appropriate interpersonal social-psychological web that makes 2. true. But even given that social-psychological web, it may well be that there is no group subject of the shared intention.

This returns us to a point from Chapter 4 about a Lockean aspect of both individual and shared agency. The basic thesis highlights both referential interlocking and commonality of content of the intentions of the different participants in modest sociality. In this respect, according to the basic thesis, the social glue characteristic of modest sociality at a time to some extent parallels the Lockean structure of individual planning agency over time. This social glue is quasi-Lockean. And this might make the idea of a group subject in modest sociality more tempting. But I think that this would be a mistake. Even given these interpersonal quasi-Lockean interrelations in modest sociality, it still seems incorrect, for reasons noted, to suppose that there is, in general, a group subject in such modest sociality.

Granted, if a group has a shared intention to bring about an untoward effect and succeeds in doing that, we may want in some sense to hold that group accountable. But then what we need is an interpretation of such accountability (something I will not attempt here) that does not require a group subject (though it may require a group agent in the weak sense we have been discussing).

I noted earlier that in Margaret Gilbert's view whenever there is shared intentional activity there is a "plural subject" of the involved shared intentions.[17] I have been arguing that in standard cases of modest sociality what makes it true that there is a shared intention does not in general suffice for there being a subject of the shared intention. Am I thereby in disagreement with Gilbert?

It depends on how we are to interpret Gilbert's talk of a plural subject.[18] On a robust interpretation, Gilbert's talk of a plural subject is sufficiently analogous to our talk of an individual subject that it engages the idea of a center of a moderately holistic mental web.[19] And my claim is that modest sociality does not require a plural subject in this robust sense. So if this is how we are to interpret Gilbert, then Gilbert and I are indeed disagreeing. On a more deflationary reading, however, Gilbert's talk of a plural subject is only a shorthand for talk of a set of persons who are, in her sense, jointly committed with respect to a specific joint action. The substantive metaphysics of modest sociality lies entirely in such joint commitments—commitments that can be quite local and quite limited. So interpreted, Gilbert is *not* claiming that there is a plural subject over and above specific joint commitments, in the way in which there is an individual subject over and above specific intentions of that subject. On this interpretation, the appeal to the idea of a plural subject does no further philosophical work in Gilbert's theory, and Gilbert and I are not disagreeing about the need for a plural subject in shared intentionality. Our disagreement is, rather, about how precisely to understand the specific interrelations among participants that constitute specific cases of shared intentionality.

Now, in correspondence Gilbert has indicated her preference for this second reading, citing her *A Theory of Political Obligation*, where she says:

> It is useful to have a label for those who are jointly committed with one another in some way. I have elsewhere used the label 'plural subject' for the purpose and shall use it that way here. To put it somewhat formally: A and B (and . . .) (or those with feature F) constitute a plural subject (by definition) if and only if they are jointly committed to doing something as a body—in a broad sense of 'do'."[20]

So that is how I will understand Gilbert's view. But we then need to go back to a point, in Chapter 5, about the very idea of joint commitment. I noted there that though Gilbert sees the idea of a joint commitment as a primitive, she does want to make substantive and informative claims about joint commitments. She wants to offer claims that will to some extent help us to understand what this primitive phenomenon is. As we have seen, one of these substantive claims is that mutual obligations inhere in joint commitments; and this is a claim I have examined at some length. But it might also have seemed that a second substantive claim was that joint commitments induce plural subjects. However, for this to add something substantive to the theory, we cannot say that talk here of a plural subject is just a *façon de parler*.

As I noted earlier, one question we can have about the very idea of joint commitment is: in what does the *joint-ness* of the commitment consist? What makes it *our joint* commitment and not merely a concatenation of commitments of each? The basic thesis understands the joint-ness or shared-ness of shared intention as consisting in a multi-faceted web of interrelations among relevant plan states with common social contents. In contrast, Gilbert sees joint commitment as a primitive relational phenomenon. Still, without seeking a reduction of joint commitment to other things, we can ask whether anything substantive and informative can be said about the nature of such

joint-ness. And here it might have seemed that the appeal to the idea of a plural subject could be a part of Gilbert's answer to this question. But on the
second—privileged—interpretation of Gilbert's talk of a plural subject, this
cannot be so. This might exert pressure to return to the first, more robust interpretation of this talk of a plural subject; but I have argued against the claim
that plural subjects, so interpreted, are present in all cases of modest sociality.

In discussing a view of shared action that is broadly in the spirit of my
view, Philip Pettit and David Schweikard observe that this view "fails to point
us to a single collective subject that is causally responsible for the action"; but
they also go on to say that they

> see no metaphysical reason why a joint intentional action has to be the
> product of a single agent or a single state of intending. . . .
> 	[we do not need] the joint construction of a novel center of inten-
> tional attitude and action.[21]

I am here agreeing with Pettit and Schweikard that we need not suppose that
in modest sociality there is a "novel center of intentional attitude"—a subject
of the shared intention. But I think that Petersson is right to point us to the
idea that there can nevertheless be, in a weak sense, a "single agent"—though
not "a single collective subject"—that is, in the words of Pettit and Schweikard, "causally responsible for the action." This agent is the internally structured group—where that group consists of the appropriately structured
collection of the participants (and where the basic thesis is a thesis about what
in the present case that structure is). But, given a moderate holism of subject-
hood, in cases of modest sociality we should not expect that this group is "a
single collective subject" or "a novel center of intentional attitude." The social-
psychological organization involved in shared intention can help constitute a
group agent without constituting a group subject. In modest sociality, then,
group *agents* of a shared intentional activity—agents that are "causally responsible for the action"—are not in general *subjects* of the shared attitudes that
help make it true that there is shared intentional activity.[22]

As Joshua Cohen has emphasized (in conversation), drawing on ideas of
John Rawls,[23] we need to be careful when we try to extend our model of individual agency directly to a model of shared agency. And what we have seen is
that this thought applies to the way we think of the connection between intentional agency and subject-hood. In the case of individual intentional agency it
is plausible that the agent of the intentional activity is the subject of a web of
attitudes, some of which are part of the explanation of that activity. But what

we have seen is that when we turn to modest sociality, a correspondingly tight connection between shared intentional agency and group subject-hood is less plausible.

Return now to the purported own-action condition on intention. When I first discussed that condition in Chapter 1, I said that it seemed initially that appeal to *our* shared intention to *J*—in contrast with my intention that we *J*—satisfies that own-action condition. But now we can see that matters are more complicated. Talk of *our* intention in favor of *our* action is, to be sure, in the spirit of the own-action condition. But we have now seen that in modest sociality this talk of our intention need not treat us as the *subject* of the shared intention. There is, to be sure, a match in the dual use of the first person plural in talk of *our* intention that *we* act. But, strictly speaking, such talk need not pick out a subject of the shared intention who is one and the same as the agent of the intended action, since such talk need not pick out a subject of the shared intention. Still, if all goes well there will be a structured collection of participants that is the agent of the shared activity and also is the locus of those interconnected attitudes that constitute the shared intention in favor of that activity. So something in the spirit of the own-action condition is true about our shared intention, and there remains a relevant contrast between talk of our intention to *J* and of my intention that we *J*.

7 SHARED DELIBERATION, COMMON GROUND

1. Shared deliberation and shared intention[1]

I now turn to shared deliberation as an element in modest sociality. Examples might include our deliberating about the division of roles, or the color of paint, as part of our shared activity of painting the house together; a search committee's deliberations as part of its shared search activities; a quartet's shared deliberations about the details of a performance; a scientific research team's shared deliberations about the target of research, and when and what to publish; an admissions committee's shared deliberations as part of its efforts to decide whom to admit; yours and my shared deliberation about our route as part of our shared activity of walking together; a gang's shared deliberation as part of its shared activity of dominating a neighborhood; a start-up's shared deliberation as part of its business activities; and so on.

I want to highlight three features of such shared deliberation. First, it is embedded in an ongoing shared intentional/shared cooperative activity of the group. Second, shared deliberation is itself a shared intentional activity on the part of the group.[2] A third feature distinguishes shared deliberation from ordinary bargaining.[3] In ordinary bargaining we each bring to bear considerations that matter to each of us without assuming that the very same considerations directly matter to the others. In shared deliberation, in contrast, we reason together in a way that involves a *common ground* of *shared* commitments to treating certain considerations as mattering in our shared deliberation.[4]

Mattering in what way? A central case is when we have a shared commitment to giving more or less weight to certain considerations in our shared reasoning. We might, for example, have a shared commitment to giving a certain weight to environmental concerns in our shared activity of house building. But there are other ways in which certain considerations might be taken to matter. In our shared building of the house we might take the zoning laws to provide substantive side-constraints on how we proceed, rather than consider-ations to be weighed alongside other considerations, such as economic efficiency. We might take a norm of consensus in our decision making to be a procedural side-constraint on our shared reasoning. We might take certain promises as providing something like what Joseph Raz calls "exclusionary rea-sons": these promises block our consideration of certain other considerations that might otherwise have been taken to have relevant weight in the circum-stances.[5] Or we might have shared commitments to norms that codify "defaults," together with norms that codify relevant "defeaters" of those defaults as well as potential "under-cutters" of those defeaters, along the lines recently developed by John Horty. We might, for example, have a shared com-mitment to conforming to certain environmental constraints in the absence of certain more or less articulated defeating conditions that are not them-selves undercut.[6]

There are significant questions here about the exact interrelations between these and perhaps other structures of practical reasoning. I put these issues aside here. What I will do is work primarily with the central idea of shared commitments to more or less articulated relative weights. I will sketch a model of shared deliberation in which something like such shared commit-ments to weights plays a central role; though in developing this model I will draw somewhat on ideas that are broadly in the spirit of Raz's appeal to exclu-sionary reasons and Horty's and others' appeal to defeasibility. I leave for an-other occasion the possibility of further extensions of this model to other structures of practical reasoning.

My focus will be on garden-variety shared deliberation as it occurs in the context of ordinary shared intentional activities, given needs for mesh in social thought and action—as when we engage in shared deliberation in the pursuit of meshing sub-plans for our shared activity of building a house to-gether, or of taking a trip together, or of producing a play together, or of run-ning a scientific experiment (or a philosophy department) together.[7] My focus, to borrow from J. David Velleman, is on "how we get along" (or anyway, one important way in which we get along) in garden-variety shared deliberation that is primarily concerned with supporting mesh in our thought and action, mesh that is central to our modest sociality.[8] My focus is not specifically on moral reasoning, though commonsense moral considerations will frequently to some extent be brought to bear in garden-variety shared deliberation. (There will also be cases in which recognizably moral considerations will not be prominent—a gang might engage in shared deliberation about how to ter-rorize the neighborhood.) It is a large question—one I do not try to address here—how fundamental forms of moral reasoning are related to the sort of social, shared deliberation I seek to model here.[9]

My question, then, is how we might plausibly construct a model of such shared deliberation, a model that draws on the basic thesis and is, in the relevant sense, continuous with the planning theory of individual agency. And my proposal will be that we make progress in understanding shared deliberation by articulating a trio of interrelated forms of functioning of relevant shared intentions.

An initial point is that shared deliberation is framed by shared intention in two ways. First, since shared deliberation is part of an overall shared intentional activity, and since such shared intentional activity is guided by relevant shared intentions, shared deliberation will be in part guided by those shared intentions. Second, since shared deliberation is itself a shared intentional activity it will itself be guided by a relevant shared intention. And in each case the relevant shared intentions, and their guidance, can be understood by appeal to the basic thesis.

This takes us to the third feature of shared deliberation: the role in such deliberation of shared commitments to weights. Reflection on this aspect of shared deliberation will uncover a third important role of shared intention. And, as anticipated, this will lead us to the view that our shared deliberation characteristically involves interplay between three forms of shared intention. In this way the model of shared intention provided by the basic thesis provides important elements of a model of shared deliberation.

2. Shared commitments to weights

Let's begin with some examples of shared commitments to weights. Perhaps we share a commitment within our shared painting of the house to our giving substantial weight to environmental concerns as we decide which paints to use, and how to dispose of various materials. Or perhaps we are engaged in a shared intentional activity of building a house and we deliberate together about sub-plans in a way that brings to bear our shared commitment to giving weight to certain standards of earthquake safety, or certain aesthetic standards. An admissions committee might have a shared commitment to its giving weight to legacy considerations in its admissions decisions. A scientific research team might have a shared commitment to its giving weight to the short-term public benefits of science, or to earning lucrative patents, in its decisions about the direction of its research. A dramatic team might share a commitment to give weight to highlighting certain political issues in its production of a certain play. An academic department might have a shared commitment to its giving weight to collegiality in making faculty appointments. A start-up enterprise might have a shared commitment to giving more weight to market share than to short-term profits. A gang might have a shared commitment to giving weight to terrorizing the local population. And (to return to Gilbert's example) you and I, in walking together, might share a commitment to giving weight to beautiful scenery as we jointly settle on a route.[10]

Consider a Philosophy department that has a shared commitment to its giving weight to issues of sub-field in its searches for new faculty.[11] This shared commitment will normally be grounded to some extent in judgments of the participants about what makes a good department. But this shared commitment may go beyond such prior judgments about value, and does not require agreement in those judgments. In participating in such a shared commitment one need not suppose that it is the best such shared commitment. One may think there is no single best; or one may think that a different shared commitment would have been better. Indeed, each member of the department may have a different view of what the best shared commitment would have been, and yet the department may arrive at a shared commitment that, at least prior to that shared commitment, no one sees as best. Such shared commitments nevertheless help structure shared deliberation and shared planning.

In some cases particular shared commitments concerning what to treat as having weight in certain contexts of shared activity are more or less central to or definitive of the group or team. If you are going to be a member of a certain scientific research team, you may need to participate in a shared commitment to giving weight, in discussions of the direction of the research, to the potential for lucrative patents. Central to certain groups may be a shared commitment to giving weight to conformity to particular religious texts or traditions or rituals. Members of a club might have a shared commitment to giving weight to religious affiliation, or gender or race, in shared deliberation about membership; and that may be why you do not want to be a member of that club.

As these examples suggest, such shared commitments about weights in shared deliberation will normally be part of a larger package of shared intentions. A group might have both a shared intention to worship together each Saturday, and a shared commitment to giving weight to associated rituals and traditions on those occasions of shared worship. And a scientific research team might have a shared intention to engage in a certain line of research, together with shared commitments to weights that are relevant to the group's associated deliberations about what and when to publish. In each case participation in the relevant shared intentional activities of religious worship or scientific research involves as well participation in related shared commitments about weights. And such shared commitments about weights can help tie a group together even in the face of some divergence of view concerning particular courses of action.[12]

3. Shared policies about weights

What account should we give of this phenomenon of shared commitments to weights? We might try saying that such shared commitments are a matter of converging judgments of value in a context of common knowledge: our shared commitment to our giving weight to X consists in our each judging that X is valuable, in a context of common knowledge of these judgments. The problem, however, is that sameness of value judgment, in a context of common knowledge, seems neither sufficient nor necessary for a corresponding shared commitment to weights in shared deliberation. Perhaps each of us thinks earthquake safety in construction is a good thing and these judgments are common knowledge, yet we still do not have a shared commitment to give weight to earthquake safety in our shared deliberations concerning our construction project. Perhaps some of us resist such a commitment because, though earthquake safety is a good thing, it would stand in the way of higher profits, or speed of construction.

Further, even if there is a public consensus with respect to certain value judgments, we might share a commitment *not* to appeal to those judgments in our shared deliberation in certain domains. Perhaps each of us judges that conforming to certain religious injunctions is a good thing, yet we share a commitment to screen out appeal to these religious values in certain domains of our shared civic activities. Or perhaps each of us in a scientific research team thinks that achieving scientific fame would be a good thing, but we have a shared commitment not to appeal to that value in our deliberations about the direction of our research.

So, public convergence of value judgments need not ensure a relevant shared commitment to associated weights. The next point is that such a public convergence of value judgment is also not necessary for a corresponding shared commitment to weights. We could have a shared commitment to, for example, our giving weight to collegiality in our hiring decisions, or to legacies in admissions decisions, even if some of us are to some extent skeptical about the associated values but participate in the shared commitment as part of a social compromise. Further, even if we do each judge that X is a good, and do go on to a shared commitment to giving weight to X in our shared deliberation, the relative weight involved in our shared commitment need not strictly correspond to a common, relative weight in our value judgments. After all, there might be no such common, relative weights in our value judgments. So, public convergence of a relevant comparative value judgment in favor of X over relevant alternatives is not necessary for a shared commitment to giving X such a weight.

Granted, each person's participation in our shared commitment to give a certain positive weight to X will normally involve some judgment that there is something to be said in favor of X.[13] And the social route to the shared commitment may involve appeals to such judgments. However, this does not entail that our shared commitment to give X a certain weight involves a public convergence of corresponding, specific evaluative judgments.

A shared commitment to weights seems then to be a different phenomenon than that of a public convergence of value judgment. Sharing a commitment to certain weights seems closer to a kind of shared intention than to a common value judgment. This suggests that our shared commitment to weights is better modeled not as a common evaluative judgment but as a shared intention that favors our giving weights to certain considerations in relevant shared deliberation.[14] In participating in such a shared intention concerning weights, each person will normally have some sort of supporting evaluative judgment. But such background judgments need not interpersonally converge, and need not strictly correspond to what is favored by the shared intentions concerning weights. Here, as elsewhere, what is central to our sociality is the sharing of intentions and plans, and not agreement in belief or judgment. This is an aspect of the primacy of intention for our sociality.

To play their role in shared deliberation these shared intentions about weights need to provide a settled, public common ground that serves as a framework for relevant social thought and action; social thought and action that normally extends over time. For this to work these shared intentions about weights need to help support the reliability and predictability of the relevant contributions of each to the shared deliberation. In the shared deliberation in our search committee, for example, each needs to be confident that each would reliably apply our shared intention about weights in similar ways in relevant contexts, both now and into the future. I need to be confident that you will reliably apply the relevant standard, in ways that are similar to how I would apply it, when you are screening files both now and later, and both when we are face to face and when you are in the privacy of your office. And similarly for you. And these reliable, convergent applications of our shared intention concerning weights will need to be grounded in, and be explanatorily intelligible in the light of, that shared intention.[15]

So there is a web of social pressures in favor of explanatorily intelligible, predictable, and reliable similarity of application of the shared intention about weights. And a basic way to respond to those social pressures will involve generality in the content of the shared intention: it will be a shared intention not just about a specific weight right now in this temporally local particular situation, but rather a shared intention to give weight to a certain kind of consideration—collegiality, say—on various occasions that may arise in our ongoing shared deliberation. This is to respond to these social pressures by appeal to shared, general *policies* about weights.[16]

Now our primary focus is on the provision of sufficient conditions for robust forms of modest sociality. So, when we come to shared deliberation, there is good reason to highlight a construction within which a central role is played by shared intentions concerning weights that are shared policies about weights. This does not by itself show that such generality is strictly necessary for shared deliberation. The claim is only that such generality helps support central forms of reliability, predictability and intelligibility, and so is reasonably incorporated within our construction of shared deliberation.

I noted in Chapter 1 that an individual planning agent may have policies about weights for her deliberation, policies that go beyond her prior judgments of value. An example noted there is the policy of the young man, in Sartre's example, in favor of giving significantly more weight to the political interests of the Free French than to the interests of his mother. This policy might be formed in the face of an apparent noncomparability of these conflicting interests, or in the face of interpersonal disagreements that sensibly undermine confidence in corresponding full-blown comparative evaluative judgments. In each case the individual has a policy about weights that goes beyond his prior evaluative judgment. And the suggestion now is that we understand shared commitments to weights as a shared version of such individualistic policies about weights.

In the individual case, policies about weights can give determinateness to the agent's practical thinking in the face of underdetermination by that agent's prior judgments about the right and the good, an underdetermination that may be a matter of supposed noncomparability or of a modesty of intersubjectively accountable judgment in the face of interpersonal divergence of judgment. In the shared case both pressures for turning to nonjudgment policies about weights remain in play, but there is now also a further, distinctively social pressure. This is a pressure that derives from the need, in our modest sociality, for interpersonal convergence on modes of shared reasoning in the face of both potential divergence in the judgments of each and potential commitments to screen out certain forms of consensus of evaluative judgment from a given domain of shared deliberation.

So let us model shared commitments about weights as shared policies about weights in shared deliberation. We can then apply our plan-theoretic constructivist approach to intention sharing to the case of shared commitments to weights. We thereby extend the architecture of the basic thesis to the common ground of shared commitments to weights.[17]

On this approach, a shared commitment to give weight to R is a shared policy to give weight to R in relevant shared deliberation. According to the basic thesis, this shared policy consists, in large part, in public interlocking and interdependent general intentions, on the part of each, in favor of our giving weight to R in relevant shared deliberation by way of relevant mutual responsiveness. And the rational functioning of such a shared policy about weights will emerge from that of its interconnected individualistic constituents. Each interdependently intends that they give weight to R in relevant deliberative contexts, and each intends that this proceed by way of the relevant intentions of each, mutual responsiveness and so meshing sub-plans. So each is interdependently set to participate in and support such policy-guided reasoning within the shared deliberation, where for each this is guided by accepted norms of individual intention rationality. In this way we extend the constructivist architecture of the planning theory of shared intention to a kind of shared commitment to weights that is central to shared deliberation.

Such policies about weights can be defeasible.[18] Perhaps our shared policy to give weight to scenic beauty as we settle on routes for our walking together would, by our own lights, sensibly be blocked by certain nonstandard emergency conditions. Nevertheless, such a defeasible policy of giving weight to scenic beauty can normally play the needed social roles in our shared deliberation: it can help support the normal reliability, predictability, and explanatory intelligibility of relevant social thought and action, both at a time and over time. Or at least, it can play these roles if there is at least a rough consensus concerning what would count as a defeating condition.

Shared policies about weights in shared deliberation can, in complex ways, recognize and build on relevant agreement in evaluative judgment, when such there be. But such shared policies can instead screen out certain kinds of evaluative consensus. And such shared policies can also go beyond prior evaluative consensus to further shared commitments about weights in order to make shared deliberation more determinate and more likely to support needs for mesh in our modest sociality.

Further, as in the general case of shared intention in favor of shared action,[19] the reasons for which each participates in these shared policies can diverge. Perhaps some on a college admissions committee participate in their shared policy of giving weight to legacy considerations because they think giving such weight is an effective fundraising tool, whereas others participate because they think their institution has made an implicit promise to its alumni to provide this benefit to their children. Members of the committee participate for different reasons; but their shared policy about weights nevertheless establishes a common—albeit, partial—framework for their shared deliberation.

I think it is a virtue of our theory that it helps us model such partial but substantial social unity in the face of divergent evaluative judgment and different reasons for which each participates. Much of our sociality is partial in this way, given the pressures for shared agency in the face of such differences, pressures and differences that are characteristic of, in particular, a pluralistic, liberal political culture. We manage to reason together in the pursuit of shared projects despite significant background differences of judgment and of reasons for which each participates. Our model of shared commitments to weights as shared policies about weights aims to provide in a clear way for these important phenomena. And it does this in a way that highlights the central role of intention in our sociality.

In response to characteristic practical pressures, then, we might go beyond what consensus in evaluative judgment there is and reach a more extensive policy-like convergence concerning weights for our shared deliberation. This would be puzzling if we thought that what we would be directly arriving at is a belief or judgment about which weights are the correct weights. We do not normally think of belief or judgment as rationally responding directly to these kinds of practical pressures:[20] the formation of belief for these kinds of practical reasons is, normally, wishful thinking. But in participating in a shared policy about weights despite our prior evaluative differences, I need not be directly changing my beliefs or judgments about these weights. I need only be guided by a relevant policy in certain social contexts.[21]

This is important, since convergence in belief or judgment about relative weights is frequently difficult and unlikely to be achieved. So we want to model forms of shared agency and shared deliberation that need not depend on and do not include a demand in favor of such convergence.[22] And this is, again, an aspect of the primacy of intention in our sociality.

A shared policy to give weight to R differs from a case in which it is simply true and publically known that each favors giving weight to R in the relevant context. First, in the case of such a shared policy each not only favors his own activity of giving weight to R; each has a policy that favors the group's giving weight to R. Second, each not only takes note of the other's attitude in favor of their giving weight to R. Each interdependently intends that they give weight to R in this context; and each intends that this proceed by way of each participant's so intending and by way of mutual responsiveness and meshing. These interdependent and interlocking intentions in favor of the group's giving weight to R constitute a shared commitment to give weight to R, one that helps to induce and to stabilize this pattern of weights.[23]

Such shared policies about weights can, then, be a sensible solution to a fundamental problem for our sociality: the need for relevant social unity in the reasoning that lies behind our shared activities, despite divergence in (and perhaps bracketing of) judgments about the right and the good. And such shared policies are a solution that remains within the metaphysics of shared attitudes as constructions of interconnected attitudes of the participants.[24]

4. Where the group stands

We now need to address a worry. When these shared policies about weights are not specifically supported by corresponding evaluative judgments on the part of the participants, they may seem to be merely useful coordination devices for use in shared reasoning, rather than commitments that are substantially internalized within the psychic economies of the participants.[25] They may seem to be, as Jonathan Dancy has put a related idea, "something like a set of traffic regulations."[26] Is shared deliberation of the sort of interest here merely the reflection of some such useful coordinating devices?

Well, shared policies are real structures of interrelated intentions of the participants. These interrelated intentions are practical commitments that will, as a matter of their characteristic roles, exert rational pressures on relevant thought and action. And this will be true even if there is divergence in relevant evaluative judgment of the participants and in the reasons for which each participates.

But there is also, potentially, further support for these shared policies, a support that may be shared despite the divergence in relevant specific judgments of the right and the good. Once the shared policies are in place, their functioning can help realize relevant forms of sociality. And the participants may converge in their positive evaluation of those forms of sociality, despite

their more specific evaluative differences. So these shared policies can sometimes involve a sensible reflexivity: they can sometimes sensibly say to give
weight to X in part because of the acknowledged value of the forms of sociality
that are partly constituted by this social role of those policies.[27]

Perhaps our policy about weights in our admissions decisions is a compromise solution, given a divergence of judgments of each. Nevertheless, we may
well have public and common views of the importance of teamwork—of
working together to solve such practical problems in running a university.
And our sharing of such policies of weights helps support that valued sociality. When, as part of our intended mutual responsiveness, I criticize you for
failing to conform to our shared policy of weights concerning admission
decisions, I can appeal not just to this inconsistency with a policy of ours (and
so of yours and of mine), but also to a tension with the value that we each
acknowledge in our acting together in shared ways in such contexts.

How exactly do such shared policies about weights support such valued
sociality? An initial answer appeals to the support such shared policies provide for forms of social responsiveness, coordination, and mesh in temporally
extended social thought and action. In this way such shared policies about
weights play instrumental roles in our shared agency.

It is important, however, that these policies may also play a distinctive, constitutive role. Many times it will be by virtue of our shared policies about weights
that there will be something that counts as where *we* stand on certain relevant
issues—where we stand on, say, the importance of legacies, or of accessibility to
institutions of higher education, or of environmental constraints, or the relative
significance of long-term and short-term social benefits of science. Our shared
policies about weights are, in such cases, not merely useful coordination devices; they are, as well, partly constitutive of what we can plausibly call the *standpoint of the group* on relevant matters. If, with Dancy, we want an analogy with
the legal order, such shared policies about weights can be more like important,
central shared legal standards than traffic regulations. And when our shared
thought and action is appropriately guided by where we stand on relevant matters, there is a significant kind of group self-governance.[28] Further, many times
we will publically converge on a judgment that such group self-governance is
itself a good thing.[29] In such cases, public criticism of divergence from such
shared policies about weights can appeal, *inter alia*, to the way in which such
divergence baffles the group's shared governance of relevant shared activities—
where we agree about the importance of this shared self-governance.[30]

These shared policies about weights involve policies of each that favor the
group's relevant reasoning. These policies of each interlock, are interdependent,

and favor relevant mutual responsiveness: there is not merely a concatenation of approvals of each, approvals that happen to coincide. And this supports the idea that these shared policies about weights do not just speak for each; they speak for the group.[31]

As anticipated, this can support a common and sensible reflexivity in such shared policies about weights. Our shared policy can sometimes sensibly be to give a certain weight to X in part because of the role of this very shared policy in the socially acknowledged good of our shared self-governance. And such reflexive shared policies about weights can guide our shared deliberation.

We have now arrived, as promised, at the idea that, at least in a theoretically central case, shared deliberation is embedded within a three-fold structure of shared intention. Shared deliberation takes place within a shared activity that is guided by a shared intention in favor of that activity. The shared deliberation is itself a shared intentional activity that is guided by a relevant shared intention. And in the substantive shared reasoning, shared policies about weights play central, intended roles. All three forms of shared intention involve structures of interlocking and interdependent intentions of the participants, structures of the sort described by the basic thesis.

This network of shared intentions constitutes a broad common ground. This network goes beyond (though it involves) common knowledge of thought and action, structures shared thought and action, and supports shared deliberation even while allowing for substantial divergence in evaluative judgment and reasons for which each participates. Guidance by this common ground can be a form of shared self-governance. And this common ground is primarily a structure of shared intentions, rather than of public sameness of judgment. Here, as elsewhere in our agency, our thought and action is substantially and rationally shaped by our will, both individual and shared.

5. Interdependence in policies about weights

Shared commitments to weights are (at least in a theoretically central case) shared policies about weights. One aspect of such sharing, according to the basic thesis, is interdependence in persistence between the relevant policies of each in favor of their giving such weights in shared deliberation. In many cases such persistence interdependence will be in some way grounded in a recognized need, in the pursuit of relevant social unity, to fix on a group policy concerning weights despite divergence in relevant prior value judgments of the individuals. Drawing on our discussion in Chapters 3 and 5, we can distinguish between three different (though potentially overlapping) forms of such interdependence: desirability-based, feasibility-based, and obligation-based.

Suppose the members of the admissions committee converge on a policy about the weight to be given to legacy considerations. Each intends that they give such weights in their shared deliberation. Suppose further that one aspect of this joint practice that each finds desirable, and so treats as part of his or her reason for favoring this practice, is that the practice involves this convergence in the relevant policies of each. And, let us also suppose, neither would find desirable a practice of giving these weights that involved by-passing the conflicting policies of one of the other members, even if such a practice were feasible. On natural assumptions this will be a desirability-based interdependence; and in this respect it would be like the interdependence of Romeo's and Juliet's intentions that they flee together.[32]

In contrast, sometimes the interdependence might be only feasibility-based. Perhaps you and I each have a policy that supports our giving weight, in the context of our joint construction project, to certain environmental concerns. We each recognize that if the other did not have this policy then, other things equal, it would not be feasible for us to deliberate together in relevant ways; that is why our policies are persistence interdependent. But neither of us sees the other's policy as contributing to the desirability of our giving such weights: each favors our giving these weights solely because of what he sees as the importance of these environmental issues, not because of a social value of interpersonal convergence in policy. Nevertheless, what each of us intends (namely, that *we* reason in this way) involves the contributions of both. And we each recognize that the policy of the other is, other things equal, a condition of the feasibility of such joint reasoning. That is why our policies are interdependent. So this is a feasibility-based but not desirability-based interdependence; and in this respect it is like the interdependence of Alex's and Ben's intentions that they go to NYC together.[33]

Finally, the persistence interdependence might be grounded in mutual moral obligations that are the issue of prior interactions. Perhaps earlier one of the participants indicates that she accepts a policy in favor of the group's giving certain specified weights, where this is grounded in part in her confidence that others will respond by converging on that very policy of weights. Or perhaps she indicates that she accepts this policy conditional on the nonconditional acceptance of that policy by others, and the others indicate their nonconditional acceptance of that policy. If all goes well, such interactions can result in a shared policy about weights. The resulting interdependencies among the policies of each in favor of such weights might be desirability-based, feasibility-based, or both. But such interactions can many times also induce relevant assurance-based or reliance-based obligations of each to each. And these obligations can support the cited persistence interdependence between the policies of each about weights. In such cases the persistence interdependence among the policies of each in favor of such weights would be, *inter alia*, obligation-based.

6. Partiality and depth of shared policies about weights

Shared commitments to weights are (at least in a basic case) shared policies about weights in relevant shared deliberation. These shared policies will normally be to some extent responsive to relevant judgments of value on the part of the various participants. Nevertheless, and as we have noted, these shared policies do not require convergence in supporting value judgments.

This is another aspect of the pervasiveness of partiality in our sociality. I have emphasized that shared intention in favor of shared action need not involve commonality of reasons for participating in the sharing: a shared intention can involve a convergence on the shared activity that is grounded in diverging background reasons. And we have seen that this point extends to shared commitments to weights. To return to our earlier example: Perhaps some on a college admissions committee participate in their shared policy of giving weight to legacy considerations because they think this is an effective fundraising tool; whereas others participate because they think their institution has made an implicit promise to its alumni to provide this benefit to their children. Members of the committee participate for different reasons: their sharing is in this way partial. But their shared policy about weights nevertheless establishes a common and interlocking—albeit, partial—framework for their shared deliberation.

That said, the theory also leaves room for shared efforts to reach a deeper and more extensive convergence on the background rationale for such sharing. Such efforts may involve further agreements concerning what is to have weight within relevant shared deliberation. These efforts may themselves be shared intentional activities that are guided by a shared intention to achieve such further depth of convergence—in response, perhaps, to concerns about the determinateness of shared deliberation in hard cases.[34]

Indeed, as Seana Shiffrin has noted in conversation, if our shared policy about weights also involves a common, substantive background rationale (over and above general reasons for such sociality) we will likely be in a better position to respond to complexities about how to proceed in hard cases than we are when there is divergence in the reasons for which we each participate. If, for example, our shared policy of giving weight to legacy considerations is grounded in a shared policy of giving weight to creating loyalty among potential donors (rather than a supposed promissory obligation to alumni), we would probably be in a better position to resolve certain disputes in hard cases. In a case involving conflict between legacy considerations and other considerations that we value—economic diversity in the student population, for example—we might be able to settle disputes in part by appeal to a shared policy about the background reasons for the shared policy in favor of legacies. In contrast, if our common framework is a thin one that consists entirely of our shared policy of giving weight to legacies—where we each have different background reasons for our participation in this common framework (over and above general reasons for these forms of sociality)—we will not have available this potential contribution to conflict resolution.

Granted, in a particular case it may not be possible for us to go beyond such a thin common framework. Indeed, there may in certain cases be substantive reasons for us *not* to go beyond such a relatively shallow commonality, but rather to retain a kind of neutrality with respect to these differences. These may include certain cases of what Cass Sunstein calls "incompletely theorized agreements."[35] However, Shiffrin's point is that if this is the kind of shared framework in which we are participating, then there is a significant risk that we will have difficulties in applying the shared framework to hard cases. And that might be why we aim to reach further convergence in the substantive background for our shared policy about the weight of legacy considerations.

7. Shared policies of acceptance

According to our model, shared policies about weights involve interlocking and interdependent policies of each in favor of giving certain relative weights to certain considerations in relevant shared deliberation. The participants need not believe that these are the correct weights; they need only be committed to taking them as given in the relevant context of shared deliberation.

When there is such a shared policy about weights, the participants together have a policy of accepting these weights in relevant shared contexts. This involves a shared commitment to taking these weights as given in those contexts and so to drawing on them in relevant shared deliberation. The shared policy constitutes a *shared policy of acceptance* of those weights, with respect to relevant contexts of shared deliberation.[36] Such shared policies of acceptance of weights will sometimes be a reasonable response to a recognized need for determinateness of shared normative or evaluative background in the face of divergence in normative or evaluative judgment.[37]

And now the point to note is that this solution applies generally to cases of sociality in which we need determinateness of shared background despite divergence in judgment or belief. We have been focusing on the case in which the divergence is in value judgment or the like, and the social solution has been a shared policy about weights. But there can also be divergence in relevant beliefs about matters that are not explicitly evaluative-—about, for example, what is possible and what would be effective. Here, too, shared deliberation and shared agency frequently require a determinate shared background. We can sometimes respond to this need for determinateness of shared background by way of a shared commitment to take certain propositions as given in our shared deliberations, where this need not involve a convergence in our beliefs about these matters. And we can model such a shared commitment as a shared policy of acceptance.

I noted in Chapter 1, section 7, that shared intentions and plans will be held against a cognitive background that concerns, roughly, what is possible and what is effective. To simplify my discussion, I initially assumed that the participants have the same beliefs about these matters. And I appealed to this simplifying assumption in expressing, in a rough way, the norms on shared intention of social consistency and social coherence. We are now in a position to deepen this aspect of the theory.

The basic point is that sometimes in shared agency we can, in the face of differences of belief concerning relevant matters of possibility or effectiveness, arrive at a shared policy to treat a relevant proposition as given in the context of our shared deliberations. Perhaps we are engaged in a shared project of building a house together, but we disagree about the likely costs of certain elements of the project. We might agree to take certain estimates of the costs as given for our shared deliberation—estimates that perhaps do not match anyone's actual beliefs.[38] We thereby come to have a shared policy in favor of taking these estimates as given in the context of our relevant shared deliberation. This shared policy is a shared policy of acceptance of these estimates, with respect to these deliberative contexts.

The target of this shared policy of acceptance is not an evaluative or normative proposition about weights, but a garden-variety factual proposition. Nevertheless, it seems plausible to understand this shared policy of acceptance in terms of ideas we used to understand shared policies about weights. We appeal to the idea that we each intend that we take p as given in relevant shared deliberation. We appeal to the idea that the policy-like intentions of each, concerning what we are to take as given in our shared deliberation, are appropriately interdependent and interlocking. And so on. In this way we extend the architecture of the basic thesis to the phenomenon of shared policies of acceptance.

Once we bring onboard such shared policies of acceptance we can also allow for shared policies that screen out certain things that are publically believed by each. For example, as a result of instructions from the judge (a kind of catalyst of convergence) a jury might have a shared policy that screens out from its shared deliberations certain evidence even if that evidence happens to be publically believed by each of its members.

Shared policies of acceptance play a framework-providing role in shared deliberation. We understand these framework-providing shared policies of acceptance by extending the architecture of the basic thesis. And by appealing to forms of shared policy—rather than of common judgment or belief—we make better sense both of the shared-ness of this framework and of the practical pressures on this shared framework.

This leads to a generalization of a point made in sections 3 and 4 about the difference between shared policies about weights and a concatenation of similar attitudes about weights in a context of common knowledge. A shared policy in favor of taking p as given in a certain deliberative context is not just a matter of common knowledge of the fact that each treats p in this way in relevant contexts. When there is such a shared policy, each interdependently intends that they treat p in this way, and each intends that this proceed by way of the cited intentions of each, mutual responsiveness, and so meshing subplans. The common treatment of p is something each intends, rather than simply takes note of; and these intentions are interdependent and interlock. As a result there will normally be an intention-supported stability of this pattern of treatment of p, an intention-supported stability that may not be ensured simply by common knowledge of what happens to be a common treatment of p. And these features of shared policies of acceptance help support the idea that they speak for the group and so have a characteristic role to play in that group's self-governance.[39]

So we have, at the individual level, intentions and plans concerning individual activities, and policies concerning weights; and we have, at the shared level, shared intentions concerning shared activities and shared policies concerning weights and, more generally, shared policies of acceptance. These various intention-like attitudes, both individual and shared, play fundamental roles in the cross-temporal and social organization of our thought and action.

They do this in part by responding to pressures for determinateness in thought and action in the face of underdetermination by relevant judgments of the individuals and, in the social case, also in the face of interpersonal divergence in such judgments.

Return now to the norms on shared intention of social consistency and social means-end coherence. When I first described these norms, I made the simplifying assumption of sameness of belief concerning what is possible and effective. But we have noted that sometimes there is divergence in these beliefs of the participants. So we need to know how to apply the norms of social consistency and coherence in these contexts. The initial answer is that if there is sufficiently deep divergence it will be unclear how to apply these social norms. A group engaged in shared deliberation concerning national economic policy, for example, might be stymied by fundamental differences in relevant empirical belief. But in such cases the participants can sometimes solve this problem for their sociality by arriving at a relevant shared policy of acceptance. If, in fact, there are relevant shared policies of acceptance, they will supplement—and, if there is divergence in belief, displace—the corresponding beliefs of the individuals, for purposes of assessing social consistency and social coherence.[40]

Our ability to arrive at such shared policies of acceptance enhances our ability to reason and to act together in contexts of divergence in relevant individual belief and judgment. Such shared policies of acceptance provide part of the background with respect to which relevant forms of social consistency and coherence are assessed. And such shared policies of acceptance provide elements of the common framework within which shared deliberation can, if all goes well, successfully proceed.

8. Shared policies of social rationality

The emergence of modest sociality involves, in part, the emergence of an explanatory role of norms of social rationality of intention: norms of social consistency, social agglomeration, social coherence, and social stability. I have so far discussed two such (as I called them) explanatory modes of social rationality. There is, first, the fundamental case in which each participant guides her thought and action in light of accepted, basic norms of individual intention rationality and in which, given the special social contents and interrelations of the intentions involved in modest sociality, there is thereby rational pressure for conformity to the cited social norms. And there is, second, the case in which the individual participants each proceed individually to accept these norms of social rationality themselves.

We are now in a position to describe yet a third explanatory mode of social rationality: the participants might not just individually accept these norms of social rationality; they might share a policy in favor of these social rationality norms. And these will be shared policies of the sort we have been exploring. Each might interdependently have a policy that they conform to the social norm; each might have a policy in favor of conformity to the social norm by way of the policy of each that they conform, and by way of associated mutual responsiveness; and so on. And since these shared policies are themselves— as shared plan states—subject to these very norms, we will want to see them as implicitly reflexive: these shared policies favor norm conformity by relevant plan states, including these very policies.

Such shared policies of social rationality will be limited in their scope. They are not focused on the "overall rational unity" of the group,[41] where that includes unity of belief and judgment. Their focus is only on relevant forms of social rationality of intention: this is another reflection of the priority of intention in modest sociality. Nor is this step to shared policies of social rationality itself a step to shared norms of mutual obligation. Nevertheless, these shared policies of social rationality can serve as a basis for associated advice and criticism concerning conformity to these norms of social rationality; and this would lend further support to conformity to these social rationality norms. And guidance by such shared policies of social rationality would be an element in shared self-governance. So, given the recognized value of such shared self-governance, such shared policies of social rationality can sometimes sensibly support conforming to these very norms in part because of the role of such norm-guidance in shared self-governance.

So such shared policies of social rationality will normally be reflexive in two ways. First, they will apply to shared plan states generally, and so to themselves. Second, they will support conformity to the relevant norms in part because of the socially recognized value of the shared self-governance that their guidance in part constitutes. And such doubly reflexive shared policies of social rationality would be a further rational mechanism in support of conformity to norms of social rationality of intention.

CONCLUSION

INTERCONNECTED PLANNING AGENTS

My central questions have been: How should we understand small-scale modest sociality and its relation to individual agency? On what resources—conceptual, metaphysical, and normative—should we draw? Is there a basic discontinuity in the step from individual agency to modest sociality?

I have tried to answer these and related questions by building on the planning theory of individual human agency rather than by appealing to some new, unanalyzable practical primitive. There is independent reason—grounded in the diachronic organization of our temporally extended agency—to see planning structures as basic to our individual agency. And once these planning structures are on board we can expect them to play central roles in our sociality. The planning theory of individual agency highlights distinctive roles and norms of intentions, understood as plan states. And the conjecture is that appeal to these planning structures enables us to provide adequate resources—conceptual, metaphysical, and normative—for an account of sufficient conditions for modest sociality. This is an aspect of the fecundity of planning structures. And it is the sense in which our capacity for planning agency, a capacity that is at the bottom of our capacity for distinctive forms of temporally extended agency, is also at the bottom of our capacity for distinctive forms of social agency. Our capacity for planning agency is a common core that lies behind aspects of both the temporal and the social structure of our lives.

I have tried to develop these ideas by way of a version of the Gricean methodology of creature construction. I have aimed at a construction that is conservative in the sense that it does not require basic metaphysical, conceptual, or normative elements that go beyond those available within the planning theory of individual agency. And I have seen such a conservative construction as supporting a deep continuity between individual planning agency and modest sociality.

In pursuit of this conservative construction of shared intention and modest sociality, I have argued that the basic thesis provides relevant sufficient conditions. It does this by drawing on a web of ideas that is broadly continuous with the resources of the planning theory. These include ideas of intending the joint activity, interlocking intentions, interdependent intentions, intended and actual mutual responsiveness and mesh, effectiveness of intention, and common knowledge.[1] Returning in particular to the compressed version of the basic thesis, the claim is that the following provides sufficient conditions for our shared intention to J:

A. *Intention condition*: We each have intentions that we J; and we each intend that we J by way of each of our intentions that we J (so there is interlocking and reflexivity) and by way of relevant mutual responsiveness in sub-plan and action, and so by way of sub-plans that mesh.

B. *Belief condition*: We each believe that if the intentions of each in favor of our J-ing persist, we will J by way of those intentions and relevant mutual responsiveness in sub-plan and action; and we each believe that there is interdependence in persistence of those intentions of each in favor of our J-ing.

C. *Interdependence condition*: There is interdependence in persistence of the intentions of each in favor of our J-ing.

D. *Common knowledge condition*: It is common knowledge that A.-D.

And there is shared intentional activity, and so modest sociality, when:

E. *Mutual responsiveness condition*: our shared intention to J leads to our J-ing by way of public mutual responsiveness in sub-intention and action that tracks the end intended by each of the joint activity by way of the intentions of each in favor of that joint activity.

And **E** specifies what counts as relevant mutual responsiveness in **A** and **B**.

Suppose then that you and I are singing a duet together and that this is a shared intentional (indeed, a shared cooperative) activity. On the model, each intends that we sing the duet, and each intends that this proceed by way of the intentions of each in favor of our duet singing and by way of relevant mutual responsiveness and meshing. Each has relevant beliefs about the effectiveness and interdependence of our intentions in favor of our duet singing. These intentions are, indeed, appropriately interdependent. The duet singing emerges, as intended, from relevant mutual responsiveness and meshing between us that tracks the end intended by each of the duet singing by way of the intentions of each in favor of that. And all this is out in the open.

Such modest sociality involves, then, the rational functioning of planning structures of individual agents, structures that involve appropriately interrelated intentions and beliefs with appropriate contents, all in a context of common knowledge. Modest sociality emerges, both functionally and rationally, from these structures of interconnected planning agency.

The appeal here is to intentions; and intentions are distinctive. These intentions need to have appropriate contents and to be interpersonally interconnected. Some of these interconnections are built into the contents themselves: the intentions interlock and favor mutual responsiveness and so meshing sub-plans. Beliefs about certain interconnections—namely, relevant persistence interdependence—support the ability of these intentions each to satisfy a settle condition. And at least in robust cases of modest sociality these beliefs will be true.

These various interpersonal intention interconnections involve knowledge of each of the minds of the others, but go beyond a solely cognitive interrelation, as in common knowledge. These interconnections do not essentially involve mutual obligations between the participants, each to the other, or even beliefs of the participants about such mutual obligations. However, mutual moral obligations will frequently emerge. Such mutual moral obligations will sometimes ground relevant persistence interdependence. And such mutual obligations can help stabilize the shared intention.

We understand such structures of interconnected planning agency in part by appeal to central norms of individual intention rationality: norms of consistency, agglomeration, coherence, and stability. Proper functioning of such structures involves guidance by each agent's at-least-implicit acceptance of these norms of individual rationality. Corresponding social norms of social consistency, social agglomeration, social coherence, and social stability are anchored in the interaction of these norms of individual rationality with the distinctive intention-contents cited by the basic thesis. And the participants may each also go on to internalize these social norms, and (even further) to arrive at a shared policy in their favor.

Within such modest sociality shared intention plays a characteristic explanatory role: relevant intentions of each work their way through, as intended, to shared action by way of relevant mutual responsiveness. In such modest sociality it is because there is such a shared intention that there is relevant, coordinated joint activity, related coordinated planning, and (in many cases) related bargaining. In contrast, the presence of associated mutual obligations need not ensure that such an explanatory structure is in place. After all, people sometimes have no intention to do what they recognize they have an obligation to do, and people sometimes have obligations they do not recognize.

There may also be associated shared deliberation in modest sociality, shared deliberation that draws on a relevant common ground. Central to such a common ground will be relevant shared policies about weights. Such shared policies about weights are a special case of shared policies of acceptance, and these shared policies are understood in a way that extends the architecture of the basic thesis. Further, the guidance by such shared policies about weights can make it true that there is something that counts as the group's relevant standpoint.[2] And the participants might well converge in their judgment that there are good reasons for constituting and being guided by such a group standpoint, given the role of such a standpoint in a group's self-governance.

Let's try to locate this model of modest sociality within the space of some of the main theoretical options that have helped frame our discussion:

(a) The basic thesis agrees with both Gilbert and Searle that the kind of sociality we are after should be distinguished from mere strategic interaction and equilibrium in a context of common knowledge. The basic thesis claims— contrary to objections from Petersson, and from Gold and Sugden—that it does indeed provide sufficient conditions for modest sociality, in contrast with mere strategic interaction.

(b) The basic thesis emphasizes the central role of relevant intentions of each of the individual participants. Here it agrees with a similar emphasis in Searle's view.[3] And here it rejects Gilbert's "disjunction condition" according to which there can be shared intention in the absence of "correlative personal intentions of the individual parties" (though it grants that there can be relevant mutual obligations in the absence of "correlative personal intentions").

(c) The intentions to which the basic thesis refers are plan states explained by the planning theory of our individual agency, plan states with distinctive contents and interrelations. This contrasts with Searle's appeal to a new and nonreducible attitude of we-intention.[4] Indeed, we can see the intention condition of the compressed basic thesis as pointing to reductive sufficient conditions for something analogous to a Searle-type we-intention.

(d) The basic thesis agrees with Gilbert that modest sociality essentially involves interpersonal interconnections that go beyond common knowledge. And this emphasis on relevant interpersonal interconnections goes beyond Searle's appeal to special attitudes of each of the individuals. In contrast with Gilbert, however, the basic thesis tries to understand these interconnections primarily in terms of resources made available by the planning theory of individual agency, and without an essential appeal to relations of mutual obligation, or even to beliefs about such obligations.[5] Of special importance here are appeals, within the basic thesis, to the interlocking of intentions, intended and actual mutual responsiveness and mesh, persistence interdependence of intentions in favor of the joint activity, and beliefs about that persistence interdependence.

(e) The basic thesis can nevertheless recognize the significance to many cases of modest sociality of familiar forms of mutual obligation. In particular, the persistence interdependence involved in shared intention can sometimes be grounded in relevant forms of mutual moral obligation induced by characteristic interactions among the participants: persistence interdependence is contingently morally realizable. This is true even though such mutual obligations are neither necessary nor sufficient for relevant explanatory structures involved in shared intention.

(f) For Gilbert, the fundamental phenomenon is joint commitment. And her view is that the joint-ness of a joint commitment is itself a primitive, one that does not admit of further reductive analysis. It is not analyzed in terms of the idea of a plural subject since, on the privileged reading of Gilbert's view, the idea of a plural subject is, at bottom, the idea of a joint commitment. And it is not analyzed in terms of relevant mutual obligations, since joint commitments are seen as grounding such obligations. In contrast, the basic thesis aims at providing reductive sufficient conditions for the joint-ness or shared-ness at work in modest sociality, sufficient conditions that are continuous with the resources provided by the planning theory of individual agency. These purported sufficient conditions involve a complex web of conditions, including intentions concerning the joint activity, interlocking intentions, interdependence of intentions, and intended and actual mutual responsiveness and mesh. This reductive but multifaceted model of joint-ness and shared agency contrasts with Gilbert's nonreductive, single-faceted model.

(g) In an analogous way, the reductive, multifaceted model of joint-ness and shared agency provided by the basic thesis contrasts with Searle's single-faceted, nonreductive appeal to we-intention.

(h) The basic thesis grounds the norms of social rationality that are central to modest sociality in norms of individual intention rationality.[6]

(i) At the bottom of (a)-(h) is the way in which the basic thesis draws on the planning theory of individual agency, a theory for which there is independent support in the diachronic organization of our agency. The basic thesis supports the idea that there is a deep continuity—conceptual, metaphysical, and normative—between individual planning agency and modest sociality. There is this continuity even though it is possible for there to be planning agents who do not have the capacity to participate in modest sociality, and even though aspects of shared intention can sometimes be supported by or realized by recognized mutual moral obligations. Both Gilbert and Searle, in different ways, see the step from individual to shared agency as bringing with it a fundamentally new conceptual and metaphysical (and, in Gilbert's case, normative) element, one that goes beyond common knowledge. In contrast, the basic thesis claims to provide sufficient conditions for modest sociality by appeal to a multiplicity of plan-theoretic factors and without appeal to a new practical primitive. If this claim of the basic thesis is correct then there is a defeasible Ockham's Razor presumption against supposing that there is such a fundamentally new practical phenomenon.

Having located the basic thesis within this solution space, let me close by briefly highlighting some further themes.

The basic thesis emphasizes the central role of intention-like attitudes in modest sociality: the participants have shared intentions, plans, and policies, but many times they can do without convergence in relevant judgments or beliefs, including judgments or beliefs about the right and the good. This is the primacy of intention for modest sociality.

These shared intention-like attitudes will frequently be partial in the sense that they so far leave matters open that will need to be resolved as time goes by. And they will frequently be partial in the further sense that there is only partial agreement among the participants in their reasons for participating in the sharing.[7] This is the pervasiveness of partiality in our sociality.

When there is such modest sociality there will be at least a weak kind of group agent of the shared action. It will be true, say, that we paint the house, where 'we' refers to an internally organized structure of the participants, a structure that is a causal source of the painting and to which relevant downstream effects can be causally attributed. This structure involves a relevant shared intention to paint. But given a moderate holism of subject-hood, it does not follow, and it is not generally true, that there is a group subject of this shared intention.

Our shared intention to paint the house will many times frame our bargaining in the pursuit of mesh in sub-plans. It can also help frame shared deliberation. When we engage in such shared deliberation our thinking to-gether involves various shared commitments to treating certain consider-ations as mattering within the shared deliberative context. In a central case these will be commitments to treat those considerations as having weight within that shared context. We can model this shared commitment to weights as a shared policy to give such weights in such shared deliberation. And we can apply the basic thesis to such shared policies. Such shared policies about weights need not be accompanied by a corresponding convergence in evalua-tive or normative judgment (though of course they may). And such shared policies about weights can help constitute the group's standpoint on relevant matters.

There can also be shared policies of acceptance concerning what is pos-sible and what would be effective. Shared policies about weights are a special case of shared policies of acceptance. And there can also be shared policies in favor of social norms of intention rationality, shared policies that add further support to conformity to those norms.

All this supports the idea that the move from individual planning agency to modest sociality, while both demanding and of great importance, does not require fundamentally new practical resources—conceptual, metaphysical, or normative. The deep structure of at least a central case of modest sociality is constituted by elements that are continuous with those at work in the plan-ning theory of individual planning agents who know about each other's minds.

NOTES

CHAPTER 1

1. See Michael Tomasello et al., "Understanding and Sharing Intentions: The Origins of Cultural Cognition," *Behavioral and Brain Sciences* 28, no. 5 (2005): 675–91; Henrike Moll and Michael Tomasello, "Cooperation and Human Cognition: The Vygotskian Intelligence Hypothesis," *Philosophical Transactions of the Royal Society of London B* 362, no. 1480 (April 29, 2007): 639–48; Michael Tomasello and Malinda Carpenter, "Shared Intentionality," *Developmental Science* 10, no. 1 (January 2007): 121–25.

2. See my *Intention, Plans, and Practical Reason* (Cambridge, MA: Harvard University Press, 1987, reissued by CSLI Press, 1999), and my *Faces of Intention* (New York: Cambridge University Press, 1999). My initial thinking about planning agency benefitted greatly from Gilbert Harman's groundbreaking essay, "Practical Reasoning," first published in 1976 and reprinted in his *Reasoning, Meaning, and Mind* (Oxford: Oxford University Press, 1999), 46–74.

3. I develop this overall theme of the fecundity of planning agency in my "Agency, Time, and Sociality," *Proceedings and Addresses of the American Philosophical Association* 84, no. 2 (2010): 7–26; and in my "The Fecundity of Planning Agency," in *Oxford Studies in Agency and Responsibility*, Volume 1, ed. David Shoemaker. (Oxford: Oxford University Press, 2013), 47–69.

4. Indeed, a central conjecture of Tomasello's is that the great apes are planning agents who know about the minds of other apes but do not have a capacity for shared intentional activity. See Michael Tomasello, *Why We Cooperate* (Cambridge, MA: MIT Press, 2009).

5. This is an important theme from Harry Frankfurt. See e.g., Harry Frankfurt, "Identification and Wholeheartedness," as reprinted in his *The Importance of What We Care About* (Cambridge: Cambridge University Press, 1988).

6. Jennifer Rosner, ed., *The Messy Self* (Boulder, CO: Paradigm Publishers, 2007).

7. A standard offensive basketball play.

8. A recent treatment broadly in the spirit of this idea is Sara Rachel Chant and Zachary Ernst, "Group Intentions as Equilibria," *Philosophical Studies* 133, no. 1 (November 8, 2006): 95–109. For an overview of game theory see Don Ross,

"Game Theory," *The Stanford Encyclopedia of Philosophy*, ed. Edward N. Zalta, 2011 edition, http://plato.stanford.edu/entries/game-theory/

9. Classic statements are in David Lewis, *Convention* (Cambridge, MA: Harvard University Press, 1969), 52–60; and Stephen Schiffer, *Meaning* (Oxford: Oxford University Press, 1972). See also Jon Barwise, "Three Views of Common Knowledge," in *Proceedings of the Second Conference on Theoretical Aspects of Reasoning About Knowledge*, ed. Moshe Y. Vardi (Los Altos, CA: Morgan Kaufman, 1988), 365–79; and Gilbert Harman, "Review of Bennett, *Linguistic Behavior*," *Language* 53 (1977): 417–24, and "Self-reflexive Thoughts," *Philosophical Issues* 16 (2006): 334–45, esp. p. 342. For an overview see Peter Vanderschraaf and Giacomo Sillari, "Common Knowledge," *The Stanford Encyclopedia of Philosophy*, ed. Edward N. Zalta, 2009 edition, http://plato.stanford.edu/entries/common-knowledge/. For a helpful discussion of Lewis's theory see Robin P. Cubitt and Robert Sugden, "Common Knowledge, Salience and Convention: A Reconstruction of David Lewis' Game Theory," *Economics and Philosophy* 19, no. 2 (October 2003): 175–210. (Thanks to Olivier Roy for this reference.) Cubitt and Sugden highlight the role in Lewis's theory of the idea of (as they call it) a "reflexive common indicator" as an answer to the question, from Brian Skyrms, "where does all the common knowledge come from?" (see pp. 182, 188). For appeal to a related idea of a "mutual cognitive environment," see Daniel Sperber and Diedre Wilson, *Relevance*, 2nd ed. (Cambridge, MA: Harvard University Press, 1995), 38–46.

10. As Joshua Cohen once put it (in conversation), such common knowledge is, in this respect, more like a competence than a performance.

11. See Margaret Gilbert, "Walking Together: A Paradigmatic Social Phenomenon," *Midwest Studies In Philosophy* 15, no. 1 (1990): 1–14.

12. This example was suggested by comments by Paul Weirich at the 2008 University of Missouri workshop on shared agency.

13. See e.g., Margaret Gilbert, "Shared Intention and Personal Intentions," *Philosophical Studies* 144, no. 1 (2009): 167–87, and Margaret Gilbert, *A Theory of Political Obligation* (Oxford: Oxford University Press, 2006), section 7.4.

14. For this last distinction see H.L.A. Hart, *The Concept of Law*, 2nd ed. (Oxford: Oxford University Press, 1994).

15. For an effort to do this in understanding law, given substantial revisions in the underlying theory of shared agency, see Scott Shapiro, *Legality* (Cambridge, MA: Harvard University Press, 2011), and Scott Shapiro, "Massively Shared Agency," in *Rational and Social Agency: Essays on the Philosophy of Michael Bratman*, ed. Gideon Yaffe and Manuel Vargas (New York: Oxford University Press, forthcoming). For some caveats see Matthew Noah Smith, "The Law as a Social Practice: Are Shared Activities at the Foundations of Law?," *Legal Theory* 12, no. 3 (2006). In her *Liberal Loyalty: Freedom, Obligation, and the State* (Princeton: Princeton University Press, 2009), chap. 7, Anna Stilz seeks an extension to the theory of democracy. For a systematic effort to extend an account of small-scale shared

agency to larger institutions see Seamus Miller, *Social Action: A Teleological Account* (Cambridge: Cambridge University Press, 2001).

16. Complex individual planning agency will, I take it, involve something like language; but perhaps simpler forms of planning agency need not essentially involve language, though language capacities, if present, would be supportive. And similarly concerning modest sociality. There are large questions here, and there is much debate about the relation between various forms of thinking and language. My hope is to develop an approach to shared agency that would be available to a wide range of views about this matter. For a helpful overview of current work on the role of natural language in human thinking see Peter Carruthers, "Language in Cognition," in *The Oxford Handbook of Cognitive Science*, ed. Eric Margolis, Richard Samuels, and Stephen P. Stich (Oxford: Oxford University Press, 2011).

17. For a version of this image see Saul Kripke, *Naming and Necessity* (Cambridge, MA: Harvard University Press, 1972), 153. While this thought experiment helps to point to the kind of continuities with which I am concerned, I make no claims about the actual etiology of our sociality. Further, and as noted, this conjecture leaves room for actual creatures who are planning agents with knowledge of the minds of others but who do not have the further capacities involved in modest sociality. The continuity thesis is not that no further capacities are needed for the step from planning agency to modest sociality, but rather that these further capacities need not involve fundamentally new elements.

18. Searle insists that "we-intentions are a primitive phenomenon." See John R. Searle, "Collective Intentions and Actions," in *Intentions in Communication*, ed. Philip R. Cohen, Martha E. Pollack, and Jerry Morgan (Cambridge, MA: MIT Press, 1990), 406. Searle later expresses a version of this as the view that "the forms of collective intentionality cannot be eliminated or reduced to something else." See John R. Searle, *The Construction of Social Reality* (New York: Free Press, 1995), 37.

19. Gilbert, "Shared Intention and Personal Intentions."

20. Searle, *The Construction of Social Reality*; Gilbert, *A Theory of Political Obligation*.

21. Given my cited assumption about common knowledge.

22. Ludwig Wittgenstein, *Philosophical Investigations*, ed. P.M.S Hacker and Joachim Schulte, 4th ed. (Oxford: Wiley-Blackwell, 2009), par. 621; though Wittgenstein himself was wary of this question.

23. Though, as I argue elsewhere, it is not true quite generally that when I *A* intentionally my action is explained by my intention specifically *to A*. See my *Intention, Plans, and Practical Reason*, chap. 8. I think there will be analogous complexities in the shared case, but given the concern with sufficient conditions for shared intentional activity (see below, section 9) we can put these complexities aside here.

24. The example of a swarm of bees comes from Bjorn Petersson, "Collectivity and Circularity," *The Journal of Philosophy* 104, no. 3 (2007): 138–56. I return to this essay below in chapters 4 and 6.

25. Shapiro, "Massively Shared Agency."

26. A classic statement of this desire-belief model is in Donald Davidson, "Actions, Reasons, and Causes," in *Essays on Actions and Events*, 2nd ed. (Oxford: Oxford University Press, 2001). A more recent defender is Michael Smith, *The Moral Problem* (Oxford: Blackwell, 1994), chap. 4. In a later paper, "Intending," (in his *Essays on Actions and Events*) Davidson tried to move away from a simple desire-belief theory. In my "Davidson's Theory of Intention," (reprinted in my *Faces of Intention*) I argue that his efforts did not fully come to terms with the role of intention in planning.

27. Or, in the case of fairly simple agents, conative and cognitive analogues of desire and belief.

28. Shapiro's approach to the law is in this spirit. As he says "we are able to create law because we are able to create and share plans" (Shapiro, *Legality*, 181). And Allan Gibbard sees planning structures as at the heart of normative thinking quite generally. See his Allan Gibbard, *Thinking How to Live* (Cambridge, MA: Harvard University Press, 2003). In this respect the views of each are in the spirit of the thesis of the fecundity of planning agency.

29. A main target of my *Intention, Plans, and Practical Reason* was our temporally extended agency. A main target of my *Structures of Agency* was our individual self-governance. And below in Chapter 7 I turn to shared self-governance.

30. So the conjecture of the fecundity of planning agency includes the idea that our planning capacities support aspects of both the temporally extended and the social structures of our lives.

31. Hilary Putnam, "The Meaning of 'Meaning'," in *Mind, Language, and Reality*, vol. 2 (Cambridge: Cambridge University Press, 1975).

32. Tyler Burge, "Individualism and the Mental," *Midwest Studies in Philosophy* 4, no. 1 (September 1979): 73–121.

33. But these matters get more complex upon further analysis. See Chapter 6.

34. Versions of this worry, addressed to my initial essays on this subject, were voiced in Annette C. Baier, "Doing Things with Others: The Mental Commons," in *Commonality and Particularity in Ethics*, ed. Lilli Alanen, Sara Heinämaa, and Thomas Wallgren (London: MacMillan, 1997); Frederick Stoutland, "Why Are Philosophers of Action so Anti-Social?," in *Commonality and Particularity in Ethics*, ed. Lilli Alanen, Sara Heinämaa, and Thomas Wallgren (London: MacMillan, 1997); and J. David Velleman, "How To Share An Intention," in *The Possibility of Practical Reason* (Oxford: Oxford University Press, 2000). I respond to these challenges in my "I Intend that We *J*"—a response to which I return in Chapter 3. (Velleman graciously acknowledges the cogency of my response in his "How to Share an Intention," note 11.) See also Neil Roughley's review of my *Faces of Intention* in *International Journal of Philosophical Studies* 9 (2001): 265–70, 268–69.

    Stoutland has returned to this issue on at least two occasions. In his review of my *Faces of Intention*, in *Philosophy and Phenomenological Research* 65, no.

1 (2002): 238–40, he adds a further argument for the own-action condition. I assess that argument in Chapter 3. In his "The Ontology of Social Agency," *Analyse & Kritik* 30 (2008): 533–51, he reiterates his conviction that the own-action condition is inviolable.

35. Searle, "Collective Intentions and Actions."

36. As noted earlier, Searle asserts that "we-intentions are a primitive phenomenon." (406) And he says that "we-intentions are a primitive form of intentionality." (407) He then goes on to say that we-intentions are "not reducible to I-intentions plus mutual beliefs." (p. 407) This might suggest that he is only rejecting a specific reduction of "we-intentions," one he attributes to an early essay of Tuomela and Miller. But when Searle sketches his own positive theory his formal apparatus explicitly distinguishes, among intentions in action, those involved in individual intentional activity, and "collective" intentions in action; and this seems to embed a flat-out claim of non-reducibility (p. 412). For a study of these views of Searle see Kirk Ludwig, "Foundations of Social Reality in Collective Intentional Behavior," in *Intentional Acts and Institutional Facts*, ed. Savas L. Tsohatzidis (Dordrecht: Springer, 2007).

37. This is my reconstruction of Searle's appeal to isomorphism in his informal response to my presentation at the Konstanz Conference, June 2011.

38. For this general picture, see my *Intention, Plans, and Practical Reason*. My formulation of the agglomeration principle here has benefited from Gideon Yaffe, "Trying, Intending and Attempted Crimes," *Philosophical Topics* 32 (2004): 505–32, 510–22. The temporal qualification in the norm of means-end coherence is important, since it is normally rationally permissible to leave means-end gaps in one's future-directed plans if one supposes that there will be time later to fill in those plans. This contrasts with the consistency norm: a present inconsistency in plans for the future will violate that norm even if there remains time to sort this out before the need to act. I discuss the idea of a norm of diachronic stability in my "Time, Rationality, and Self-Governance," *Philosophical Issues* 22 (2012): 73–88. I discuss the nature and ground of these norms on intention further in my "Intention, Belief, Practical, Theoretical," in *Spheres of Reason*, ed. Simon Robertson (New York: Oxford University Press, 2009), "Intention, Belief, and Instrumental Rationality," in *Reasons for Action*, ed. David Sobel and Steven Wall (Cambridge: Cambridge University Press, 2009), and in "Intention, Practical Rationality, and Self-Governance," *Ethics* 119, no. 3 (2009): 411–43. In these essays I argue, in particular, that these norms are best seen as distinctively practical norms, rather than as, at bottom, theoretical norms on the beliefs that are purportedly involved in intending.

39. In talking about the individual agent's acceptance of these norms I lean on Allan Gibbard's discussion of this idea in his *Wise Choices, Apt Feelings* (Cambridge, MA: Harvard University Press, 1990). See also Peter Railton, "Normative Guidance," in *Oxford Studies in Metaethics*, ed. Russ Shafer-Landau, vol. 1, 2006. And

see H.L.A. Hart's ground-breaking discussion of the "internal aspect of rules" in his *The Concept of Law*, esp. pp. 55–57.

40. Talk of "normative discussion" comes from Gibbard, *Wise Choices, Apt Feelings*, who emphasizes the social coordinating roles of norm acceptance. My claim in the text is that for the case of acceptance of norms of individual intention rationality, we should not be led by reflection on the social roles of norm acceptances to the view that simply in appealing to the acceptances of these norms of individual intention rationality we are already drawing on the very idea of shared intentional action.

41. This distinction between explanatory role and normative force is in the spirit of Timothy Schroeder's distinction between a "categorization scheme" of a norm and a "force-maker" of that norm. See Timothy Schroeder, "Donald Davidson's Theory of Mind Is Non-Normative," *Philosophers' Imprint* 3, no. 1 (2003). And see John Broome, "Is Rationality Normative?," *Disputatio* 2, no. 23 (2007).

42. For a version of this worry see Niko Kolodny, "Reply to Bridges," *Mind* 118, no. 470 (2009): 369–76.

43. See my "Intention, Practical Rationality, and Self-Governance."

44. I discuss these matters further in my "Rational and Social Agency: Reflections and Replies," in *Rational and Social Agency: Essays on The Philosophy of Michael Bratman*, ed. Manuel Vargas and Gideon Yaffe.

45. See e.g., Daniel Kahneman, Paul Slovic, and Amos Tversky, eds., *Judgments Under Uncertainty: Heuristics and Biases* (Cambridge: Cambridge University Press, 1982). For a discussion of related issues see Jennifer M. Morton, "Toward an Ecological Theory of the Norms of Practical Deliberation," *European Journal of Philosophy* 19, no. 4 (2011): 561–94.

46. Which is not to say that we have it in our power simply to abandon our planning agency.

47. In claiming that intentions are not ordinary beliefs I put aside theories that maintain that intentions are a special kind of belief or, perhaps, a special belief-like attitude. For example, Kieran Setiya holds that an intention to do something later is a "desire-like belief that one is hereby *going to*" do that. (Kieran Setiya, *Reasons Without Rationalism* (Princeton: Princeton University Press, 2007), 49.) And David Velleman holds that intention is a special belief, or belief-like attitude. (The identification with belief is in his J. David Velleman, *Practical Reflection* (Stanford, CA: CSLI Press, 2007) (originally published in 1989). However, as Velleman indicates in his "Introduction" to the 2007 re-issue of *Practical Reflection* at p. xix, what is most important to his view is only identification with a belief-like attitude). In his "What Good Is a Will," in *Action in Context*, ed. Anton Leist and Holger Baumann (Berlin: de Gruyter, 2007), at p. 204, Velleman expresses this as the view that an intention is "a cognitive commitment to the truth of its propositional object." I have discussed such theories elsewhere. (See, for example, my "Intention, Belief, Practical, Theoretical.") For now it suffices to make the simpler point about the contrast between intention and ordinary belief.

48. Jean-Paul Sartre, "Existentialism Is a Humanism," in *Existentialism from Dostoevsky to Sartre*, ed. Walter Kaufmann, rev. and expanded (New York: Meridian/Penguin, 1975), 345–69, at 354–56.

49. Frank Stockton, "The Lady or the Tiger?" in *The American Short Story*, ed. Thomas K. Parkes (New York: Galahad Books, 1994), 202–7.

50. Herbert Simon, *Reason in Human Affairs* (Stanford, CA: Stanford University Press, 1983).

51. I discuss such personal policies and their characteristic defeasibility in my *Intention, Plans, and Practical Reason*, 87–91, and in my "Intention and Personal Policies," *Philosophical Perspectives* 3 (1989): 443–69.

52. I first appealed to such policies in my "Reflection, Planning, and Temporally Extended Agency," reprinted in *Structures of Agency*, (New York: Oxford University Press, 2007) where I called them self-governing policies. (As I note there, there are important similarities between this idea and Robert Nozick's idea of weight-bestowing decisions. See Robert Nozick, *Philosophical Explanations* (Cambridge, MA: Harvard University Press, 1981), 294–316. I discuss these views of Nozick's in my "Nozick on Free Will," as reprinted (with added appendix) in my *Structures of Agency*, 106–36.) In this early discussion I focused on self-governing policies that are hierarchical in the sense that they concern the role in practical reasoning and deliberation of the agent's own first-order conative attitudes. This was in part because my concern in that essay was primarily with the Frankfurtian idea of identification with first-order conative attitudes. Later it became clear (in part by way of discussions with Agnieszka Jaworska and Samuel Scheffler) that policies about weights need not always be hierarchical in this way. So that is how I treated such policies in "Three Theories of Self-Governance," reprinted in *Structures of Agency* (New York: Oxford University Press, 2007), where I considered the general case of policies in favor of giving weight to a certain consideration. However, I also argue there (pp. 240–43) that there are practical pressures of self-management and coordination in response to which such policies about weights will tend to involve policies that are in part about the agent's own first-order conative attitudes.

    Such policies about weights are similar to what Keith Frankish calls "premising policies," though I want to leave open the possibility that these policies about weights may sometimes function in the background rather than by providing an explicit premise. See Keith Frankish, *Mind and Supermind* (Cambridge: Cambridge University Press, 2004), esp. chap. 4.

53. See my "Three Theories of Self-Governance" at 235–38 and 252, where I focus on humility of judgment in response to what Joshua Cohen has called "full awareness of the fact of reflective divergence." Note that my present concern is not with a case in which the young man already has a relevant judgment and is concerned with how he should adjust it in light of disagreement with others. My present concern is, rather, with a case in which the young man does not yet have a

relevant judgment and is reflecting on the significance of the fact of disagreement among others. Further, I am not claiming that such epistemic modesty is the uniquely rational response to such disagreements among others, only that it can sometimes be a sensible response. That said, there are large issues here concerning the epistemology of peer disagreement, issues I am not trying to sort out here. See for example, David Christensen, "Epistemology of Disagreement: The Good News," *The Philosophical Review* 116, no. 2 (2007): 187–217; and Richard Feldman and Ted Warfield, eds., *Disagreement* (Oxford: Oxford University Press, 2010). (In thinking about peer disagreements I have been much aided by discussions with Han van Wietmarschen.)

54. In Chapter 7 I develop a related idea of *shared* policies about weights.

55. Harman, "Practical Reasoning;" Gilbert Harman, *Change in View: Principles of Reasoning* (Cambridge, MA: MIT Press, 1986), chap. 8; Gilbert Harman, "Desired Desires," in *Value, Welfare, and Morality*, ed. Ray Frey and Chris Morris (Cambridge: Cambridge University Press, 1993); Alan Donagan, *Choice: The Essential Element in Human Action* (London: Routledge & Kegan Paul, 1987), 88; John R. Searle, *Intentionality* (Cambridge: Cambridge University Press, 1983); Velleman, *Practical Reflection*; Abraham Sesshu Roth, "The Self-Referentiality of Intentions," *Philosophical Studies* 97, no. 1 (2000): 11–51; and Setiya, *Reasons Without Rationalism*, pt. one. For an important critique see Alfred R. Mele, *Springs of Action: Understanding Intentional Behavior* (Oxford: Oxford University Press, 1992), chap. 11.

56. Here I am assuming a model of self-governance along the lines sketched in my "Three Theories of Self-Governance." The basic idea is that plan-like commitments to weights play a central role in the practical thinking of a planning agent, and help tie together that agent's thought and action synchronically and diachronically. In the absence of relevant conflict, these plan-like commitments to weights speak for the agent, and when they guide the agent governs.

57. Such reflexive policies involve a kind of supposed bootstrapping: one sees the policy itself as supporting a reason of self-governance for following through on that very policy. But this limited form of bootstrapping seems acceptable, in contrast with a very general view that every intention grounds a new reason for so acting. I criticize such a general view in *Intention, Plans, and Practical Reason* at 24–27.

58. I discuss limitations on such reflexive support in my "A Desire of One's Own," reprinted in *Structures of Agency* (New York: Oxford University Press, 2007), 154–56. For a different approach to related matters see Ruth Chang, "Commitment, Reasons, and the Will," in *Oxford Studies in Metaethics*, Volume 8, ed. Russ Shafer-Landau. Oxford: Oxford University Press (2013): 74-113. In Chapter 7 section 4, I discuss a parallel possibility of reflexivity of shared policies about weights.

59. I owe the term "snowball effect" to John Etchemendy. See *Intention, Plans, and Practical Reason*, 82.

60. See my "Agency, Time, and Sociality" and my "Time, Rationality, and Self-Governance."

61. The idea that goals need not be subject to the agglomerativity constraints characteristic of intentions is a lesson of the video-games case I discuss in *Intention, Plans, and Practical Reason* chap. 8.

62. John Locke, *An Essay Concerning Human Understanding*, ed. Peter H. Nidditch (Oxford University Press, 1975) bk. 2, chap. 27. And see H. P. Grice, "Personal Identity," *Mind* 50, no. 200 (1941): 330–50; Anthony Quinton, "The Soul," *The Journal of Philosophy* 59, no. 15 (1962): 393–409; John Perry, "Personal Identity, Memory, and the Problem of Circularity," in *Personal Identity*, ed. John Perry (Los Angeles: University of California Press, 1975); John Perry, "The Importance of Being Identical," in *The Identities of Person*, ed. Amelie Oksenberg Rorty (Los Angeles: University of California Press, 1976), 67–90; and Derek Parfit, *Reasons and Persons* (Oxford: Oxford University Press, 1984).

63. I briefly discuss the relation between these comments and Derek Parfit's Lockean theory of personal identity in my "Reflection, Planning, and Temporally Extended Agency," at 28–30.

64. This remark about conceptual openness owes to conversation with Keith Lehrer.

65. In *Intention, Plans, and Practical Reason*, chap. 10, I explore some of the complexities of putting together a story of the deliberation that leads to intention with my story of the downstream roles of intention.

66. H. P. Grice, "Method in Philosophical Psychology (From the Banal to the Bizarre)," *Proceedings and Addresses of the American Philosophical Association* 48 (1974–1975): 23–53.

67. See my "Valuing and the Will," reprinted in *Structures of Agency* (New York: Oxford University Press, 2007). Herbert Simon's work has been enormously influential in focusing our attention on the fundamental significance of such limits. See for example, his *Reason in Human Affairs*. And for an application of some of these ideas to issues in artificial intelligence, see Michael E. Bratman, David J. Israel, and Martha E. Pollack, "Plans and Resource-Bounded Practical Reasoning," *Computational Intelligence* 4, no. 3 (1988): 349–55.

68. Concerning the roles of intention-like attitudes in response to temptation see my "Toxin, Temptation, and the Stability of Intention," reprinted in *Faces of Intention* (New York: Cambridge University Press, 1999) and my "Temptation Revisited," reprinted in *Structures of Agency* (New York: Oxford University Press, 2007). And see Richard Holton, *Willing, Wanting, Waiting* (Oxford: Oxford University Press, 2009), chap. 4–7.

69. Indeed, as Mark Turner noted in conversation, the evolutionary story of our individual psychic economies may well need to appeal to ways in which they support sociality.

70. My earlier discussion of the roles characteristic of shared intention appealed to related bargaining but did not appeal, as I do here, to shared deliberation. (See

"Shared Intention," in my *Faces of Intention* at p. 112.) Ideas leading to this addition are in my "Shared Valuing and Frameworks for Practical Reasoning," an essay that is a basis for elements of Chapter 7. Andrea C. Westlund independently emphasizes a contrast between bargaining and what she calls "joint deliberation" in her Andrea C. Westlund, "Deciding Together," *Philosophers' Imprint* 9, no. 10 (July 2009), a discussion from which I have benefitted. However, in discussing my "Shared Valuing and Frameworks for Practical Reasoning," Westlund indicates that what I describe there "is a more general phenomenon than what [she has] in mind." (p. 6)

71. See my discussion of shared deliberation in Chapter 7.

72. Natalie Gold and Robert Sugden propose instead that "the key" to what I call shared intentions lies in "the modes of reasoning in which they are formed." They also propose a specific model of the kind of reasoning involved—as they call it, "team reasoning." But the issue now is the more general issue of their proposed priority of "the modes of reasoning in which [shared intentions] are formed." And my thought, in contrast, is that in order to articulate various forms of reasoning that can legitimately issue in a shared intention we need to know what work shared intentions do, and so we need to articulate their downstream roles and associated norms. See Natalie Gold and Robert Sugden, "Collective Intentions and Team Agency," *The Journal of Philosophy* 104, no. 3 (2007): 109–37, at 137.

73. In his "Practical Intersubjectivity," in *Socializing Metaphysics: The Nature of Social Reality*, ed. Fred Schmitt (Lanham, MD: Rowman & Littlefield, 2003), 65–91, Abraham Seeshu Roth emphasizes that our sociality involves characteristic norms of interpersonal rationality. It is such norms that Roth means to refer to in his talk of practical intersubjectivity. I am here agreeing with Roth that such norms are central to our understanding of such sociality. Roth, however, argues that we cannot account for these norms within a broadly individualistic model of shared intention. In contrast, one of my main claims, to be defended below, is that we can.

74. I appeal to the second case—individual acceptance of the social norms—in section 8 below. I discuss the third case—shared acceptance of these social norms—in Chapter 7 section 8.

75. In this paragraph I benefited from a query from Gideon Yaffe.

76. Pierre Demeulenaere, "Where Is the Social?," in *Philosophy of the Social Sciences: Philosophical Theory and Scientific Practice*, ed. Chris Mantzavinos (Cambridge: Cambridge University Press, 2008).

77. As in, for example, Creature 3 in my "Valuing and the Will."

78. Such an independent impact is a challenge to a reductionist account of intention as a complex of desires and beliefs. For a defense of such a reductivism, see Michael Ridge, "Humean Intentions," *American Philosophical Quarterly* 35, no. 2 (1998): 157–78; Neil Roughley, *Wanting and Intending: Elements of a Philosophy of*

Practical Mind (Dordrecht: Springer, 2008); and Neil Sinhababu, "The Desire-Belief Account of Intention Explains Everything," *Noûs* (forthcoming).

79. This is broadly in the spirit of Philip Pettit's view that "the natural person is the ultimate center of action . . . " Philip Pettit, "Groups with Minds of Their Own," in *Socializing Metaphysics: The Nature of Social Reality*, ed. Fred Schmitt (Lanham, MD: Rowman & Littlefield, 2003), 167–93, at 190.

80. I discuss differences between these two ways of putting this point in "I Intend that We J" in *Faces of Intention* at 144. I return to the possibility of multiple forms of shared intention below in section 9.

81. In this last sentence I am indebted to conversation with Michael Smith.

82. This is broadly in the spirit of what Scott Shapiro calls the "constructivist strategy" in legal philosophy. See his *Legality* at 21. A different kind of constructivism—one that neither is entailed by nor entails constructivism about shared intention—is a view about the nature of practical reason. See e.g., Christine Korsgaard, "Realism and Constructivism in Twentieth Century Moral Philosophy," *Journal of Philosophical Research* 32 (2003): 99–122.

83. A point emphasized (in conversation) by Christopher Kutz.

84. I return to such values in Chapter 7.

85. See my "I Intend that We J" at 144.

86. The argument in section 1, above, is that a straightforward desire-belief model of strategic interaction in a context of common knowledge—a model that would satisfy the (perhaps qualified) continuity constraint—does not provide such sufficient conditions. And that was one of the pressures that led me to turn to a plan-theoretic approach. Further, I think there are independent reasons for seeing the planning theory as superior to a desire-belief model of our individual agency, and so for looking for continuities with such individual planning agency. That said, I do not offer a completely general argument that it is impossible to construct an alternative, complex, desire-belief model that does provide such sufficient conditions for modest sociality. If some such model were on offer we would need to assess it along the lines indicated in the text.

87. This may be a good way to understood Christopher Kutz's appeal to participatory intentions in his Christopher Kutz, "Acting Together," *Philosophy and Phenomenological Research* 61, no. 1 (2000): 1–31. And it may also be a useful way to see Scott Shapiro's appeal to "massively shared agency" in his "Massively Shared Agency."

88. My focus here is on deception or coercion between the participants. If some third party got us to sing together by lying to us about the rewards, or threatening harm if we did not sing together, that would not normally prevent our joint singing from being a shared intentional and a shared cooperative activity.

89. Here I diverge from John Searle's thought that "the notion of . . . collective intentionality, implies the notion of *cooperation*." Searle, "Collective Intentions and Actions," 406.

CHAPTER 2

1. In my early thinking about this condition I was helped by remarks of Philip Cohen.
2. Christian List and Philip Pettit, *Group Agency: The Possibility, Design, and Status of Corporate Agents* (Oxford: Oxford University Press, 2011), 194.
3. This does not mean that the "we" in these contents cannot ever refer to a group in a yet stronger sense that does bring with it the very idea of shared intentionality. The idea is only that at this basic level of our construction we aim to avoid the use of such a stronger sense.
4. Thanks to Abraham Roth, who credits Michael Thompson, for encouraging clarification here.
5. Debra Satz emphasized this issue in conversation. Matthew Noah Smith argues that this need for conceptual convergence induces limits on the applicability of my account of shared intention to larger social phenomena. I am inclined to think that this worry can be to some extent defused by noting that in many cases there is agreement about what we are doing together at a somewhat abstract level even when there is not agreement at a more specific level. But this is a matter for another occasion. See Smith, "The Law as a Social Practice: Are Shared Activities at the Foundations of Law?"
6. See my discussion of the distinction between plan-states and goal-states in Chapter 1, section 5.
7. In his "Acting Together," Christopher Kutz provides a model of what he calls a participatory intention, where this is offered as an alternative to—because weaker than—my condition (i). Kutz says that to have a participatory intention "participants need not intend to achieve [the] collective end. It is sufficient that participants regard themselves as contributing to a collective end." (21) But if to regard oneself as contributing to an end is not to intend that end but only to believe that what one is doing will in fact contribute to that end, then one will not thereby be set to adjust in response to pressures of consistency and coherence with respect to that end. So one will not thereby be a participant in the kind of shared intention I am trying to understand.

   It may be that this difference is due to a difference of philosophical target. Kutz seeks an account of joint action in which certain institutional authorities are the source of much of the social organization ("Acting Together," section VI), whereas I have put aside cases involving such asymmetric institutional authority relations.
8. Raimo Tuomela and Kaarlo Miller, "We-Intentions," *Philosophical Studies* 53, no. 3 (1988): 367–89. Tuomela and Miller indicate (note 1) that their appeal to "we-intentions" to some extent draws on work of Wilfred Sellars. See e.g., Wilfred Sellars, "Imperatives, Intentions, and the Logic of 'Ought'," in Hector-Neri Castañeda and George Nakhnikian (eds.), *Morality and the Language of Conduct* (Wayne State University Press, 1963), 159–218; and Wilfred Sellars, *Science and Metaphysics*

(London: Routledge and Kegan Paul, 1968), chap. VII. Searle's discussion is in his "Collective Intentions and Actions."

9. Searle, "Collective Intentions and Actions," 405.

10. Searle begins his essay with an "intuition": "Collective intentional behavior is a primitive phenomenon that cannot be analyzed as just the summation of individual intentional behavior; and collective intentions expressed in the form 'we intend to do such-and-such' . . . are also primitive phenomena and cannot be analyzed in terms of individual intentions expressed in the form 'I intend to do such-and-such.'" (401) As I see it however, each half of this supposed intuition points to a false dichotomy: we can agree in each case with the rejection of the specific analysis considered, without being committed, in either case, to the purported primitiveness.

11. Raimo Tuomela, "We-Intentions Revisited," *Philosophical Studies* 125, no. 3 (2005): 327–69, note 8 and section VI.

12. Tuomela's alternative, more complex strategy (which I will not try to discuss here) is in section VI of this 2005 essay.

13. For a brief statement of this concern see Hans Bernard Schmid, *Plural Action: Essays in Philosophy and Social Science* (Dordrecht: Springer, 2009), 36–37.

14. Searle claims that "collective intentional behavior is a primitive phenomenon" and we should not seek "a reductive analysis of collective intentionality." ("Collective Intentions and Actions," at 401, 406.) And he claims that a fundamental reason for this is that "the notion of . . . collective intentionality, implies the notion of *cooperation*." (406) His view, I take it, is both that the phenomenon of collective intentional behavior is primitive, and that the "notion" or concept of collective intentionality is not reducible. In contrast, Searle does not take a similar nonreductive tack to individual intentional action. (See Searle, *Intentionality*, chap. 3.) My approach to collective intentionality is more in the spirit of Searle's approach to individual intentional action than is Searle's own approach to collective intentionality.

15. I note this parallel in "I Intend that We J," at 147. A worry about circularity in the individual case goes back at least as far as H.A. Prichard's 1945 essay "Acting, Willing, Desiring," in *Moral Writings* (Oxford: Oxford University Press, 2002), at 274–76.

16. Davidson saw his theory as a view of this kind. As he said, he saw his reductive account of acting with an intention as "not definitional but ontological." See his "Intending," 88.

17. "Shared Intention," at 114–15; "I Intend that We J" at 146–48. And see Christopher Kutz, *Complicity: Ethics and Law for a Collective Age* (New York: Cambridge University Press, 2000), 86–88. In "Collectivity and Circularity," Bjorn Petersson interprets my earlier remarks about this idea as appealing to a purely behavioral notion of our activity, a notion that does not even involve the idea that each individual acts intentionally. (See p. 150.) However, my thought is, rather, that we want an idea of our activity that is neutral with respect to *shared* intentionality but can (and normally will) involve the idea of individual intentionality.

18. This is in the spirit of what Christopher Kutz describes as "a genealogical account that shows generally how the capacity to engage in collective action emerges out of capacities explicable without reference to collective concepts." See Kutz, *Complicity*, 86.

19. Searle's view is the mirror image of this: reducibility at the level of individual intentionality, nonreducibility at the level of shared intentionality.

20. Cp. Christopher Kutz's appeal to seeing the other as "a partner in a joint enterprise." *Complicity*, 78.

21. Thomas Schelling, *The Strategy of Conflict* (Cambridge, MA: Harvard University Press, 1960), 87.

22. As indicated, this conjecture—that it is overly hasty to turn here immediately to obligation and entitlement—diverges from the approach developed by Margart Gilbert. I turn to her work below. My approach is also different in spirit from Stephen Darwall's emphasis on such reciprocal demands, claims, and entitlements. In his *The Second-Person Standpoint* (Cambridge, MA: Harvard University Press, 2006) Darwall sometimes writes as if he thinks that the move from (i) the "individual's psychic economy" to (ii) the "social," must be a move to such reciprocal demands and the like. (e.g., p. 195) Darwall associates with Hume an approach to (ii) that proceeds primarily in terms of (i). And he associates with Reid an approach to (ii) that proceeds primarily in terms of entitlements to claim and demand. Darwall does acknowledge that "it seems to be possible for individuals to share intentions . . . without" such reciprocal obligations and the like. (201 n. 34) But this acknowledgment has little resonance in Darwall's detailed approach to the social, an approach that is broadly in the spirit of Reid, as Darwall interprets him. In contrast, while I do not deny the importance of these interpersonal normative phenomena, I think that they should not enter immediately at this ground level in our theorizing about modest sociality, and that there is an important theoretical space here between Darwall's Hume and Darwall's Reid.

23. Recall that the idea of our going to NYC, as it appears in (i), is neutral with respect to shared intentionality.

24. The classic source of ideas broadly in this spirit is H. P. Grice, "Meaning," *The Philosophical Review* 66, no. 3 (1957): 377–88.

25. Miller, *Social Action: A Teleological Account*, 75.

26. Ibid.

27. In Chapter 3 I return to Miller's example to see if it poses a problem for the account of interdependence developed there.

28. Here I have benefited from discussion with Kit Fine.

29. Scott J. Shapiro, "Law, Plans, and Practical Reason," *Legal Theory* 8, no. 4 (2002): 387–441, 428.

30. In these last four sentences I have benefitted from discussion and correspondence with John Campbell, Victor Caston, and Webb Keane.

31. Such arbitration would be framed by our shared intention. This contrasts with a case in which an external agent manages our interactions in a way that does not go through our shared intention.

32. For a different approach to related matters see Roth, "Practical Intersubjectivity," 78–79.

33. A question from Abraham Roth.

34. Here I draw from a related but somewhat different example sketched by Facundo Alonso in correspondence.

35. See Searle, "Collective Intentions and Actions," 413–14.

36. This point in hand, return to the mafia case that motivated the introduction of (ii-initial). In this case, might the two gang members share an intention to go together to NYC in a way that involves competition about how this is to happen (that is, who throws whom into which car trunk)? Well, such a case is possible. But this would require both that each intends that they go to NYC in this competitive way, and (as we will see) that these intentions of each are out in the open. But many cases of mutual threatened coercion will not be framed by such a shared intention in favor of a competitive shared activity: the participants will be more like opposing soldiers than opposing boxers in a rule-regulated game of boxing. And in my discussion of the mafia case I have assumed that it is not framed by a shared intention in favor of such a competitive shared activity. (Thanks to Gideon Yaffe for raising this issue.)

37. Nicholas Bardsley, "On Collective Intentions: Collective Action in Economics and Philosophy," *Synthese* 157, no. 2 (2007): 145. Bardsley rejects the idea, in my next sentence, that what I intend really does include your action. See his p. 152.

38. This is a revision of my discussion of the case of the unhelpful singers in my "Shared Cooperative Activity" in *Faces of Intention* at 103–5. I was helped here by discussions with Facundo Alonso.

39. My argument here has been an appeal to the downstream functioning of a shared intention. Margaret Gilbert also appeals to a common knowledge condition for "joint commitment," and so for shared intention. But her idea is rather that common knowledge is needed in the normal etiology of a joint commitment. (See Margaret Gilbert, "What Is It for *Us* to Intend?," in *Sociality and Responsibility: New Essays in Plural Subject Theory* (Lanham: Rowman & Littlefield Publishers, Inc., 2000), 21. Facundo Alonso notes this contrast in his "Shared Intention, Reliance, and Interpersonal Obligations," *Ethics* 119, no. 3 (2009): 444–75, at note 45. In Chapter 3 I draw on the common knowledge condition to support relevant interdependence between the intentions of each in (i). This role of common knowledge is closer to the role highlighted by Gilbert.

40. I skip to (vii) to leave room for further conditions, to be discussed below.

41. See Harry Frankfurt, "The Faintest Passion," in *Necessity, Volition, and Love* (Cambridge: Cambridge University Press, 1999), 101, quoting from Shakespeare, *Henry IV Part I*.

42. Sydney Shoemaker, "Self-Reference and Self-Awareness," in *Identity, Cause, and Mind* (Cambridge: Cambridge University Press, 1984), 7.
43. I explore some implications of this point in my "Intention, Belief, Practical, Theoretical."

CHAPTER 3

1. I will briefly return later to this issue as it arises for (ii) and (iii).
2. See Wayne Davis, "A Causal Theory of Intending," *American Philosophical Quarterly* 21, no. 1 (1984): 43–54; and Bruce Vermazen, "Objects of Intention," *Philosophical Studies* 71, no. 3 (1993): 223–65 (esp. section IX where Vermazen argues for the importance of what he calls "non-act" intentions). The example to follow of the composer intending that the finale be grand is from Davis's essay.
3. In these initial examples the mechanism by way of which the intention is to lead to its realization involves a kind of asymmetric authority on the part of the intender. As we will see below in section 2, however, the coherence of the intentions that we *J* in condition (i) does not in general depend on such asymmetric authority.
4. For a subtle development of a view in this spirit, see Michael Thompson, *Life and Action: Elementary Structures of Practice and Practical Thought* (Cambridge, MA: Harvard University Press, 2008), Part Two.
5. Stoutland, "Critical Notice of *Faces of Intention*," 241.
6. Or anyway to quasi-moralize, since there may be relevant, nonmoral forms of accountability.
7. See Michael E. Bratman, "Two Faces of Intention," *The Philosophical Review* 93, no. 3 (1984): 375–405, and my *Intention, Plans, and Practical Reason*, 124–25. And see Joshua Knobe, "The Concept of Intentional Action: A Case Study in the Uses of Folk Psychology," *Philosophical Studies* 130, no. 2 (2006): 203–31.
8. Harry Frankfurt makes a closely related point in his "Freedom of the Will and the Concept of a Person," in *The Importance of What We Care About* (Cambridge: Cambridge University Press, 1988), at p. 25 note 10.
9. The expression "anticipate experiencing" comes from J. David Velleman, "Self to Self," first published in 1996, as reprinted in his *Self to Self* (Cambridge: Cambridge University Press, 2006), 194. In this discussion Velleman articulates something like the worry I am trying to address here. He says that "framing an intention . . . entails representing the intended action from the point of view of the agent who is to perform it." (Though I appeal not simply to "the point of view of the agent" but to the experience of acting from the perspective of the agent.) And he goes on to say that "the agent who is to perform any action that I intend must be me, since I can't intend the actions of others." (196) But he gives up on this in his later "How to Share an Intention," (first published in 1997 and reprinted in his *The Possibility of Practical Reason* (Oxford: Oxford University Press, 2000) at 205), and then in his review of my *Faces of Intention* in *The Philosophical Quarterly* 51, no. 202 (2001): 119–21.

10. In saying this I am accepting the premise that there is no such thing as the group's experience of acting, but rejecting the inference to skepticism about intending that we *J*. Hans Bernhard Schmid might well reject the cited skepticism concerning a group's experience. (See Hans Bernard Schmid, "Shared Feelings: Towards a Phenomenology of Collective Affective Intentionality," in *Plural Action: Essays in Philosophy and Social Science* (Dordrecht: Springer, 2009).) But then we would still be faced with skepticism that this is an experience I could anticipate having.

11. So it is not accurate to say—as does Frederick Stoutland—that my appeal to intending that we *J* "simply *postulates* a technical notion of intention whose point is just to permit" the kind of account I am sketching. Rather, my theory embeds the phenomenon of intending that we *J* within the plan-theoretic structures of roles and norms in terms of which intention is, quite generally, to be understood. And those structures help us understand what an intention that we *J* is. See Stoutland, "The Ontology of Social Agency," 541.

12. A point that Randolph Clarke once emphasized (in conversation). In this sense, the idea that intentions are "conduct controlling" pro attitudes remains apt (*Intention, Plans, and Practical Reason* at 16). And this is my reply to a concern from Roughley in his review of *Faces* at 268.

13. I will also conditionally intend to help you if you need it; though I might not unconditionally intend to help you, since I might fully expect that you will not need my help.

14. I am responding here to queries from Luca Ferrero and Pamela Hieronymi.

15. J. David Velleman, "How to Share an Intention." As noted earlier, however, Velleman acknowledges in this paper that my reply to this challenge in my essay "I Intend that We *J*"—a reply I am here recounting and extending—is successful. See his note 11; and see his review of my *Faces of Intention*.

16. "How to Share an Intention," 203.

17. "How to Share an Intention," 205.

18. Stoutland does not challenge this claim. See his review of *Faces of Intention* at 240. What Stoutland thinks, rather, is that an appeal to this settle condition "misses the distinctive point of the own-action condition." (240) That distinctive point is, he thinks, the connection—discussed earlier—between intending and taking full responsibility. But I have argued that there is not a sound argument here in favor of the own action condition. Neil Roughley also does not challenge this claim about the settle condition, but thinks, as does Stoutland, that there is independent reason nevertheless to hold onto a strict own-action condition, though he does not try to spell out that reason (Roughley, "Review of Bratman, *Faces of Intention*," 268–69). I have argued, however, that two main lines of argument in the literature for a strict own-action condition do not work.

19. I explain this qualification below, in section 3.

20. Responsiveness to these norms, but perhaps not full conformity to these norms. Recall the case of the weak-willed lovers who share an intention to have an affair.

Each intends that they have the affair, and each is set to change that intention if the other were to drop out. Such a change, in response to knowledge that the other has dropped out, would be responsive to norms of plan consistency and coherence, even though there would remain a violation of a norm that requires that one's intentions not violate one's judgment of the best. The intentions of these lovers can be interdependent in the sense I am after even though they are weak-willed.

21. Part of the explanation of why this proceeds in accordance with the connection condition will normally be that there are, as well, intentions of the sort alluded to in (ii). For now, however, we can focus just on the supposed truth of (c).

22. I do not say that we each only have the *conditional* intention that we *J* if the other so intends. On the model I am proposing each (non-conditionally) intends that we *J*, but the persistence of this intention is dependent on the other's so intending. For a critical discussion of an appeal here to conditional intentions see Abraham Sesshu Roth, "Shared Agency and Contralateral Commitments," *The Philosophical Review* 113, no. 3 (2004): 359–410, at 373–80.

23. This does not mean that each *infers* that he intends that we *J* by noting that the other so intends. As Abraham Sesshu Roth emphasizes, that would normally be an overly theoretical attitude towards one's own intention. [See Abraham Sesshu Roth, "Prediction, Authority, and Entitlement in Shared Activity," *Noûs* (forthcoming)]. Instead, in a normal case each arrives at his intention that we *J* by way of practical reasoning; but each is nevertheless in a position to note the dependence of the persistence of that intention on the persistence of the intention of the other, an intention that one's own intention, formed through practical reasoning, supports.

24. Velleman elsewhere points out that this conclusion is in the spirit of the idea— one he attributes to John Searle—that "*what is intended* . . . is whatever the state represents itself as causing and thereby tends to cause." (Velleman, "Review of Bratman, Faces of Intention," 121; and for the attribution to Searle see Velleman's "How to Share an Intention," 207). This indicates that, as suggested earlier, Searle's basic approach to intentionality can be seen as compatible with my view about intending that we *J* as ordinary intention with a special content, even though Searle himself thinks we need here to appeal to a fundamentally different attitude of we-intention. In this respect I agree with Velleman's astute observation that "Searle's account of shared intention is not entirely faithful to his own conception of what an intention is" ("How to Share an Intention," 202).

25. Annette Baier writes: "one cannot intend what one does not take oneself to control." See Baier, "Doing Things with Others: The Mental Commons," 25. In this discussion Baier seems to be revising her earlier endorsement of an own-action condition in her "Act and Intent," *The Journal of Philosophy* 67, no. 19 (1970): 648–58, at 649.

26. I am responding here to issues raised by Ned Block and Christopher Peacocke in discussion and in correspondence.

27. Robert C. Stalnaker, "Common Ground," *Linguistics and Philosophy* 25, no. 5–6 (2002): 701–21, at 708. I am here assuming that the wonderfulness—and not just, say, the loudness—of the concert can be "manifest."

28. There can also be cases in which you would retain your intention that we applaud so long as I intend to applaud. See the discussion below.

29. Recall that we are assuming condition (vii)—a common knowledge condition—is satisfied; so we can assume that relevant changes in my intention would be known by you, and vice versa.

30. There will also be cases in which my intention that we applaud would drop out once I knew that you no longer intend that we applaud even if you substitute an intention to applaud. I might see the desirability of our applauding as depending on your also so intending, even though I see that it is feasible that we applaud given only your intention to applaud. I turn to this distinction between desirability-based and feasibility-based interdependence below in section 4.

31. See Chapter 2 section 2.

32. I am assuming that I would know that my intention that we build the tunnel, together with your intention to build halfway, would together lead to our building it. I am also assuming that I don't see the desirability of our building the tunnel as depending on your intending that we build it.

33. The example to follow is courtesy of Luca Ferrero.

34. And that you are not going to return to the fold in a timely way, and your intention that we *J* is not replaced by a relevant substitute.

35. As noted earlier, there can be cases in which this interdependence is supported by a kind of mutual rational support even though this involves some sort of divergence from fully rational functioning. An example of this is the case of the weak-willed lovers and their shared intention in favor of their affair. I put such cases aside here.

36. This is a contrast with the mafia case in Chapter 2 section 2.

37. This distinction between a condition that makes the joint action desirable and a condition that makes it feasible is in the spirit of the distinction between reasons for an action and enabling conditions for that action that I once drew in discussing Donald Davidson's account of conditional intentions. See my "Davidson's Theory of Intention," 217–19. Jonathan Dancy, in his *Ethics Without Principles* (Oxford: Oxford University Press, 2004), at 39–41, appeals to a related but different distinction between a reason that favors an action and a condition that enables that reason to favor that action. My distinction between a condition that makes the joint action desirable and a condition that makes that joint action feasible does not depend on the viability of Dancy's distinction.

38. To return one more time to Miller's example of the tunnel builders: A natural interpretation of this example is that the interdependence is feasibility-based but not desirability-based. That is why one of the builders would retain his intention that they build the tunnel even if the other substituted an intention to dig halfway (given the former's knowledge that his intention that they build the tunnel,

together with the other's intention to dig halfway, would suffice for the tunnel-building).

39. Chapter 1, section 5.

40. Facundo Alonso independently discusses and endorses a similar, though some-what different idea—as he calls it, a "virtuous circle of mutual reinforcement"—in his "Shared Intention, Reliance, and Interpersonal Obligations" (Ph.D. Thesis, Stanford University, 2008), Chapter 7.

41. For this concern see Roth, "Shared Agency and Contralateral Commitments," 373–80. My response to follow draws from, and goes beyond, my discussion in "I Intend that We J" at 154–60.

42. This is a variant of an example from Margaret Gilbert, though I use it to make a different point than she aims to make. See Margaret Gilbert, "The Nature of Agreements: A Solution to Some Puzzles About Claim-Rights and Joint Intention," in Manuel Vargas and Gideon Yaffe, eds., *Rational and Social Agency: Essays on The Philosophy of Michael Bratman* (New York: Oxford University Press, forthcoming).

43. Much, though not all, of my discussion here of persistence interdependence derives from my 1998 essay "I Intend that We J." I argued in that essay, as I do here, that appeal to such interdependence helps explain how intentions of each that we J can satisfy a plausible settle condition. However, in that essay I did not go on to ask whether we should directly and explicitly build such an interdependence condition into our construction of shared intention. In this section I ask that question, and answer in the affirmative. As we will see in Chapter 5, this affects how precisely we should characterize the relation between shared intention and mutual obligation.

44. In a moment I will argue against requiring that the beliefs in (iv) be true; so it would be a mistake to render (iv) as a knowledge condition.

45. Recall that in defending the coherence of (ii) I also appealed (at the end of section 2 of this chapter) to

(e) if we do both intend as in (d), then we will J by way of those intentions (and in accordance with the connection condition).

[Recall that (d) says: that we each intend that we J by way of the intentions of each that we J and in a way that satisfies the connection condition.]

Applied to our specific case of our going to NYC, this is the condition that

(e-NYC) if we do both intend as in (ii), then we will go to NYC by way of those intentions (and in accordance with the connection condition).

Here the antecedent is more demanding that the antecedent of the beliefs in (iv). So if (iv) is true then, given the common knowledge condition, each will be in a position also to believe (e-NYC). So in this part of its effort to ensure the co-herence of both (i) and (ii), our construction can rest content with (iv).

46. See *Intention, Plans, and Practical Reason*, at 37–38.

47. Note that (v) shares with (b) the strategy of framing relevant conditions in terms of an abstract interrelation of interdependence, even though, as we have seen, such interdependence can take several different forms.

48. Thanks to Abraham Roth for helpful questions here.
49. For some theoretical purposes we might find it useful also to appeal to a condition that these beliefs are epistemically justified; but that is not a matter we need to pursue here.
50. Robert Nozick, *Philosophical Explanations* (Harvard University Press, 1981), esp. chaps. 3 and 4; though my use of this term does not precisely correspond to his.
51. Luis Cheng-Guajardo highlights closely related ideas in unpublished work.
52. Thomas Schelling, *The Strategy of Conflict* (Harvard University Press, 1980), 87.
53. I do not say "tracks the intended end of each of: the joint activity by way of relevant intentions of each in a way that satisfies the connection condition." That way lays a threat of circularity.
54. Chapter 2, section 3.

CHAPTER 4

1. One adjustment, noted at the end of Chapter 3, is that we now read our account of the connection condition, in terms of characteristic forms of mutual responsiveness, into the content of the attitudes in (ii) and (iv).
2. One question here is how to understand persistence interdependence for cases involving more than two participants. Well, suppose that four singers share an intention to sing a quartet together. Each intends that they sing the quartet. And there is the requisite interdependence just in case each would continue so to intend, other things equal, if but only if each of the others continued so to intend (where this is a matter of relevant rational functioning).

   Consider a different quartet (suggested by a query from David Estlund): Suppose that A, B, C, and D are a firing squad. Each intends that they together kill E. Suppose that if, counterfactually, D were to drop out then each of A, B, and C would intend that the remaining three of them together kill E. Does this mean that in the actual situation there is not the relevant persistence interdependence among the intentions of each of A, B, C, and D in favor of the quartet's killing of E? No. After all, if D were to drop out, each of A, B, and C would no longer intend that the quartet (of A, B, C, and D) kill E; what they each would intend, rather, is that the trio (of A, B, and C) together kill E.
3. So, with the possible exception of common knowledge, the cited attitudes, contents, and interrelations are, at least in basic cases, available within our model of individual planning agency.
4. For talk of "the glue that binds team members together" see Philip R. Cohen, Hector J. Levesque, and Ira A. Smith, "On Team Formation," in *Contemporary Action Theory*, ed. G. Holmstrom-Hintikka and Raimo Tuomela, vol. 2 (Dordrecht: D. Reidel, 1997), 89.
5. Searle, "Collective Intentions and Actions," 414.
6. And see Alonso's discussion of a "virtuous circle of mutual reinforcement" in his "Shared Intention, Reliance, and Interpersonal Obligations," (2008) chap. 7.

7. As noted by Samuel Asarnow and by Luca Tummolini.

8. This last example owes to Christopher Potts.

9. So I reject the thought, from Raimo Tuomela, that the agents in the kind of sociality of interest here, and characteristic of a world of multiple and diverging background reasons and values, "have their intentions of the form 'I intend that we J' (for each participant) necessarily because of a group reason . . ." Raimo Tuomela, *The Philosophy of Sociality: The Shared Point of View* (Oxford: Oxford University Press, 2007), 100–101.

10. In Chapter 7 I explain how shared intention also can structure shared deliberation.

11. Again, putting aside the exact status of a common knowledge condition. Having noted this qualification several times I will, for the remainder of this book, take this qualification as read.

    We can see an evolutionary proposal from Michael Tomasello and Malinda Carpenter as an analogue of this proposal about the conceptual, metaphysical, and normative continuities in the step from planning agency to modest sociality. Tomasello and Carpenter write:

    "The emergence of these skills and motives for shared intentionality during human evolution did not create totally new cognitive skills. Rather, what it did was to take existing skills . . . and transform them into their collectively based counterparts of joint attention, cooperative communication, collaborative action . . . Shared intentionality is a small psychological difference that made a huge difference in human evolution . . ." (Tomasello and Carpenter, "Shared intentionality," 124)

    This evolutionary proposal has a structure that is similar to that of my conservative constructivism, though I am not making an evolutionary claim, and though Tomasello and Carpenter speak of various "existing skills" where I speak of individual planning agency. While I do not see my conservative constructivism as depending on the truth of some such evolutionary story, this constructivism might be of use in articulating and assessing that evolutionary story, by providing a model of what is involved in the transformation to "collectively based counterparts." (Though, for a complexity, see this chapter, note 36.)

12. This contrasts with a case in which the stranger has no preference as between these different mechanisms, and is not set to promote an alternative mechanism if that were possible. As I indicated in Chapter 2, in discussing Miller's example of the tunnel builders, in the absence of some such preference and disposition, he might still intend that your actual intention be efficacious.

13. This seems to be a problem for Nicholas Bardsley's proposal in his "On Collective Intentions: Collective Action in Economics and Philosophy" that what is basic is that "given the right kinds of *expectation* about the other, one may be said to intend joining-in with him, so long as this is an action which can be performed if the expectations are correct." (152, emphasis added) Bardsley would respond that on his account what each expects is not just the actions of the

others "but their disposition to act on team considerations." (156) But if all that we say is that each *expects* this, then we have not yet ensured that each intends to support it. I might believe you are disposed to act on such considerations but not be set to filter options of mine that are inconsistent with your so acting. The same point can be made in response to Bardsley's condition that each participant expects the other's actions "to flow from an intention like their own." (158) I can expect that but still aim to prevent it. The lesson is that expectation is not a sufficiently practical commitment to play the needed role in our model of shared intention.

14. "Collectivity and Circularity," 140–41. Petersson refers to my "Shared Cooperative Activity," and my "I Intend that We *J*."

15. Though, in fairness to Petersson, in the earlier essay of mine to which he refers, "Shared Cooperative Activity," the condition of being set to help you if needed is cited as a condition on shared cooperative activity but not as a condition on intending that we *J*—though the disposition to filter incompatible alternatives is there cited as a condition on intending that we *J*.

16. Chapter 3 section 4.

17. Gold and Sugden, "Collective Intentions and Team Agency," at 112.

18. "Collective Intentions and Team Agency," p. 109. (An earlier version of this challenge is in Michael Bacharach (edited by Natalie Gold and Robert Sugden), *Beyond Individual Choice* (Princeton: Princeton University Press, 2006), at 139.) In putting the point this way Gold and Sugden are glossing over the distinction between intentions of individuals that are essential to shared collective activity, and collective intentions in the sense of intentions of a collective. The latter would be an analogue of my talk of shared intention, the former an analogue of Searle's talk of we-intentions in the heads of individuals. Since the latter reading is needed for their discussion to provide the intended criticism of my view, I will take it that their objection to the basic thesis is that it does not distinguish "intentions that lie behind Nash equilibrium behavior" from shared intention.

19. A sign of this is their remark that "Bratman might object that it is too glib to interpret P1's intending that J come about 'because of' P2's intention as the idea that P1 believes that P2 has the corresponding intention and acts on the basis of this belief. But his expansion of it . . . is opaque" (115). On my view, as I have indicated, this proposed identification of intending with belief is a mistake. As Marc Pauly once remarked, it may be that this mistake is rooted in a failure fully to appreciate the significance of the introduction of distinctive planning structures, over and above desire-like and belief-like structures, within the theory of individual agency. This is the ghost of the desire-belief (or, utility-probability) model.

Though I will not develop the point here, I also suspect that some such overly cognitive conception of intention is at work in the approach that Gold and Sugden take to "identification." They write: "*i identifies with* G if *i* conceives of G as a unit of agency, acting as a single entity in pursuit of some single objective." (125) And they see such identification as central to the explanation of why the agent is guided by her team preference ordering (where G is the relevant team) rather than by her individual preference ordering, and so engages in "team reasoning." But simply *conceiving* of G in this way does not seem to suffice for this explanatory job; one might, after all, *conceive* of G as a "unit of agency" while wanting and intending that G not function in this way. In contrast, if one were to *intend* that G function in this way that would explain why one is guided in that direction in one's thought and action. But now we would be appealing to something like the intention that we *J*, as highlighted by the planning theory. And the planning theory has a systematic explanation of the guiding role of such intentions.

20. Searle writes: "all intentionality, whether collective or individual, could be had by a brain in a vat . . ." ("Collective Intentions and Actions," 407). Strictly speaking, this is not yet to say that modest sociality—where this includes shared intentional and shared cooperative activity—is *solely* a matter of what could be had by a brain in a vat. But since Searle's entire theory of "collective intentionality" is a theory of the we-intentions that could be had by a brain in a vat, it seems that he at least implicitly endorses this stronger thought. And it is this stronger thought that the basic thesis rejects. John Hund also reads Searle in this way, and makes a similar point in his "Searle's The Construction of Social Reality," *Philosophy of the Social Sciences* 28, no. 1 (1998): 122–31, 129. (Thanks to Facundo Alonso for this reference, and to Vance Ricks for highlighting this aspect of Searle's view in conversation.)

21. *An Essay Concerning Human Understanding*, Book II, chap. XXVII, paragraph 9.

22. "Self to Self," 172. In Chapter 3 I cautioned against the overextension of this idea to all cases of intending, but this is not to reject the importance of this idea to a Lockean view of personal identity.

23. "Self to Self," 192.

24. Quinton, "The Soul," section 2. Related and more complex ideas are in H. P. Grice, "Personal Identity." A more extended treatment of social networks might exploit the further complexities of inter-relation highlighted by Grice in this essay.

25. Miller, *Social Action: A Teleological Account*, 13. Miller sees such cases of "intergenerational joint projects" as posing a problem for a theory like mine; but I think that a treatment of such cases by way of the idea of a social network seems promising.

26. But what if the building of the cathedral, or the research project, comes to a complete stop for several generations, and then the project is rediscovered and people begin it anew and complete it? This kind of case might motivate an extension of the idea of a social network, one that allows that some of the "links" across time may not themselves be ones of modest sociality.

27. I do not claim that my theory is uniquely positioned to do this. For example, and as Luca Ferrero has observed, we could consider an extension of Gilbert's theory

that focuses on overlapping strands of joint commitment. My concern here is only to indicate how my theory would treat these matters, not to argue that these are matters that could not be theorized within other frameworks.

28. Thanks to Abraham Sesshu Roth for pointing to this line of reply to Korsgaard's objection.

29. This is a possibility anticipated in Chapter 1, section 10. The deception and coercion in these last two cases might also affect the interpersonal obligations that are triggered by the sharing. I return to this matter in Chapter 5.

30. Aspects of this section derive from thoughts triggered by several discussions with Christine Korsgaard.

31. For one version of this worry see Elisabeth Pacherie, "Framing Joint Action," *Review of Philosophy and Psychology* 2, no. 2 (2011): 180. Martin Stone once raised this issue in conversation. My discussion in this section has benefited from very helpful written comments from Stephen Butterfill.

32. For example, Bart Geurts argues that a similar charge of psychological implausibility that is commonly leveled against a Gricean model of implicature may well be mistaken. See Bart Geurts, *Quantity Implicatures* (New York: Cambridge University Press, 2011), chap. 4. (Thanks to Stephen Butterfill for this reference.)

33. Philip Pettit, *A Theory of Freedom* (Cambridge: Polity, 2001), 38–39.

34. Here I am responding to a query once posed by Alison Gopnik.

35. Work broadly in this spirit includes: Stephen A. Butterfill and Natalie Sebanz, "Joint Action: What Is Shared?," *Review of Philosophy and Psychology* 2, no. 2 (2011): 137–146; Stephen A. Butterfill, "Joint Action and Development," *The Philosophical Quarterly* 62, no. 246 (2012): 23–47; Deborah Perron Tollefsen, "Let's Pretend! Joint Action and Young Children," *Philosophy of the Social Sciences* 35, no. 1 (2005): 75–97.

36. Recall the appeal, by Tomasello and Carpenter (this chapter, note 11), to "the emergence of these skills and motives for shared intentionality during human evolution" and to the idea that these "skills and motives for shared intentionality" made a "huge difference in human evolution." Our multifaceted model of shared intentionality points to complex questions here about the extent to which these purported evolutionary impacts are traceable primarily to the overall package of building blocks highlighted by the basic thesis or rather to certain individual building blocks, or sub-combinations of such building blocks. Further (and as emphasized by Samuel Asarnow in conversation) our multifaceted model also points to a question concerning the hypothesis that the great apes are planners without the capacity for shared intentionality: which of these further building blocks are absent in the case of the great apes?

37. For relevant discussions see Deborah Perron Tollefsen, "Let's Pretend! Joint Action and Young Children," and Stephen Butterfill, "Joint Action and Development," As Christopher Kutz has emphasized in conversation, however, we also need to keep a lively sense of the differences between the shared activities of 4-year-old humans and the swarming of bees.

38. David Lewis, *Counterfactuals* (Oxford: Basil Blackwell, 1973), 87. Thanks to Manuel Vargas for noting the connection of these issues with this aspect of Lewis's work.

39. As Pacherie puts it, on my theory "the materials [for the construction] come cheap . . . but their assemblage is costly." Pacherie, "Framing Joint Action," 180.

40. Lewis, *Counterfactuals*, 87. It is of course a further question whether we should agree with the specific use to which Lewis puts this idea in his defense of realism about possible worlds.

CHAPTER 5

1. See for example her essays "What Is It for *Us* to Intend?" and "A Theoretical Framework for the Understanding of Teams," in *Teamwork: Multi-disciplinary Perspectives*, ed. Natalie Gold (New York: Palgrave MacMillan, 2005); "The Structure of the Social Atom: Joint Commitment as the Foundation of Human Social Behavior," in *Socializing Metaphysics: The Nature of Social Reality*, ed. Frederick F. Schmitt (Lanham, MD: Rowman & Littlefield, 2003); and "Shared Intention and Personal Intentions." Abraham Sesshu Roth sketches a somewhat related view in his "Shared Agency and Contralateral Commitments," but here I will mostly concentrate on Gilbert's theory.

2. See Chapter 3 section 4.

3. For appeals to the reinforcement of reliance see Alonso, "Shared Intention, Reliance, and Interpersonal Obligations" (2009).

4. See my "Shared Intention," 126–27 (where I discuss the case of, as we might say, the Ayn Rand singers). As I note there, David Lewis makes this point in his *Convention*, at 34. Daniel Markovits (in conversation) noted that such cases are analogues of the doctrine of "employment at will" in American law.

5. This is in the spirit of Lewis's observation that "an exchange of declarations of present intention will be good enough, even if each explicitly retains his right to change his plans later." (*Convention*, 34)

6. This example comes from my "Dynamics of Sociality," 7. Facundo Alonso to some extent challenges my thought that there need be no mutual obligation in such a case; but his challenge is limited to, as he says, "cases of shared intention that, instrumentally or intrinsically, matter to us." (Facundo Alonso, "Shared Intention, Reliance, and Interpersonal Obligations," (2009) p. 471, note 76.) But it seems to me likely that there will be cases of, as we might say, accidental shared intentions that are too trivial or minimal to "matter to us" in a way that supports such obligations. Indeed, it is plausible that any induced or reinforced reliance in such a case is a source of an associated obligation only if the person who relies would suffer something like what T. M. Scanlon calls a "significant loss" if one did not follow through. But in cases such as the one described there may well be no such threatened significant loss: what is at stake may not be important to any of the parties. But lack of importance need not block shared intention. [See T. M. Scanlon, *What We Owe to*

Each Other (Cambridge, MA: Harvard University Press, 1998), chap. 7, pp. 300–301. Facundo Alonso, "Shared Intention, Reliance, and Interpersonal Obligations," (2009) 470. Also see Alonso's discussion of the idea of a "significant" loss at note 76.]

7. In my "Shared Intention and Mutual Obligation" I try to point to some of the relevant principles by appealing to principles of moral obligation defended by T. M. Scanlon, "Promises and Practices," *Philosophy & Public Affairs* 19, no. 3 (1990): 199–226. [And see T. M. Scanlon, *What We Owe to Each Other* (Harvard University Press, 1998), chap. 7.] While I see this appeal to Scanlon's work as a promising strategy, the view of modest sociality that I am developing here is open to a range of different approaches to relevant principles of moral obligation. (Facundo Alonso also explores a Scanlon-type approach to relevant obligations, but explicitly notes that there may well be other plausible approaches. [Alonso, "Shared Intention, Reliance, and Interpersonal Obligations," (2009) 473.])

8. In "Shared Intention and Mutual Obligation" I described my strategy as follows: "first to describe a social-psychological web of interlocking attitudes that plays the roles definitive of shared intention. We then go on to ask about further normative consequences of that web." ("Shared Intention and Mutual Obligation" in *Faces of Intention* at 140). In introducing the idea that persistence interdependence is both a building block of shared intention and contingently morally realizable, I need to change that last quoted sentence to: We then go on to ask about *possible normative realizations of, or* further normative consequences of that web.

9. See her "What Is It for *Us* to Intend?"

10. Gilbert, "What Is It for *Us* to Intend?", 21.

11. In this respect, and as I have noted before, there is a kind of agreement between Gilbert and Searle: both appeal to a fundamental, primitive idea/phenomenon. However, whereas for Gilbert this primitive is a special relation between individuals, for Searle it is a special attitude of individuals. I seek to avoid either form of appeal to a practical primitive.

12. Gilbert, "What Is It for *Us* to Intend?", 22.

13. As will emerge there, on the reading of this idea of a plural subject that is favored by Gilbert, it turns out that this claim about the connection between a joint commitment and a plural subject does not, in the end, add anything of substance to the account of joint commitment.

14. "What Is It for *Us* to Intend?", 25.

15. A point highlighted by Jules Coleman.

16. Gilbert, "Shared Intention and Personal Intentions," 169–73. An earlier version of my discussion of this essay of Gilbert's was part of my presentation at the University of London/University of Manchester 2009 workshop on "Joint action, Commitment and Agreement."

17. Granted, an agreement that is sincere on the part of each would normally generate a shared intention; but that is in part because it would normally involve relevant intentions on the part of each.

18. Could one respond by saying that there is, strictly speaking, no agreement if there is the cited insincerity on the part of either participant? Well, if this is how we understand the idea of an agreement then we cannot appeal (as Gilbert does at p. 172) to the phenomenon of agreement to support the disjunction condition, since agreements in this special sense do not conform to the disjunction condition.

19. As Paul Tulipana has highlighted.

20. I return here to a theme introduced in Chapter 1 section 9.

21. In his "Shared Agency and Contralateral Commitments," Abraham Sesshu Roth seeks a theory that is broadly in the spirit of Gilbert's appeal to special mutual obligations, but appeals only to a weaker normative inter-relation he calls "contralateral commitment." Roth thinks that contralateral commitments between the participants in shared agency fall in the space between the rational commitments that are built into a theory along the lines of the basic thesis, and the interpersonal ties explained by appeal to substantive principles of moral obligation. Roth's understanding of these contralateral commitments involves an asymmetric exercise of authority on the part of one of the participants to settle what the other does. And Roth aims to explain this by appeal to the idea that one participant can act "directly" on the intention of the other that settles what is to be done. I myself am skeptical that such an asymmetry is a general feature of shared agency. And if the argument of this book is successful it gives us reason to believe that we do not need to appeal to such purported, asymmetric authority in order to provide sufficient conditions for modest sociality. (See Roth, "Shared Agency and Contralateral Commitments," section 6, and the further discussion in Abraham Sesshu Roth, "Prediction, Authority, and Entitlement in Shared Activity.")

CHAPTER 6

1. "Collectivity and Circularity," 148. Petersson credits Tim Crane for this term. See Tim Crane, "The Efficiacy of Content: A Functionalist Theory," in *Human Action, Deliberation, and Causation*, ed. Jan Bransen and Stefan E. Cuypers (Dordrecht: Kluwer, 1998), at 220.

2. "Collectivity and Circularity," 149.

3. "Collectivity and Circularity," 148.

4. We might see this as in the spirit of Donald Davidson's proposal that "we may take the accordion effect as a mark of agency." (Donald Davidson, "Agency," in *Essays on Actions and Events*, 2nd ed. (Oxford: Oxford University Press, 2001), 53–54. The term "accordion effect" is due to Joel Feinberg.) Davidson expresses this proposal by saying that "an agent causes what his actions cause" (that is the accordion effect) and that this is a "mark of agency." We can express this as the view that if X causes what its actions cause (where that is the accordion effect) then X is an agent (and its actions are thereby accurately so-called). And Petersson's idea is that a group is a group agent when *it* causes what its actions cause

(and its actions are thereby accurately so-called). The swarm of bees, for example, causes what its stings cause. (If the victim dies then the swarm causes the victim's death.)

It is worth noting, however, that this proposal about the accordion effect as a mark of agency is in tension with Davidson's view, in this same essay, about the necessary relation between agency and intentional agency: "a person is the agent of an event if and only if there is a description of what he did that makes true a sentence that says he did it intentionally." ("Agency," 46) The problem in putting these two Davidsonian ideas together is that the accordion effect is tied to matters of causation, rather than to matters of intention. Davidson seems to have his eye on this tension when he claims that "the accordion effect is not applicable if there is no intention present." (54) But it is not clear that we should agree with Davidson about this limit on the accordion effect. If I non-voluntarily lose my balance and fall, and my falling causes your vase to break and that causes you to be upset, then I have broken your vase and I have thereby upset you. We seem here to have the accordion effect in the absence of intention.

5. "Collectivity and Circularity," 152–53. I have omitted parts of this passage that are tied to the further point that we might also refrain from seeing the bees in this way, and even if we do see them this way we might have different substantive theories of the internal structure. While I would also agree with these further points, they can safely be omitted here.

6. "Collectivity and Circularity," 155. Emphasis and bracketed phrase added.

7. "Collectivity and Circularity," 146; though it is important that I would say: intertwined *individually intentional* acts. See next note.

8. "Collectivity and Circularity," 155. Emphasis added. Petersson says here that the kind of action description I have in mind can include only "a behavioral description like 'their arms move'." But as I have noted earlier, this is not correct. I allow that the descriptions may well involve concepts of individual intentionality. What is crucial is that they not involve the concept of shared intentionality. In the discussion to follow I will assume that this correction has been made.

9. Recall that in Chapter 2 section 1, in reflecting on the concepts needed in the contents of the relevant intentions of the participants, I distinguished between a concept of our activity that is (a) neutral with respect to shared intentionality, and one that (b) can also be articulated using the conceptual resources of the planning theory of individual agency. In this discussion of Petersson's proposal I am returning, as promised, to the issue of whether our theory of the intentions of the participants can work, at the basic level, with a concept of our activity that satisfies both (a) and (b), or must instead involve a concept that satisfies (a) but not (b).

10. "Collectivity and Circularity," 153.

11. Ibid, 151.

12. Ibid, 151.

13. Some of the thoughts in this section derive from my reactions to detailed and very helpful comments, both oral and written, from Carol Rovane.

14. Donald Davidson, "Mental Events," in *Essays on Actions and Events*, 2nd ed. (Oxford: Oxford University Press, 2001). And see also Carol Rovane, *The Bounds of Agency: An Essay in Revisionary Metaphysics* (Princeton: Princeton University Press, 1998).

15. This trio of sentences (and my similar remarks in Chapter 4, section 4) is in the spirit of List and Pettit, *Group Agency*, 34.

16. This possibility is a central concern of List and Pettit, *Group Agency*. And for a suggestive, earlier treatment of related ideas see Carol Rovane, *The Bounds of Agency*. List and Pettit argue that in certain cases, issues raised by "discursive dilemmas" will sensibly lead members of a group to construct overall group positions in a way that bears only a complex relation to the attitudes of each of the individuals and that conforms to conditions of a Davidsonian group subject. They thereby bring it about that the group has "a single, robustly rational body of attitudes" (75) and is a "unified rational agent." (vii) However, List and Pettit also explicitly allow for the kind of modest sociality that is the target of my theory here—indeed, they build their model of group agency and group subject-hood on the top of structures of (what I am calling) modest sociality, structures that themselves need not involve a group subject. They call such modest sociality cases of joint intention and joint action. And they write: "a group of individuals may . . . form a joint intention to become a group agent. They each intend that they together act so as to form and enact a single system of belief and desire, at least within a clearly defined scope." (34) And I take it that on their view, such an originating joint intention need not itself have a group subject, since they explain group agents and group subjects as the outcome of such joint intentions. Since my target is limited to such modest sociality, I will not try here to assess their claim that in some special cases, ones in which discursive dilemmas loom large and there are practical pressures to resolve them in a systematic way, there really does emerge a unified, rational group agent that is a Davidsonian group subject. That said, I will discuss, in Chapter 7 section 4, a way in which a theory like mine can model a group standpoint without appeal to the strong idea of "a single, robustly rational body of attitudes."

17. "What Is It for *Us* to Intend?," 19, 22.

18. J. David Velleman notes this interpretive issue in his "How to Share an Intention," 201. Velleman himself seeks a theory in the spirit of the first, more ambitious interpretation. (My discussion in this paragraph draws on my discussion in "Modest Sociality and the Distinctiveness of Intention," 163–64.)

19. Philip Pettit and David Schweikard interpret Gilbert in this way in their "Joint Actions and Group Agents," *Philosophy of the Social Sciences* 36, no. 1 (2006): 18–39, at 32.

20. The correspondence is December 2008. The quoted passage is *in A Theory of Political Obligation*, at 144–45.

21. Pettit and Schweikard, "Joint Actions and Group Agents," 30. As noted, Pettit and Schweikard interpret Gilbert as asserting that there is such a "novel center" in joint intentional action.

22. As the quotations above from Pettit and Schweikard indicate, they are assuming a tight connection between group agent-hood and group subject-hood. And the assumption that a group agent is a group subject is also central to List and Pettit, *Group Agency*. But I do not see reason to think that these philosophers would need to reject the claim I am making, in following Petersson, that there is a weaker kind of group agency that does not require subject-hood though it does require appropriate internal organization of the group.

23. Cp. Rawls's discussion of classical utilitarianism in John Rawls, *A Theory of Justice* (Cambridge, MA: Harvard University Press, 1971) at 22–27.

CHAPTER 7

1. Portions of this chapter draw on my earlier discussion in "Shared Valuing and Frameworks for Practical Reasoning."

2. So shared deliberation is something we do together as a shared intentional activity. It is not simply a concatenation of the reasoning of each, in a context of common knowledge, about what would be best from the point of view of the group (as understood by the individual engaged in the reasoning). So the shared deliberation that is my target here contrasts with "team reasoning," as understood in recent work by Michael Bacharach, Natalie Gold and Robert Sugden. See Sugden, "Team Preferences," *Economics and Philosophy* 16, no. 2 (2000): 175–204; Gold and Sugden, "Collective Intentions and Team Agency;" Bacharach, *Beyond Individual Choice*. For a helpful discussion of Bacharach's views see Pacherie, "Framing Joint Action." And see above, Chapter 4 note 19.

3. As noted in Chapter 1, this distinction between bargaining and shared deliberation is in the spirit of a similar distinction made by Westlund in her "Deciding Together." Westlund also focuses on our shared activity of reasoning together; but her primary concern is our effort to arrive *at* a "shared perspective" of "reasons for us," whereas my primary concern is with the shared activity of deliberating *from* some such shared perspective. Further, Westlund focuses on shared deliberation that is in a significant way constrained by "mutual, non-instrumental concern" of each for each (p. 9; but see p. 15). In contrast, I do not in the same way treat such cases as paradigmatic of shared deliberation, though such a mutual concern may be a feature of some cases of shared deliberation. Finally, in contrasting bargaining and shared deliberation I aim to leave room for forms of reasoning together that do not fit comfortably within either category. (In this last sentence I am responding to queries from Niko Kolodny and Christopher Kutz.)

4. I borrow the expression "common ground" from Robert Stalnaker, who gets it from Paul Grice. (Stalnaker refers to H. P. Grice, *Studies in the Way of Words*

(Cambridge, MA: Harvard University Press, 1989), 65 and 274.) However, as I explain below (this chapter, note 39) my concern is with a somewhat different phenomenon than the one on which Stalnaker focuses. See Stalnaker, "Common Ground," 716. (Thanks to Joshua Armstrong for pointing me to this essay.)

5. Joseph Raz, *Practical Reason and Norms* (Princeton: Princeton University Press, 1990, originally published 1975), esp. chaps. 1 and 2.

6. John F. Horty, "Reasons as Defaults," *Philosophers' Imprint* 7, no. 3 (2007): 1–28; and John F. Horty, *Reasons as Defaults* (Oxford: Oxford University Press, 2012). (Horty sees Razian exclusionary reasons as a special form of defeater of a default. And Horty also sees his appeal to defaults, defeaters and under-cutters as capturing the ideas built into Jonathan Dancy's ideas of "intensifiers" and "attenuators" of reasons. See "Reasons as Defaults," pp. 14–15.) For related ideas see Mark Norris Lance and Margaret Little, "From Particularism to Defeasibility in Ethics," in *Challenging Moral Particularism*, ed. Mark Norris Lance, Matjaz Potrc, and Vojko Strahovnik (New York: Routledge, 2008).

7. As Scott Shapiro would say ("Law, Plans, and Practical Reason," 428), in these contexts our shared deliberation is a potential "mesh-creating mechanism."

8. J. David Velleman, *How We Get Along* (Cambridge: Cambridge University Press, 2009). Though my model of relevant forms of getting along differs importantly from Velleman's, we are both interested in, as he says, "our mundane ways of muddling through together." (p. 1)

9. For skepticism about a tight connection between moral reasoning and social, shared deliberation, see Dancy, *Ethics Without Principles*, at pp. 83, 133–34.

10. As some of these examples indicate, this phenomenon sometimes is embedded within larger institutional structures of the sort that I have been trying to put to one side for present purposes. So we need to be careful that we identify features of this phenomenon that do not essentially depend on such an institutional embedding.

11. For related examples see Velleman, "How to Share an Intention," and Christopher Kutz, "The Judicial Community," *Philosophical Issues* 11 (2001): 442–69. In keeping with the cited caution about institutions, I am here ignoring the authority of the chairperson of the department (as do most philosophers).

12. A point emphasized by Joseph Shieber (in conversation).

13. Maike Albertzart has emphasized this point.

14. There are concerns here about circularity, given the appeal to shared deliberation within the content of the cited shared intention. In response, I would deploy the approach to issues of circularity discussed in Chapter 2; but in order to keep the discussion manageable, I put these complexities aside here.

15. This is in the spirit of the emphasis on explanatory intelligibility in Velleman, *How We Get Along*, chap. 3, and in Adam Morton, *The Importance of Being Understood: Folk Psychology as Ethics* (New York: Routledge, 2003).

16. Brad Hooker explores a related but different idea about the connection between practical predictability and generality. (See Brad Hooker, "Moral Particularism and

the Real World," in *Challenging Moral Particularism*, ed. Mark Norris Lance, Matjaz Potrc, and Vojko Strahovnik (New York: Routledge, 2008).) Hooker's concern is with the relation between (a) predictability of moral judgment and (b) the role of general principles in moral reasoning. He thinks that (1) the substantive moral conclusions of other agents concerning what is morally right will be more predictable if they are known to reach those conclusions by way of moral reasoning that draws on general principles about *pro tanto* moral considerations, and we know what those principles are. Further, he thinks that (2) "in the special case of choosing between moral theories that are otherwise equally plausible, a difference in how predictable people who accepted these theories would be does seem . . . to count in favor of the theory whose adherents would be more predictable agents." (28) And Hooker believes (2) because of the social roles of moral judgment in our "cooperation and co-ordination." (18)

In contrast, my concern is with the predictability of the contributions of each to our shared deliberation, rather than with the predictability of, in particular, each contributor's moral judgments. My claim is that such predictability of contribution is central to our shared deliberation, not that it would tilt in favor of a specific moral theory. And my claim does not address the need for general principles in specifically moral reasoning. My claim concerns, instead, the virtue of generality of policies about weights in supporting relevant predictability in shared deliberation. So my claims about the connection between predictability and generality do not require Hooker's claims (1) and (2), though they are compatible with those claims.

17. Such shared policies about weights are plausibly classified as a kind of shared valuing. See my "Shared Valuing and Frameworks for Practical Reasoning."

18. I made the parallel point about individualistic policies about weights in Chapter 1, section 5.

19. See Chapter 4 section 2.

20. Here I am agreeing with K. Brad Wray, "Collective Belief and Acceptance," *Synthese* 129, no. 3 (2001): 319–33, at 325.

21. Kevin Toh appeals to a related phenomenon of "shared acceptance of a norm" as fundamental to central forms of legal reasoning. However, Toh thinks that we should understand such shared norm acceptances as forms of shared normative *judgment*. And a concern about this is that we do not normally see judgment as sensibly subject to these kinds of pragmatic pressures. See Kevin Toh, "Legal Judgments as Plural Acceptances of Norms," in *Oxford Studies in Philosophy of Law Volume 1*, ed. Leslie Green and Brian Leiter, (2011): 107–37, esp. 131–33.

22. This is related to a central theme in John Rawls's political philosophy. See his discussion of "the fact of pluralism" in his "The Domain of the Political and Overlapping Consensus," in *John Rawls: Collected Papers* (Cambridge, MA: Harvard University Press, 1999). Blain Neufeld discusses related issues in his Blain Neufeld, "'The Power of Free and Equal Citizens as a Collective Body'—Public Reason and the Scope of Distributive Justice" (unpublished manuscript).

23. So there is not merely—as H. L. A. Hart once expressed a related idea, due to Ronald Dworkin—a public "consensus of independent *conviction*", or (in the terms of our present discussion) a public consensus of independent intentions in favor of weights. (See H. L. A. Hart, *The Concept of Law*, 2nd ed., at 255.) Instead, the participants *share* a practical commitment to common weights, where this shared practical commitment consists in the cited structure of inter-dependent and interlocking policies. As we will see in section 4, this helps support a central role of these weights in the group's relevant standpoint.

24. In both respects there is a contrast with views of Christian List and Philip Pettit. First, List and Pettit focus on a specific type of problem that a group can face. This is, roughly, the problem that arises when a simple majority rule procedure for arriving at a group view would lead to different outcomes if the group proceeded in a "conclusion-driven" way, rather than a "premise-driven" way. In contrast, I have focused on the more general problem of, roughly, the need for relevant social unity despite divergence in individual judgment. Second, List and Pettit want to highlight the *discontinuity* between a group's solutions to such, as they call them, "discursive dilemmas"—solutions in the form of group judgments or preferences—and the attitudes of the individual participants. This is part of their argument that there is in some such cases a group subject and a group mind (see Chapter 6). In contrast, on my proposal there remains a deep *continuity* between the group solution—in the form of a shared policy about weights—and the attitudes of the participants. After all, these shared policies are constituted primarily by interconnected intentions of those participants—though there can be a kind of discontinuity between the shared policy and specific judgments of the participants about the right and the good. See List and Pettit, *Group Agency*, esp. chaps 2–3; and for a helpful discussion, Abraham Sesshu Roth, "Indispensability, the Discursive Dilemma, and Groups with Minds of Their Own," in *From Individual to Collective Intentionality*, ed. Sara Rachel Chant, Frank Hindriks, and Gerhardt Preyer (Oxford: Oxford University Press, forthcoming).

25. Andrea Westlund articulates this worry as follows:

"a reasoning-governing policy may be shared even while each of us holds at arm's length the considerations we treat as reasons under that very policy. While we are each committed to giving these considerations a justificatory role in our deliberations and planning, neither of us need regard the purported reasons themselves as in any sense deeply shared." ("Deciding Together," 6)

26. Dancy, *Ethics Without Principles*, 83.

27. This would parallel a potential reflexivity of individual policies about weights noted in Chapter 1 section 5.

28. Here, as in Chapter 1, I take as given the approach to self-governance sketched in my "Three Theories of Self-Governance" (see Chapter 1 note 56). Now, however, I am extending this approach to cases of shared self-governance. (In unpublished work Arthur Lau also appeals to a related idea of the group's self-governance.)

This extension to shared self-governance is a further aspect of the fecundity of planning agency.

29. There can be this convergence in value judgment despite divergence in more specific judgments. This convergence in evaluative judgment does not preclude the need for shared policies about weights. Instead, it supports the importance of such shared policies. (I am responding here to remarks from A. J. Julius.)

30. This appeal to a reason of shared self-governance for the group to take a relevant stand is in the neighborhood of a central idea in List and Pettit, *Group Agency*, the idea that participants might jointly form a group with a rationally unified structure of cognitive and conative attitudes in response to pragmatic problems posed by discursive dilemmas (see Chapter 6 note 16). But, in contrast with this idea of List and Pettit, structures of shared policies about weights are normally limited and partial, and need not involve "a single, robustly rational body of attitudes" of the group. (*Group Agency*, 75) Further, the basic thesis sees these shared policies as each consisting of structures of inter-related attitudes of the individual participants. As I noted above (this chapter, note 24), this contrasts with the kind of "autonomy" of the group agent and subject, with respect to the individual agents and subjects who are members of the group, that List and Pettit are concerned to explain and defend. (*Group Agency*, Chap. 3) (This is not offered as an argument against the List-Pettit model of such a rationally unified group subject; it is only a clarification of the differences between the two models of a group standpoint.)

31. See above note 23.

32. See Chapter 3, section 4.

33. See Chapter 3, section 4. The participants in such a feasibility-based interdependence might be to some extent like Scott Shapiro's "fundamentalists": their basic reason for favoring such weights does not involve the fact that the other does as well (Shapiro, *Legality*, 109–10). Nevertheless, their policies are feasibility-interdependent, and so they may be an element in shared policies about weights. That said, and as we observed in section 4, participants may value the kind of sociality in which there is such shared deliberation, and this will exert pressure toward a kind of desirability-based interdependence.

34. For talk of "hard cases" see Ronald Dworkin, "Hard Cases," in *Taking Rights Seriously* (Cambridge, MA: Harvard University Press, 1977).

35. Cass R. Sunstein, "Incompletely Theorized Agreements," *Harvard Law Review* 108 (1994): 1733–1772.

36. In putting the point this way I was helped by discussion with Facundo Alonso. I discuss context-relative acceptance in my "Practical Reasoning and Acceptance in a Context," reprinted in *Faces of Intention* (New York: Cambridge University Press, 1992). And see Robert C. Stalnaker, *Inquiry* (Cambridge, MA: MIT Press, 1984); L. J. Cohen, *An Essay on Belief and Acceptance* (Oxford: Oxford University Press, 1992); and Frankish, *Mind and Supermind*, esp. chap. 4.

37. And similarly with respect to underdetermination of a shared perspective that is due primarily to the partiality and incompleteness of the evaluative judgments of the individual participants. Here, however, I focus on cases of interpersonal divergence.

38. I discuss a version of this example in "Practical Reasoning and Acceptance in a Context," at 24–25.

39. Robert Stalnaker offers a model of "common ground" for a conversation, a model that appeals to common belief in a pattern of acceptances: "It is common ground that ϕ in a group if all members *accept* (for the purpose of the conversation) that ϕ, and all *believe* that all accept that ϕ, and all *believe* that all *believe* that all accept that ϕ, etc." ("Common Ground," 716) My remarks in this paragraph point to differences between shared policies of acceptance and a common ground in Stalnaker's sense. I do not say that Stalnaker's account of common ground is not apt for his purposes of analyzing important features of conversation. My purpose is to provide a helpful model of shared deliberation; and not all conversation is shared deliberation.

40. See my discussion of the "context-relative adjusted cognitive background" in "Practical Reasoning and Acceptance in a Context," 29–30.

41. The quoted phrase is from Rovane, *The Bounds of Agency*, 136. Nor do these shared policies focus on what List and Pettit call "a single system of belief and desire." (34)

CONCLUSION

1. Though, as noted, I leave open precisely how common knowledge is related to the planning model of individual agency.

2. As noted earlier (Chapter 7, note 30), this is a weaker notion of a group standpoint than idea of a "single, robustly rational body of attitudes" of the group, an idea that is at work in the model of group agents provided by List and Pettit (*Group Agency*, 75).

3. In this respect there is also agreement with the views of Raimo Tuomela. See his *The Philosophy of Sociality*.

4. There is here also a contrast with Tuomela's view in his 2007 book, given his emphasis on what he calls "we-mode mental states," together with his view that "the we-mode is not reducible to the I-mode." *The Philosophy of Sociality*, 9–10.

5. Nor is there an essential appeal to asymmetric authority relations of the sort to which Abraham Sesshu Roth appeals in his "Shared Agency and Contralateral Commitments."

6. As noted, Abraham Sesshu Roth expresses reservations about this strategy of deriving relevant social rationality norms from norms of individual intention rationality in his "Practical Intersubjectivity."

7. As noted in Chapter 4, note 9, this last point contrasts with the view of Raimo Tuomela in his *The Philosophy of Sociality*.

BIBLIOGRAPHY

Alonso, Facundo M. "Shared Intention, Reliance, and Interpersonal Obligations." Ph.D. Diss. Stanford University (2008).

Alonso, Facundo M. "Shared Intention, Reliance, and Interpersonal Obligations." *Ethics* 119, no. 3 (2009): 444–75.

Bacharach, Michael. *Beyond Individual Choice.* Edited by Natalie Gold and Robert Sugden. Princeton: Princeton University Press, 2006.

Baier, Annette C. "Act and Intent." *The Journal of Philosophy* 67, no. 19 (1970): 648–58.

Baier, Annette C. "Doing Things with Others: The Mental Commons." In *Commonality and Particularity in Ethics,* edited by Lilli Alanen, Sara Heinämaa, and Thomas Wallgren. London: MacMillan, 1997.

Bardsley, Nicholas. "On Collective Intentions: Collective Action in Economics and Philosophy." *Synthese* 157, no. 2 (2007): 141–59.

Barwise, Jon. "Three Views of Common Knowledge." In *Proceedings of the Second Conference on Theoretical Aspects of Reasoning About Knowledge,* edited by Moshe Y. Vardi, 365–79. Los Altos, CA: Morgan Kaufman, 1988.

Bratman, Michael E. "Agency, Time, and Sociality." *Proceedings and Addresses of the American Philosophical Association* 84, no. 2 (2010): 7–26.

Bratman, Michael E. "A Desire of One's Own." In *Structures of Agency.* New York: Oxford University Press, 2007.

Bratman, Michael E. "Davidson's Theory of Intention." In *Faces of Intention.* Cambridge: Cambridge University Press, 1999.

Bratman, Michael E. "Dynamics of Sociality." *Midwest Studies in Philosophy: Shared Intentions and Collective Responsibility* XXX (2006): 1–15.

Bratman, Michael E. *Faces of Intention.* New York: Cambridge University Press, 1999.

Bratman, Michael E. "The Fecundity of Planning Agency." In *Oxford Studies in Agency and Responsibility,* Volume 1, edited by David Shoemaker. Oxford: Oxford University Press (2013): 4–69.

Bratman, Michael E. "I Intend That We J." In *Faces of Intention.* New York: Cambridge University Press, 1999.

Bratman, Michael E. "Intention, Belief, and Instrumental Rationality." In *Reasons for Action,* edited by David Sobel and Steven Wall. Cambridge: Cambridge University Press, 2009.

Bratman, Michael E. "Intention, Belief, Practical, Theoretical." In *Spheres of Reason*, edited by Simon Robertson. New York: Oxford University Press, 2009.

Bratman, Michael E. "Intention and Personal Policies." *Philosophical Perspectives* 3 (1989): 443–69.

Bratman, Michael E. *Intention, Plans, and Practical Reason*. Cambridge, MA: Harvard University Press, 1987. Reissued by CSLI Publications 1999.

Bratman, Michael E. "Intention, Practical Rationality, and Self-Governance." *Ethics* 119, no. 3 (2009): 411–43.

Bratman, Michael E. "Modest Sociality and the Distinctiveness of Intention." *Philosophical Studies* 144, no. 1 (2009): 149–65.

Bratman, Michael E. "Nozick on Free Will" (and Appendix). In *Structures of Agency*. New York: Oxford University Press, 2007.

Bratman, Michael E. "Practical Reasoning and Acceptance in a Context." In *Faces of Intention*. New York: Cambridge University Press, 1992.

Bratman, Michael E. "Rational and Social Agency: Reflections and Replies." In *Rational and Social Agency: Essays on The Philosophy of Michael Bratman*, edited by Manuel Vargas and Gideon Yaffe. New York: Oxford University Press, forthcoming.

Bratman, Michael E. "Reflection, Planning, and Temporally Extended Agency." In *Structures of Agency*. New York: Oxford University Press, 2007.

Bratman, Michael E. "Shared Agency." In *Philosophy of the Social Sciences: Philosophical Theory and Scientific Practice*, edited by Chris Mantzavinos. Cambridge: Cambridge University Press, 2009.

Bratman, Michael E. "Shared Cooperative Activity." In *Faces of Intention*. New York: Cambridge University Press, 1999.

Bratman, Michael E. "Shared Intention." In *Faces of Intention*. New York: Cambridge University Press, 1999.

Bratman, Michael E. "Shared Intention and Mutual Obligation." In *Faces of Intention*. New York: Cambridge University Press, 1999.

Bratman, Michael E. "Shared Valuing and Frameworks for Practical Reasoning." In *Structures of Agency*. New York: Oxford University Press, 2007.

Bratman, Michael E. *Structures of Agency*. New York: Oxford University Press, 2007.

Bratman, Michael E. "Temptation Revisited." In *Structures of Agency*. New York: Oxford University Press, 2007.

Bratman, Michael E. "Three Theories of Self-Governance." In *Structures of Agency*. New York: Oxford University Press, 2007.

Bratman, Michael E. "Time, Rationality, and Self-Governance." *Philosophical Issues* 22 (2012): 73–88.

Bratman, Michael E. "Toxin, Temptation, and the Stability of Intention." In *Faces of Intention*. New York: Cambridge University Press, 1999.

Bratman, Michael E. "Two Faces of Intention." *The Philosophical Review* 93, no. 3 (1984): 375–405.

Bratman, Michael E. "Valuing and the Will." In *Structures of Agency*. New York: Oxford University Press, 2007.

Bratman, Michael E., David J. Israel, and Martha E. Pollack. "Plans and Resource-Bounded Practical Reasoning." *Computational Intelligence* 4, no. 3 (1988): 349–55.

Broome, John. "Is Rationality Normative?" *Disputatio* 2, no. 23 (2007).

Burge, Tyler. "Individualism and the Mental." *Midwest Studies in Philosophy* 4, no. 1 (September 1979): 73–121.

Butterfill, Stephen A. "Joint Action and Development." *The Philosophical Quarterly* 62, no. 246 (2012): 23–47.

Butterfill, Stephen A., and Natalie Sebanz. "Joint Action: What Is Shared?" *Review of Philosophy and Psychology* 2, no. 2 (2011): 137–46.

Carruthers, Peter. "Language in Cognition." In *The Oxford Handbook of Cognitive Science*, edited by Eric Margolis, Richard Samuels, and Stephen P. Stich. Oxford: Oxford University Press, 2011.

Chang, Ruth. "Commitments, Reasons, and the Will." In *Oxford Studies in Meta-ethics*, Volume 8, edited by Russ Shafer-Landau. Oxford: Oxford University Press (2013): 74–113.

Chant, Sara Rachel, and Zachary Ernst. "Group Intentions as Equilibria." *Philosophical Studies* 133, no. 1 (November 8, 2006): 95–109.

Christensen, David. "Epistemology of Disagreement: The Good News." *The Philosophical Review* 116, no. 2 (2007): 187–217.

Cohen, L. J. *An Essay on Belief and Acceptance*. Oxford: Oxford University Press, 1992.

Cohen, Philip R., Hector J. Levesque, and Ira A. Smith. "On Team Formation." In *Contemporary Action Theory*, edited by G. Holmstrom-Hintikka and Raimo Tuomela. Vol. 2. Dordrecht: D. Reidel, 1997.

Crane, Tim. "The Efficacy of Content: A Functionalist Theory." In *Human Action, Deliberation, and Causation*, edited by Jan Bransen and Stefan E. Cuypers. Dordrecht: Kluwer, 1998.

Cubitt, Robin P., and Robert Sugden. "Common Knowledge, Salience and Convention: A Reconstruction of David Lewis' Game Theory." *Economics and Philosophy* 19, no. 2 (October 2003): 175–210.

Dancy, Jonathan. *Ethics Without Principles*. Oxford: Oxford University Press, 2004.

Darwall, Stephen. *The Second-Person Standpoint*. Cambridge, MA: Harvard University Press, 2006.

Davidson, Donald. "Actions, Reasons, and Causes." In *Essays on Actions and Events*. 2nd ed. Oxford: Oxford University Press, 2001.

Davidson, Donald. "Agency." In *Essays on Actions and Events*. 2nd ed. Oxford: Oxford University Press, 2001.

Davidson, Donald. *Essays on Actions and Events*. 2nd ed. Oxford: Oxford University Press, 2001.

Davidson, Donald. "Intending." In *Essays on Actions and Events*. 2nd ed. Oxford: Oxford University Press, 2001.

Davidson, Donald. "Mental Events." In *Essays on Actions and Events*. 2nd ed. Oxford: Oxford University Press, 2001.

Davis, Wayne. "A Causal Theory of Intending." *American Philosophical Quarterly* 21, no. 1 (1984): 43–54.

Demeulenaere, Pierre. "Where Is the Social?" In *Philosophy of the Social Sciences: Philosophical Theory and Scientific Practice*, edited by Chris Mantzavinos. Cambridge: Cambridge University Press, 2008.

Donagan, Alan. *Choice: The Essential Element in Human Action*. London: Routledge & Kegan Paul, 1987.

Dworkin, Ronald. "Hard Cases." In *Taking Rights Seriously*. Cambridge, MA: Harvard University Press, 1977.

Feldman, Richard, and Ted Warfield, eds. *Disagreement*. Oxford: Oxford University Press, 2010.

Frankfurt, Harry. "The Faintest Passion." In *Necessity, Volition, and Love*. Cambridge: Cambridge University Press, 1999.

Frankfurt, Harry. "Freedom of the Will and the Concept of a Person." In *The Importance of What We Care About*. Cambridge: Cambridge University Press, 1988.

Frankfurt, Harry. "Identification and Wholeheartedness." In *The Importance of What We Care About*. Cambridge: Cambridge University Press, 1988.

Frankfurt, Harry. *The Importance of What We Care About*. Cambridge: Cambridge University Press, 1988.

Frankish, Keith. *Mind and Supermind*. Cambridge: Cambridge University Press, 2004.

Geurts, Bart. *Quantity Implicatures*. New York: Cambridge University Press, 2011.

Gibbard, Allan. *Thinking How to Live*. Cambridge, MA: Harvard University Press, 2003.

Gibbard, Allan. *Wise Choices, Apt Feelings*. Cambridge, MA: Harvard University Press, 1990.

Gilbert, Margaret. "The Nature of Agreements: A Solution to Some Puzzles About Claim-Rights and Joint Intention." In *Rational and Social Agency: Essays on The Philosophy of Michael Bratman*, edited by Manuel Vargas and Gideon Yaffe. New York: Oxford University Press, forthcoming.

Gilbert, Margaret. *Sociality and Responsibility: New Essays in Plural Subject Theory*. Lanham: Rowman & Littlefield Publishers, Inc, 2000.

Gilbert, Margaret. "A Theoretical Framework for the Understanding of Teams." In *Teamwork: Multi-disciplinary Perspectives*, edited by Natalie Gold. New York: Palgrave MacMillan, 2005.

Gilbert, Margaret. *A Theory of Political Obligation*. Oxford: Oxford University Press, 2006.

Gilbert, Margaret. "Shared Intention and Personal Intentions." *Philosophical Studies* 144, no. 1 (2009): 167–87.

Gilbert, Margaret. "The Structure of the Social Atom: Joint Commitment as the Foundation of Human Social Behavior." In *Socializing Metaphysics: The Nature of Social Reality*, edited by Frederick F. Schmitt. Lanham, MD: Rowman & Littlefield, 2003.

Gilbert, Margaret. "Walking Together: A Paradigmatic Social Phenomenon." *Midwest Studies In Philosophy* 15, no. 1 (1990): 1–14.

Gilbert, Margaret. "What Is It for *Us* to Intend?" In *Sociality and Responsibility: New Essays in Plural Subject Theory*. Lanham: Rowman & Littlefield Publishers, Inc, 2000.

Gold, Natalie, and Robert Sugden. "Collective Intentions and Team Agency." *The Journal of Philosophy* 104, no. 3 (2007): 109–37.

Grice, H. P. "Meaning." *The Philosophical Review* 66, no. 3 (1957): 377–88.

Grice, H. P. "Method in Philosophical Psychology (From the Banal to the Bizarre)." *Proceedings and Addresses of the American Philosophical Association* 48 (1974): 23–53.

Grice, H. P. "Personal Identity." *Mind* 50, no. 200 (1941): 330–50.

Grice, H. P. *Studies in the Way of Words*. Cambridge, MA: Harvard University Press, 1989.

Harman, Gilbert. *Change in View: Principles of Reasoning*. Cambridge, MA: MIT Press, 1986.

Harman, Gilbert. "Desired Desires." In *Value, Welfare, and Morality*, edited by Ray Frey and Chris Morris. Cambridge: Cambridge University Press, 1993.

Harman, Gilbert. "Practical Reasoning." In *Reasoning, Meaning, and Mind*. Oxford: Oxford University Press, 1999.

Harman, Gilbert. "Review of Bennett, *Linguistic Behavior*." *Language* 53 (1977): 417–24.

Harman, Gilbert. "Self-reflexive Thoughts." *Philosophical Issues* 16 (2006): 334–45.

Hart, H. L. A. *The Concept of Law*. 2nd ed. Oxford: Oxford University Press, 1994.

Holton, Richard. *Willing, Wanting, Waiting*. Oxford: Oxford University Press, 2009.

Hooker, Brad. "Moral Particularism and the Real World." In *Challenging Moral Particularism*, edited by Mark Norris Lance, Matjaz Potrc, and Vojko Strahovnik. New York: Routledge, 2008.

Horty, John F. "Reasons as Defaults." *Philosophers' Imprint* 7, no. 3 (2007): 1–28.

Horty, John F. *Reasons as Defaults*. Oxford: Oxford University Press, 2012.

Hund, John. "Searle's *The Construction of Social Reality*." *Philosophy of the Social Sciences* 28, no. 1 (1998): 122–31.

Kahneman, Daniel, Paul Slovic, and Amos Tversky, eds. *Judgments Under Uncertainty: Heuristics and Biases*. Cambridge: Cambridge University Press, 1982.

Knobe, Joshua. "The Concept of Intentional Action: A Case Study in the Uses of Folk Psychology." *Philosophical Studies* 130, no. 2 (2006): 203–31.

Kolodny, Niko. "Reply to Bridges." *Mind* 118, no. 470 (2009): 369–76.

Korsgaard, Christine. "Realism and Constructivism in Twentieth Century Moral Philosophy." *Journal of Philosophical Research* 32 (2003): 99–122.

Kripke, Saul. *Naming and Necessity*. Cambridge, MA: Harvard University Press, 1972.

Kutz, Christopher. "Acting Together." *Philosophy and Phenomenological Research* 61, no. 1 (2000): 1–31.

Kutz, Christopher. *Complicity: Ethics and Law for a Collective Age*. New York: Cambridge University Press, 2000.

Kutz, Christopher. "The Judicial Community." *Philosophical Issues* 11 (2001): 442–69.

Lance, Mark Norris, and Margaret Little. "From Particularism to Defeasibility in Ethics." In *Challenging Moral Particularism*, edited by Mark Norris Lance, Matjaz Potrc, and Vojko Strahovnik. New York: Routledge, 2008.

Lewis, David. *Convention*. Cambridge, MA: Harvard University Press, 1969.

Lewis, David. *Counterfactuals*. Oxford: Basil Blackwell, 1973.

List, Christian, and Philip Pettit. *Group Agency: The Possibility, Design, and Status of Corporate Agents*. Oxford: Oxford University Press, 2011.

Locke, John. *An Essay Concerning Human Understanding*, ed. Peter H. Nidditch (Oxford: Oxford University Press, 1975).

Ludwig, Kirk. "Foundations of Social Reality in Collective Intentional Behavior." In *Intentional Acts and Institutional Facts*, edited by Savas L. Tsohatzidis. Dordrecht: Springer, 2007.

Mele, Alfred R. *Springs of Action: Understanding Intentional Behavior*. Oxford: Oxford University Press, 1992.

Miller, Seamus. *Social Action: A Teleological Account*. Cambridge: Cambridge University Press, 2001.

Moll, Henrike, and Michael Tomasello. "Cooperation and Human Cognition: The Vygotskian Intelligence Hypothesis." *Philosophical Transactions of the Royal Society of London B* 362, no. 1480 (April 29, 2007): 639–48.

Morton, Adam. *The Importance of Being Understood: Folk Psychology as Ethics*. New York: Routledge, 2003.

Morton, Jennifer M. "Toward an Ecological Theory of the Norms of Practical Deliberation." *European Journal of Philosophy* 19, no. 4 (2011): 561–94.

Neufeld, Blain. "'The Power of Free and Equal Citizens as a Collective Body' – Public Reason and the Scope of Distributive Justice" (unpublished manuscript).

Nozick, Robert. *Philosophical Explanations*. Cambridge: Harvard University Press, 1984.

Pacherie, Elisabeth. "Framing Joint Action." *Review of Philosophy and Psychology*, no. 2 (2011): 173–92.

Parfit, Derek. *Reasons and Persons*. Oxford: Oxford University Press, 1984.

Perry, John. "The Importance of Being Identical." In *The Identities of Person*, edited by Amelie Oksenberg Rorty. Los Angeles: University of California Press, 1976.

Perry, John. "Personal Identity, Memory, and the Problem of Circularity." In *Personal Identity*, edited by John Perry. Los Angeles: University of California Press, 1975.

Petersson, Bjorn. "Collectivity and Circularity." *The Journal of Philosophy* 104, no. 3 (2007): 138–56.

Pettit, Philip. "Groups with Minds of Their Own." In *Socializing Metaphysics: The Nature of Social Reality*, edited by Fred Schmitt. Lanham, MD: Rowman & Littlefield, 2003.

Pettit, Philip. *A Theory of Freedom*. Cambridge: Polity, 2001.

Pettit, Philip, and David Schweikard. "Joint Actions and Group Agents." *Philosophy of the Social Sciences* 36, no. 1 (2006): 18–39.

Prichard, H. A. "Acting, Willing, Desiring." In *Moral Writings*. Oxford: Oxford University Press, 2002.

Putnam, Hilary. "The Meaning of 'Meaning'." In *Mind, Language, and Reality*. Vol. 2. Cambridge: Cambridge University Press, 1975.

Quinton, Anthony. "The Soul." *The Journal of Philosophy* 59, no. 15 (1962): 393–409.

Railton, Peter. "Normative Guidance." In *Oxford Studies in Metaethics*, Volume 1, edited by Russ Shafer-Landau. Oxford: Oxford University Press (2006): 3–34.

Rawls, John. "The Domain of the Political and Overlapping Consensus." In *John Rawls: Collected Papers*. Cambridge, MA: Harvard University Press, 1999.

Rawls, John. *A Theory of Justice*. Cambridge, MA: Harvard University Press, 1971.

Raz, Joseph. *Practical Reason and Norms*. Princeton: Princeton University Press, 1990.

Ridge, Michael. "Humean Intentions." *American Philosophical Quarterly* 35, no. 2 (1998): 157–78.

Rosner, Jennifer, ed. *The Messy Self*. Boulder, CO: Paradigm Publishers, 2007.

Ross, Don. "Game Theory." *The Stanford Encyclopedia of Philosophy*, 2011. http://plato.stanford.edu/entries/game-theory/.

Roth, Abraham Sesshu. "Indispensability, the Discursive Dilemma, and Groups with Minds of Their Own." In *From Individual to Collective Intentionality*, edited by Sara Rachel Chant, Frank Hindriks, and Gerhardt Preyer. Oxford: Oxford University Press, forthcoming.

Roth, Abraham Sesshu. "Practical Intersubjectivity." In *Socializing Metaphysics: The Nature of Social Reality*, edited by Fred Schmitt. Lanham, MD: Rowman & Littlefield, 2003.

Roth, Abraham Sesshu. "Prediction, Authority, and Entitlement in Shared Activity." *Noûs* (forthcoming) DOI: 10.1111/nous.12011.

Roth, Abraham Sesshu. "Shared Agency and Contralateral Commitments." *The Philosophical Review* 113, no. 3 (2004): 359–410.

Roth, Abraham Sesshu. "The Self-Referentiality of Intentions." *Philosophical Studies* 97, no. 1 (2000): 11–51.

Roughley, Neil. "Review of Bratman, *Faces of Intention*." *International Journal of Philosophical Studies* 9 (2001): 265–70.

Roughley, Neil. *Wanting and Intending: Elements of a Philosophy of Practical Mind*. Dordrecht: Springer, 2008.

Rovane, Carol. *The Bounds of Agency: An Essay in Revisionary Metaphysics*. Princeton: Princeton University Press, 1998.

Sartre, Jean-Paul. "Existentialism Is a Humanism." In *Existentialism from Dostoevsky to Sartre*, edited by Walter Kaufmann, rev. and expanded. New York: Meridian/Penguin, 1975.

Scanlon, T. M. "Promises and Practices." *Philosophy & Public Affairs* 19, no. 3 (1990): 199–226.

Scanlon, T. M. *What We Owe to Each Other*. Cambridge, MA: Harvard University Press, 1998.

Schelling, Thomas. *The Strategy of Conflict*. Cambridge, MA: Harvard University Press, 1960.

Schiffer, Stephen. *Meaning*. Oxford: Oxford University Press, 1972.

Schmid, Hans Bernard. *Plural Action: Essays in Philosophy and Social Science*. Dordrecht: Springer, 2009.

Schmid, Hans Bernard. "Shared Feelings: Towards a Phenomenology of Collective Affective Intentionality." In *Plural Action: Essays in Philosophy and Social Science*. Dordrecht: Springer, 2009.

Schroeder, Timothy. "Donald Davidson's Theory of Mind Is Non-Normative." *Philosophers' Imprint* 3, no. 1 (2003).

Searle, John R. "Collective Intentions and Actions." In *Intentions in Communication*, edited by Philip R. Cohen, Martha E. Pollack, and Jerry Morgan. Cambridge, MA: MIT Press, 1990.

Searle, John R. *The Construction of Social Reality*. New York: Free Press, 1995.

Searle, John R. *Intentionality*. Cambridge: Cambridge University Press, 1983.

Sellars, Wilfred. "Imperatives, Intentions, and the Logic of 'Ought'." In Hector-Neri Castañeda and George Nakhnikian (eds.), *Morality and the Language of Conduct* (Wayne State University Press, 1963).

Sellars, Wilfred. *Science and Metaphysics*. London: Routledge and Kegan Paul, 1968.

Setiya, Kieran. *Reasons Without Rationalism*. Princeton: Princeton University Press, 2007.

Shapiro, Scott J. "Law, Plans, and Practical Reason." *Legal Theory* 8, no. 04 (2002): 387–441.

Shapiro, Scott J. *Legality*. Cambridge, MA: Harvard University Press, 2011.

Shapiro, Scott J. "Massively Shared Agency." In *Rational and Social Agency: Essays on The Philosophy of Michael Bratman*, edited by Manuel Vargas and Gideon Yaffe. New York: Oxford University Press, forthcoming.

Shoemaker, Sydney. "Self-Reference and Self-Awareness." In *Identity, Cause, and Mind*. Cambridge: Cambridge University Press, 1984.

Simon, Herbert. *Reason in Human Affairs*. Stanford, CA: Stanford University Press, 1983.

Sinhababu, Neil. "The Desire-Belief Account of Intention Explains Everything." *Noûs* (forthcoming).

Smith, Matthew Noah. "The Law as a Social Practice: Are Shared Activities at the Foundations of Law?" *Legal Theory* 12, no. 3 (2006).

Smith, Michael. *The Moral Problem*. Oxford: Blackwell, 1994.

Sperber, Daniel, and Diedre Wilson. *Relevance*. 2nd ed. Cambridge, MA: Harvard University Press, 1995.

Stalnaker, Robert C. "Common Ground." *Linguistics and Philosophy* 25, no. 5–6 (2002): 701–21.

Stalnaker, Robert C. *Inquiry*. Cambridge, MA: MIT Press, 1984.

Stilz, Anna. *Liberal Loyalty: Freedom, Obligation, and the State*. Princeton: Princeton University Press, 2009.

Stockton, Frank. "The Lady or the Tiger?" In *The American Short Story*, edited by Thomas K. Parkes. New York: Galahad Books, 1994.

Stoutland, Frederick. "Critical Notice of Faces of Intention." *Philosophy and Phenomenological Research* 65, no. 1 (2002): 238–40.

Stoutland, Frederick. "The Ontology of Social Agency." *Analyse & Kritik* 30 (2008): 533–51.

Stoutland, Frederick. "Why Are Philosophers of Action so Anti-Social?" In *Commonality and Particularity in Ethics*, edited by Lilli Alanen, Sara Heinämaa, and Thomas Wallgren. London: MacMillan, 1997.

Sugden, Robert. "Team Preferences." *Economics and Philosophy* 16, no. 2 (2000): 175–204.

Sunstein, Cass R. "Incompletely Theorized Agreements." *Harvard Law Review* 108 (1994): 1733–72.

Thompson, Michael. *Life and Action: Elementary Structures of Practice and Practical Thought* Cambridge, MA: Harvard University Press, 2008.

Toh, Kevin. "Legal Judgments as Plural Acceptances of Norms." In *Oxford Studies in Philosophy of Law*, Volume 1, edited by Leslie Green and Brian Leiter (2011): 107–37.

Tollefsen, Deborah Perron. "Let's Pretend! Joint Action and Young Children." *Philosophy of the Social Sciences* 35, no. 1 (2005): 75–97.

Tomasello, Michael. *Why We Cooperate*. Cambridge, MA: MIT Press, 2009.

Tomasello, Michael, and Malinda Carpenter. "Shared Intentionality." *Developmental Science* 10, no. 1 (January 2007): 121–25.

Tomasello, Michael, Malinda Carpenter, Josep Call, Tanya Behne, and Henrike Moll. "Understanding and Sharing Intentions: The Origins of Cultural Cognition." *Behavioral and Brain Sciences* 28, no. 5 (2005): 675–91.

Tuomela, Raimo. *The Philosophy of Sociality: The Shared Point of View*. Oxford: Oxford University Press, 2007.

Tuomela, Raimo. "We-Intentions Revisited." *Philosophical Studies* 125, no. 3 (2005): 327–69.

Tuomela, Raimo, and Kaarlo Miller. "We-Intentions." *Philosophical Studies* 53, no. 3 (1988): 367–89.

Vanderschraaf, Peter, and Giacomo Sillari. "Common Knowledge." Edited by Edward N. Zalta. *The Stanford Encyclopedia of Philosophy*, http://plato.stanford.edu/entries/common-knowledge/.

Velleman, J. David. "How To Share An Intention." In *The Possibility of Practical Reason*. Oxford: Oxford University Press, 2000.

Velleman, J. David. *How We Get Along*. Cambridge: Cambridge University Press, 2009.

Velleman, J. David. *Practical Reflection*. Stanford, CA: CSLI Press, 2007.

Velleman, J. David. "Review of Bratman, *Faces of Intention.*" *The Philosophical Quarterly* 51, no. 202 (2001): 119–21.

Velleman, J. David. "Self to Self." In *Self to Self.* Cambridge: Cambridge University Press, 2006.

Velleman, J. David. "What Good Is a Will." In *Action in Context*, edited by Anton Leist and Holger Baumann. Berlin: de Gruyter, 2007.

Vermazen, Bruce. "Objects of Intention." *Philosophical Studies* 71, no. 3 (1993): 223–65.

Westlund, Andrea C. "Deciding Together." *Philosophers' Imprint* 9, no. 10 (July 2009).

Wittgenstein, Ludwig. *Philosophical Investigations.* Edited by P. M. S. Hacker and Joachim Schulte. 4th ed. Oxford: Wiley-Blackwell, 2009.

Wray, K. Brad. "Collective Belief and Acceptance." *Synthese* 129, no. 3 (2001): 319–33.

Yaffe, Gideon. "Trying, Intending and Attempted Crimes." *Philosophical Topics* 32 (2004): 505–32.

INDEX

acceptance. *See* norm acceptance; shared policies of acceptance

accordion effect as mark of agency (Davidson), 186n4

accountability, practices of
  and group agents vs. group subjects, 128
  for intention/intentional action, 61–62
  non-moral forms of, 174n6
  as pertaining to evaluative judgments, 20–21
  and shared intention/shared intentional action, 6–7, 27, 62
  See also obligations and entitlements, mutual

activity
  competitive, 55, 173n36
  individual ballistic and shared prepackaged, 81
  intentionally neutral vs. intentionally loaded concepts of, 45–46, 48
  shared-intention-neutral vs. shared-intention-loaded concepts of, 44, 46–48
  See also individual agency, planning theory of; modest sociality

admissions committee (case), 132, 134, 136, 140, 142, 144, 145
  See also search committee (case)

agency. *See* individual agency, planning theory of; desire-belief purposive agency; modest sociality; shared intentional vs. shared cooperative agency; temporally extended agency

agglomerativity, norm of. *See* individual rationality, norms of; social rationality, norms of

agreements
  incompletely theorized (Sunstein), 146
  insincere, 112, 116–17, 185n17, 186n18
  as sufficient for shared intention (Gilbert), 115–17
  as insufficient for shared intention but sufficient for mutual obligations, 112, 116–17, 119
  on what to give weight to or take as given (*see* shared policies about weight; shared policies of acceptance)
  See also shared commitments; shared policies of acceptance; value judgments; disagreement

Albertzart, Maike, 190n13

Alonso, Facundo M., 173n34, 173nn38–39, 178n40, 179n6, 184n3, 184n6, 185n7, 193n36

apes
  and modest sociality without mutual obligations, 113
  as planning agents (Tomasello), 159n4, 183n36

applaud together, shared intention to (case), 68–69, 73–74, 110, 177n28, 177n30

commonalities (*continued*)
  in reasons for participating in
    sharing, 91, 109, 145–46, 156
  of sensibility, 35, 89
  shallow, 146
  See also common ground for shared
    deliberation; conceptual convergence;
    partiality in sociality, pervasiveness of
competitive activities, 55, 173n36
conceptual convergence, 42, 170n5
conceptual openness, 24, 167n64
concurrence condition (Gilbert), 116–17
connection condition, 10, 50, 52, 78–83,
  86, 103
  and analogous problem for individual
    intention and intentional action,
    45–46
  in the content of relevant intentions,
    84, 179n1
  and intended mesh in sub-plans,
    54–55, 67, 83
  and mutual responsiveness
    condition, 103
connections, cross-temporal, referential
  Lockean and quasi-Lockean (*see*
    cross-temporal ties, Lockean; social
    ties, quasi-Lockean)
  and roles of intention, 23
consensus of independent conviction
  (Hart/Dworkin), 192n23
conservatism about shared intention
  and modest sociality, 4, 14–15, 26,
    31–35, 92, 151–52
  in creature construction, 31
  about group agents and concept of a
    group agent, 125
  presumption in favor of, 36–37, 156
  See also constructivism; continuity
    thesis; Ockham's razor
consistency, norm of. *See* individual
  rationality, norms of; social
  rationality, norms of

constructivism
  evolutionary analogue, 180n11
  in legal philosophy (Shapiro), 169n82
  about practical reason (Korsgaard),
    169n82
  about shared intention and modest
    sociality, 30–35, 180n11
  See also basic thesis, the; continuity
    thesis
continuities
  in attitudes (*see* cross-temporal ties,
    Lockean)
  between planning agency and modest
    sociality (*see* continuity thesis)
continuity constraint, 36, 169n86
  See also continuity thesis
continuity thesis, 3–4, 8, 151–52,
    155–56, 157, 161n17
  and basic thesis, 105, 152, 155–56
  and creature construction, 25–26,
    35, 151
  and group agents, 125–26
  and multiple realizability of shared
    intention and modest sociality, 35–37
  and own action condition, 14
  and presumption against
    discontinuous alternatives, 36–37,
    156
  qualified, 8–9
  and shared deliberation, 134
  and shared-intention-neutral
    concepts of activities, 46–47
  See also basic thesis, the; modest
    sociality
contribution to joint action, expected vs.
  intended, 56, 93, 96
control condition, 61, 64, 66–67, 88,
  176n25
control, virtual vs. active (Pettit), 104
cooperation, moralized notion of, 38, 102
  See also shared intentional vs. shared
    cooperative agency

weak-willed intentions, 19,
175–76
weak-willed lovers (case), 41, 175n20,
177n35
weakness of the will, 41
Weirich, Paul, 160n12
Westlund, Andrea C., 168n70, 189n3,
192n25
wholeheartedness (Frankfurt), 4
will, the
demystifying theory of,
25

as shaping thought and action, 143
(*see also* primacy of intention for
modest sociality)
Wilson, Diedre, 160n9
window smashing (Petersson), 93–95, 96
Wittgenstein, Ludwig, 10, 161n22
Wittgenstein's question and social
analogue, 10, 161n22
Wray, K. Brad, 191n20

Yaffe, Gideon, 102, 160n15, 163n38,
168n75, 173n36

CPSIA information can be obtained at www.ICGtesting.com
Printed in the USA
BVOW01s1953150916

462291BV00002B/18/P